THE DUKE OF NORFOLK'S DEEDS
AT ARUNDEL CASTLE

CATALOGUE 2

Properties in London and Middlesex, 1154-1917

THE DUKE OF NORFOLK'S DEEDS AT ARUNDEL CASTLE

CATALOGUE 2

Properties in London and Middlesex, 1154-1917

Edited by

Heather Warne

Phillimore

2010

Published by
PHILLIMORE & CO. LTD
Oving, West Sussex, England
www.phillimore.co.uk

ISBN 978-1-86077-613-7

Printed and bound in Great Britain

Contents

Contents

7. THE STRAND ESTATE, 1868-1917

8. NORFOLK HOUSE ESTATE, ST JAMES'S SQUARE

9. OTHER PROPERTIES

APPENDIX I

APPENDIX II

INDEX

List of Illustrations

Foreword by the Duke of Norfolk

The task of preserving and cataloguing the archives of the Dukes of Norfolk, storing and keeping them in good order as tools in the management of the estates, and also to enable their historical content to be understood, has occupied the family archivists throughout the centuries. Old reference and location notes dating from the 16th century onwards can be found written on the backs or fronts of most rolls, bundles and volumes.

One of the final goals has been to bring to the light of day the many details contained in the twelve thousand or more title deeds that have accumulated in the archives as the ducal estates grew through the centuries. This had been done in the past for small groups and collections of the deeds, and scholarship has benefited from the efforts involved. But the project embarked upon in 1994 was a greater one. All the collections of deeds would be looked at as a whole, enabling their inter-relationships, and therefore their context and their significance to the Norfolk family and local history, to be better understood.

My late father gave enormous encouragement to this work and was always delighted to learn of some new nuance of Howard family history that the cataloguing had revealed. He would have found great satisfaction, as I do, in supporting this publication, for its scholarly content and for the benefit to historical research that it will provide.

Acknowledgements

Dr John Martin Robinson, Librarian to the Duke of Norfolk and head of our Library and Archives team at Arundel, has been my guiding light in putting together this catalogue. His knowledge of the architectural history and development of London is immense and has been most helpful in organising the varied material in this collection. I have also relied heavily on the rest of the team, Sara Rodger, Margaret Richards and Sylvia Medic, who have frequently had to do more than their fair share of the routine office tasks when I was too deep into my cataloguing to help out. I thank them all warmly.

Finally, and most importantly, I would like to thank the Duke of Norfolk for his continued and valued support.

The Illustrations

I thank the Hon. Lady Roberts, Librarian and Curator of the Print Room, The Royal Collection, Windsor, for kindly supplying the view of Arundel House from the River by Wenceslaus Hollar on page xviii. All the other illustrations are from the collections comprised in the catalogue itself, or from elsewhere in the Arundel Castle Archives, as their captions indicate.

The front and back cover illustrations show the river frontage and the street layout of the Strand Estate in the mid-19th century. As today, a river frontage was desirable and this prestigious part of the Estate turned its face south to capture the view from a multitude of windows and balconies; while the raised balustrades at the ends of the three principal streets would have provided a pleasing outlook for all residents and vistors. Norfolk Street, at the heart of the estate, was developed later than the other two streets, on a more generous scale.

The drawings, which are reproduced here at much the same size as the originals, are the work of R.E. Philips, one of the Strand Estate agents. His small ink-and-colourwash floor plans of premises in the estate, which are inset in almost every lease of the 1850s and 1860s in this catalogue, also contain fine clarity of detail. (Ref. ACA/MD689.)

Heather Warne, November 2009

A General Introduction

This significant collection of deeds, leases and associated papers relates in large measure to the two ducal houses in London, the first generally known as 'the Strand Estate' and the second as 'Norfolk House'. Many other premises in which the Earls of Arundel and/or the Dukes of Norfolk had a passing interest are also represented by small handfuls of deeds in this catalogue. However, there were other London premises, such as the Charterhouse, or houses at Tower Hill and Lambeth, which had once been owned by the family, for which no deeds have survived in this archive and which therefore do not appear in this catalogue.

The Strand Estate

The vast bulk of this catalogue relates to the Strand Estate. It lay just outside the City gates in the parish of St Clement Danes on the site of the house and grounds of Hampton Place or Bathe Place, former residence of the Bishop of Bath and Wells. The estate, a rambling old house with extensive grounds reaching down to the River Thames, came into the hands of the Crown at the Reformation. It was purchased by the 12th Earl of Arundel in 1549, who immediately developed and adapted the building as his own residence and gave it a new name, Arundel House. With great debts to pay off in the 1670s the acting head of family, Henry Howard, Earl of Norwich, took drastic action and obtained an Act of Parliament for the redevelopment of the entire site, which included a cluster of pre-existing houses and inns along the Strand from Milford Lane on the east to Strand Lane on the west.

In the early 1670s, with the recent disaster of the Great Fire of London fresh in people's minds, the capriciousness of timber and thatch was to be avoided. A desire to build in brick, outside the City limits if possible, was paramount. Many families were still displaced and in need of a new start. The acting Duke was leaving no stone unturned in raising new revenues at this time, selling off distant estates and allowing vast acreages of timber in Sussex and Yorkshire to be sold off and felled. Arundel House, located just outside the Temple Bar, presented an opportunity not to be missed.

The gardens and grounds of the Earl's residence were subsequently developed as streets of terraced houses; and in the 1690s, the old house having been pulled down, further houses were inserted. The scheme was successful in that the rent income that it created went a good way to help pay off the family debts; while subsequent rounds of lease renewals raised money for significant later projects. The details of each stage of building and rebuilding from 1672 to the late 19th century can be followed in this catalogue.

The Thames river bank was a part of the estate that deserves some notice. Old Arundel House had enjoyed private access to the River – from a 'water house' and from 'Arundell Staires' at the bottom of the Earl's garden (etching, Wenceslaus Hollar, 1658). Public access to the River in 1658 was by a 'bridge' or pier at the bottom of Strond Bridge (Strand) Lane on the western bounds of the estate and 'Milford Staires' at the bottom of Milford Lane on the eastern bounds. Arundel Stairs functioned as a private wharf. In a dispute in 1659, for example, it transpired that Thomas, the 'collector Earl' (d. 1646), had previously imported stone and marble to the wharves there, to be worked upon by his men, for his own use (ACA MD1005). As the estate developed, a private wharf for the Dukes and their lessees was maintained at the bottom of Water Street, and the whole stretch of water front between Surrey Stairs and Water Street was policed by the Duke's liveried 'water men' (eg. **MXD813-14** below). A bond concerning a waterman's livery in 1690 makes it clear that the badge they wore displayed the crest of the Earls of Arundel as well as insignia of the Dukes of Norfolk (**MXD93**). Water Street itself became an area of coach houses, stables and commercial premises. In 1836 a 'barge basin' is shown lying between Arundel wharf and Milford Lane (ACA PM 190).

A strip of land along the water front was reclaimed from the tidal reach in the late 17th century, at the earliest stage of the new development (see **MXD133-4** below), and some of the grander new houses were sited there, with river views. The reclamation predated the main Victorian embankment we see today. This later scheme involved the Duke of Norfolk's agreement and his participation in developments such as the Temple Tube Station, copies of the architectural drawings of which are among the Arundel Castle Archives. When the Metropolitan Board of Works took over some of the reclaimed land at the bottom of Surrey Street in 1875, the Duke agreed to contribute half the cost of new railings – but his approval of the plans was a pre-condition (ACA MD893/3).

As well as private housing in the estate, there were shops along the Strand and inns and taverns peppering the lower streets. The 11th Duke (1786-1815) was the first to develop a pre-existing inn into a prestigious meeting place, the *Crown and Anchor Tavern*. During the 19th century the area became less residential and more commercial, trends which were capitalised upon by the 13th, 14th and 15th Dukes. As a ducal lessee, W.H. Smith built his London newspaper empire in the 1880s out of no. 183 Strand (see Section 7 below). The later 19th century saw some grand developments such as Surrey House and *Schrams Hotel* come to fruition during the watch of John Dunn, the 15th Duke's architect. His *'Norfolk Hotel'* and 'Arundel House' survive today in Surrey Street and Arundel Street/Embankment respectively, alongside their 20th-century neighbours. Many of his exquisitely drafted architectural plans are now at Arundel. A *'Howard Hotel'*, developed in the late 19th century by the 15th Duke, was subsequently extended southwards to the Embankment. The *Howard Hotel* today, with the 'Great Court' development behind it, stands at the heart of the estate. In its name it commemorates the Howard family who, in losing their private mansion, opened their doors to Londoners; and who subsequently guided their ancestral plot of central London into the modern era.

Norfolk House

Norfolk House, in St James's Square between Pall Mall and Piccadilly, became the London residence of the Dukes of Norfolk after a hiatus following the abandonment of earlier plans to build a ducal mansion within the Strand Estate itself. From earlier beginnings in 1676 as St Alban House, owned by Henry, Earl of St Alban, it was purchased by Thomas, 8th Duke of Norfolk, with adjoining properties, and was rebuilt as 'Norfolk House' by Edward, 9th Duke of Norfolk who succeeded his brother in 1732. It became the favoured residence of the Duke and of Mary, his Duchess, especially following the destruction by fire in 1761 of their rural seat, Worksop Manor in Nottinghamshire. The house continued as a family home, with attached offices for the ducal agents and surveyors throughout the 19th century, as well as the repository for the family archives. On its demolition in 1938, the archives, including the deeds which are the subject of the present catalogue, were brought to Arundel Castle. A small series of deeds in this collection (Section 9 below) relate to the acquisition and expansion of the Norfolk House complex.

Other properties

Both medieval and post-medieval deeds relating to London are included in this catalogue, mainly because there are so few of the former. They consist of a few items relating to the old premises fronting the Strand at Arundel House, three deeds relating to Knightsbridge co. Middlesex and a small but important series relating to the Nunnery of Clerkenwell. These are gifts to the nunnery of land and other rights (in Tottenham, Muswell and elsewhere), from the mid-12th century onwards. They are catalogued in Section 10 below along with other small series of deeds, or stray items, of a much later date.

The catalogue

The Duke of Norfolk's decision, in wishing to publish this series of catalogues, was to bring into easy reach of researchers a wealth of information about landscapes and persons long gone. This has been done by the long and painstaking process of extracting the substance of each lease or deed in detail. The insight thus gained into the ordering of a substantial estate like the Strand Estate will be, it is hoped, of great value to London historians. The successive waves of redevelopment in delineated plots each represent a desired standard of their day, from the earliest phase of building in the 1670s onwards. By contrast, we can glimpse a lost medieval London in the random assemblages of inns, shops, tenements and 'back houses' around the yards and alleys of the older properties. For those interested in the sanitary arrangements of the day, there are many mentions of 'the house of office' in various yards, including one that was 'built backward' in 1623; while the cutting edge of modernity was represented by Lord Teynham who, in 1619, had a pump and a *pipe and cocke of the newe Ryver water lately brought into the yard.*

Most of the material in this catalogue was created by an alliance of ducal solicitors, surveyors and estate agents, working from their various offices. The counterpart leases of the Strand Estate, a vast series, would have been kept in the agents' offices, which were variously on the Strand Estate itself or at Norfolk House in St James's Square. Other London documents not in this catalogue but listed by Dr Francis Steer between 1968 and 1975 (see Appendix I) would also have emanated from agents' offices. The earlier leases were almost certainly drafted by lawyers whose names are now lost to us, but from the early 19th century onwards, Messrs Few and Co. of Covent Garden were employed. However, it is clear that by the mid-19th century much of the routine verbiage of the Strand Estate leases was prepared by the agents themselves. Further information can be found in the introductions to the various sections throughout this catalogue.

This catalogue contains all those 'London and Middlesex' deeds formerly bundle-listed by Dr Steer prior to 1975 under the prefixes D and STD. To these have now been added the small collection of medieval and Tudor items listed under the prefix MX by H. Warne in 1992. Further items, mainly late 19th-century in date and formerly uncatalogued in any form, have also been included in the present catalogue under the prefix MXD. These were found at Arundel, either in unmarked boxes or among the unlisted papers of Messrs Few and Co., the ducal solicitors in Covent Garden. The prefix MXD has now been applied to everything in this catalogue.

This catalogue does not contain those family deeds and settlements which relate to packages of properties in several counties, including London and Middlesex. A further catalogue, in preparation, will eventually bring together these important family deeds.

Style and abbreviations

Italics are used in catalogue entries for direct quotes from the text. Abbreviations are generally not used, personal titles including, esq. (esquire) being an exception, 'doc.' for document being another. 'Occ.' and 'appurts.' are also frequently used in property descriptions. Dates have been rendered into modern style. Before 1752, the new year began on 25 March. This means, for example, that a document created on 2 January or 23 March 1700 is, by our reckoning, 2 January or 23 March 1701. In the catalogue I have put the main document date at the right-hand margin, for clarity. I have abbreviated the months to a three-letter style, for brevity.

Rents, down payments and purchase prices are all in the old-style pounds, shillings and pence, expressed in standard abbreviated form as, for example £10 15s. 6d. (10 pounds, 15 shillings and six pence). An old shilling (12 old pence) is now 5p and an old sixpence is 2½p in modern currency. So the above sum would be £10 77½p.

The few medieval deeds which exist in this collection are translated from the Latin in the same style conventions as I explained in the first volume in this series of The Duke of Norfolk's Deeds at Arundel Castle, viz. H. Warne (ed.), *The Dacre Estates in Northern Counties* (Phillimore, 2006), pp. xix-xxi; with a history of the deeds collections, pp. xv-xvii. Where other Arundel Castle Archives are referred to in the body of the catalogue, they are cited as ACA, followed by their reference number. A comprehensive list can also be found in Appendix II.

The property descriptions

'Appurts.' for appurtenances and 'occ.' for 'in the occupation of' (i.e., subtenants) are standard abbreviations used. Abuttals of properties are given, usually following a semicolon, though I have generally omitted the word 'abuttals' for entries from the 18th century onwards. The property clauses are transcribed in full topographical detail in the 17th- and early 18th-century deeds and leases and earlier, though this doesn't necessarily mean word for word. But the repetitive nature of the Strand Estate section means that fewer and fewer details are given as the centuries wear on. However, it is possible to trace the evolution of postal addresses in the Strand Estate as proper street numbering dispensed with lengthy descriptions such as 'house fronting the Strand on the east corner of Arundel Street'.

The documents were all created when imperial measurements were standard, long before metric measurements came in. Dimensions of building and house plots are given in feet and inches.

The indexes

As with the first volume in this series, it has been decided to provide, for family historians and others, a simple index of surnames of lessees, occupants and private owners of properties, rather than a full index which includes Christian names. To this is added a select subject index and the full names of certain key players. The catalogue presents the Strand Estate material in a way that follows its chronological development, and it should therefore be relatively easy to pinpoint names within a time frame. Researchers are encouraged, as always, to read through, holistically, those sections of the catalogue that interest them. The contents page gives guidance as to the places to which the deeds and leases relate.

Further research on the Dukes of Norfolk

The starting point for any study of the Howard family, Dukes of Norfolk, is the book by John M. Robinson, *The Dukes of Norfolk* (Phillimore, 1995). An overview of records available is provided by the former Historical Manuscripts Commission publication, *Guides to Sources for British History, 10, Principal family and estate collections: Family names A-K* (H.M.S.O., 1996 – look under Fitzalan-Howard). To follow up by research in the archives at Arundel one should first consult the four printed catalogues edited by archivist Dr Francis Steer, *Arundel Castle Archives*, vols I-IV (West Sussex County Council, 1968-1980). Help in finding where to consult the catalogues and, importantly, guidance to further cataloguing that has been done since 1978, can be obtained by calling the Archive department at Arundel Castle on 01903 882173 x 235 on a Tuesday or Wednesday only; or emailing ARCHIVE@ arundelcastle.org. The Castle website currently gives some details about the archives. Work is in progress to make the printed catalogues available on-line, via the Castle website.

Fig. 1 Arundel House.
This drawing by Wenceslaus Hollar, in or around 1637, looks across the River Thames to the Tudor mansion developed by the Earls of Arundel. Its attendant houses, offices and taverns crowd the skyline as far as the Strand, the great highway between the City of London and Westminster. Many details of this scene are illuminated in the first few deeds of this catalogue. The galleries in which the Earl and his Countess displayed their sculptures and other works of art extend prominently towards the River. (Ref. The Royal Collection, RL13268. Reproduced by gracious permission of HM The Queen.)

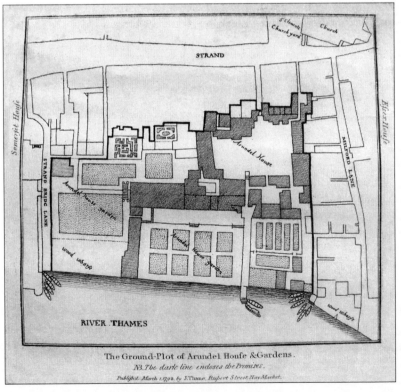

Fig. 2 The ground plot of Arundel House and gardens.
This plan, also by Hollar, is one of a series of his drawings of Arundel House, commissioned by the Earl of Arundel after he brought the artist to England in 1636. It distinguishes between the Earl's private curtilage, in heavy outline, and the area of rental properties to the north. Both were thrown together for the redevelopment scheme in the late 17th century, though the block in the north-west corner against Strand Bridge Lane did not stay with the Estate after Surrey Street had been developed. The extent of the gardens and the richness of their design can be appreciated from this plan. (Ref. ACA/MD1713, a copy published in 1792 by J. Thane.)

1. ARUNDEL HOUSE AND ITS ENVIRONS

i. Arundel House, 1545-1624

Bath Place (later Arundel House), with its flotilla of adjacent dwellings, had been seized by King Henry VIII following the Reformation. From the patents and deeds below we can trace its title from the King to Sir Thomas Seymour, and thence on his attainder to Henry, 12th Earl of Arundel, who died in 1580. It passed to his grandson (Saint) Philip, 13th Earl of Arundel, but the Crown took it back at the latter's attainder in 1589. In that year, the Queen's asset strippers entered and removed all the furniture and effects, but they allowed Philip's wife Anne to remain there as their lodger. However, after her husband's death in the Tower in 1595, she retired to her house in the country, Shifnal Manor in Shropshire, where she died 35 years later. Arundel House was not regained, in the direct line of descent, until 1607. By Act of Parliament 18 April 1604 Thomas, 14th Earl of Arundel had been restored to his late father's attainted Earldom of Arundel and Surrey and to his two grandfathers' baronies of Maltravers, Mowbray and Segrave. But the important property, Arundel House, had already been given by the King to Charles, Earl of Nottingham, a distant cousin of the Earl. The latter had had to pay Nottingham £4,000 in 1607 in order to regain his ancestral home, a transaction which is not represented by the deeds in this collection. We only have a copy of the formal ratification in 1608 whereby the King released all his interest in the premises to the Earl and his trustee Robert Cansfield.

It is likely that Arundel House came into Earl Henry's hands in 1545 little changed from the Bishop's days. The houses along the Strand and within the courtyards were part of the package. Not only did they provide an income from rent but they also housed retainers, judging from the names *the Keper's House* and *the Surveyour's chamber* below. Some tenants such as the bookbinder, haberdasher and pouchmaker may well have been in the Bishop's employ and perhaps passed seamlessly in 1545 to a new, secular master. Indeed, the chief accountant or 'receiver' of Philip, Earl of Arundel was one John Keper. The significance of a house called *the Cardinallys hatte* is not apparent to the editor, but future researchers, it is hoped, may provide the answer.

By 1608 when the King ratified the possession by Thomas, Earl of Arundel of his late great-grandfather's property, it seems clear that some modern embellishments had been made. The language of the patent (**MXD7** below) differs from all previous grants and speaks of an *atrium* (which I have perhaps translated inadequately as a 'courtyard'), and walkways including the *bowling alley*. The houses on the north side have been supplemented by further purchases whose title is cited in subsection iv below.

1

The bowling alley which was mentioned as early as 1591 was doubtless an Arundel addition.

The pleasure taken in their London house by the earls of Arundel is well documented elsewhere. It is also evidenced by the fine portraits of the 14th Earl and his Countess, Alatheia, in the long gallery overlooking the River Thames, displaying the Earl's statuary gathered from Rome and elsewhere in the ancient world. The 'Roman bath', which can be viewed today in Strand Lane, is sited just north of the Earl's western gardens and, it is thought, may have been constructed by him.

An interesting lease, **MXD14** below, gives us a glimpse into the world of 17th-century collecting when the Earl and his Countess reward a retainer for transferring a cabinet of curiosities to them. The dispersal of the Earl's statuary, and its subsequent journey to the safe havens of the Ashmolean Museum in Oxford and elsewhere, is well documented. A small further shaft of light is thrown by a lease of 1685, from which it appears that the statues, or some of them, were in Arundel Street, awaiting the Duke's attendance (**MXD148**).

MXD1	Letters patent from King Henry VIII to Thomas Seymour, knight	**29 Nov. 1545**

All that capital mansion and capital messuage called Hampton Place or Bathe Place with all its appurts. in the parish of St Clement Danes without the barres of the New Temple, London, in the county of Middlesex, late parcel of the territories and possessions of William late Earl of Southampton and formerly parcel of the lands, tenements and possessions of John, Bishop of Bath and Wells; with all the messuages, houses, buildings edifices, curtilages, gardens, barns, orchards, yards and other commodities

And additionally:

i) messuage called Le Keper's House and garden, occ. Robert Rede, between the tenements of Richard Wallaston west, Richard Hardyng, tailor east, Hampton or Bathe Place south and the highway north

ii) messuage in occ. of Oliver Moryell between the tenement once parcel of the Bishop of Bath and Wells east, the tenement of Margaret Kese west, a stable once parcel of the late bishop's possession south and the highway north

iii) messuage and garden formerly in the occ. of George Osboston, powchemaker, now of John Towerson between the tenements of Eustace Rypley, tailor east and John Edlys west, Bathe Place south and the highway north

iv) messuage of Peter Hughson between the tenements once pertaining to the late Bishop in the occ. of Oliver Moryell east and that in which William Haddeff lives, west, a stable of Bathe Place south and the highway north

v) messuage and small garden in the occ. of John Mann between Richard Jeloys east and Robert James west, a ruinous building or stable late of the said RJ south and the highway north

vi) messuage and garden in the occ. of Eustace Rypley and another, with a garden, in the occ. of John Porchett, hosier, between George Osboston, powchemaker east and Thomas Hunter, shoemaker west, Bathe Place south and the highway north

vii) messuage in the occ. of John Andrewe between a tenement once of the late Bishop now in the tenure of Thomas Semarke, gentleman east, a tenement of Richard Bonde, glasier, west, the highway north and a chamber commonly called Le Surveyour's Chamber, part of the said Bathe Place, south

viii) messuage called *The Cardynallys Hatte* in the occ. of John Sclater, between a tenement late of the Bishop in the occ. of William Potter east, a tenement late of John Lovell and since of Peter Forton, bookbinder west, the walls of Bath Place and the walls of Strande south [*sic*] and the highway north

ix) message and garden in the occ. of George Jackeson between the tenement of John Dyconson east and that of Thomas Hunter west, Bathe Place south and the highway north

x) messuage and garden in the occ. of John Andrewe between a tenement of John Andrewe once parcel of the Bishop's possessions west, the tenement called the Surveyour's Chamber once the Bishop's south, the tenement of John Te[illeg]son, haberdasher east and the highway north

xi) messuage and garden in the occ. of John Cooke between a tenement once of the Bishop in the occ. of Thomas Farlyng west, a tenement once of the Bishop in the occ. of Richard Takyll east, the wall of the capital mansion once of the Bishop south and the highway outside the same north

xii) messuage in the occ. of Thomas Hunter between a tenement once of the Bishop, now in the occ. of Henry Savell west, a tenement late of the Bishop now in the occ. of John Dykenson east, the wall of the capital mansion late of the Bishop south and the highway outside it north

xiii) Four messuages and one garden in the separate

3

occs. of John Nedys, Robert Lodyhame, Christopher Wotton and Thomas Northopp
– together with all the houses, buildings, structures, chambers, shops, cellars, solars, stables, gardens and curtilages, with all jurisdictions, commodities, emoluments and hereditaments pertaining and with all rents, annuities and profits (etc.)

For a payment of £700, the King grants to Seymour as a gift, to hold to himself and his heirs for ever as of the King and his manor of Grenewich, co. Kent, without having to pay any rent or render of any kind or to make any account of it to the King.
Great Seal appended, somewhat worn and part missing (repaired)

MXD2	Letters patent from King Edward VI to Henry, Earl of Arundel	**5 Nov. 1549**

Hampton or Bathe Place also called the Bishop of Bathe Place in St Clement Dane's (as above) late the possession of Thomas Seymour, knight, Lord Seymer of Sudley who has been attainted for High Treason with houses also in St Clement Danes:

> i) two messuages and gardens in the occ. of Thomas Northope
> ii) messuages in the separate occs. of Pharnando Desola, John Cooke, Christopher Wanton, John Aman, Richard Hugans, Peter Backe, Robert Lodyon, Roger Lyle, Rowland Browne, Katherine Thomson, Ewstace Rypley, Robert Stedman, George Jackson, William Kene, John Hardyng, Robert Rede, with all appurtenances (chambers, shops, solars etc. as above).
> **No abuttals are given**

The premises are granted to the Earl of Arundel and his heirs for a nominal sum of £41 6s. 6d. with all reversions, rents, profits, etc., to hold of the King in free socage as of his manor of Grenewich, co. Kent.
Great seal appended; good image, part missing

MXD3	Contemporary copy of **MXD2** above, on paper	**Undated, 16th-c.**

MXD4	Letters patent from Queen Mary to Henry, Earl of Arundel Confirmation of her predecessor Edward VI's grant, **MXD2** above, of Hampton or Bathe Place also called the Bishop of Bathes Place	**7 Feb. 1554**

Property described as in **MXD2** above.

Half the great seal is missing but the image is good on the remainder.
Contains a stylised copy signature of the Queen between the cords of the seal

MXD5   Grant in trust   **8 Sep. 1556**

a) Henry, earl of Arundel   b) Lady Mary his wife   c) Thomas Palmer, knight and William Sentabyn, esquire   d) Humphrey Floyde, gentleman and David Goghe, yeoman

> Capital messuage and tenement called Arundell Place in the parish of St Clement Danes without the barres of the New Temple of London; with all the houses, buildings, structures, gardens, yeards, orchards, curtilages, ways, paths, lanes and all hereditaments belonging and contained within its bounds and all other messuages, lands and rents, etc. belonging to a) in the same parish

a) grants to c) to hold to the use of a) and b) for life and after their deaths, to the use of their heirs and assigns. He appoints d) as his attorneys to deliver seisin to c).

MXD6   **Copy, made in 1737,** of letters patent dated   **10 Aug. 1603**

The King to Charles, Earl of Nottingham *our great English Admiral of outstanding faithfulness and prudence* [Lord High Admiral]

> Arundel House and all the adjacent premises as in **MXD7** below [NB: all details are exactly the same as in **MXD7** barring some different spellings of surnames and premises]

The premises were part of the possessions of Philip, late Earl of Arundel before his attainder. The King now grants them, with all their appurts. and with their annual rental value of £65 8s. 4d. to the Earl of Nottingham and his heirs for ever.

NB: **The original patent** was numbered by Francis Steer as MD2738 and is retrievable as such, but it was not catalogued.

5

MXD7   Letters patent   **6 Jan. 1608**

King James I to Thomas, earl of Arundel and Robert
Cansfield, esq.

Messuage or mansion house called Arundel House
in the parish of St Clement Danes without the
barres of the New Temple of London, with all its
appurts., including a courtyard [*atrium*] inside the
first entrance, two gardens, one orchard and all
the walkways [*ambulatores*], one being 'Le Bowling
Alley' with all the buildings, barns and stables
pertaining, all now or late in the occ. of Anne,
Countess of Arundel and all lying by the lane called
Strondlane on the west and the river Thames on
the south; together with:
i) messuages in the separate occs. of John Bell,
tailor, Francis Cutting, gentleman, and another
late in the occ. of Robert Reade, all abutting on
the highway to the north
ii) messuage late in the occ. of Ann Bright, widow
abutting west on the way leading from the mansion
called Arundel House to the common street and
south on the said mansion
iii) messuage late in the occ. of John Harden
abutting on the door of the said mansion house
west, the street north and the mansion house itself
south, and another messuage in the occ. of John
Harden or Hardyng abutting north on the street
iv) messuage in the occ. of William Wood, pewterer
abutting north on the highway
v) messuage commonly called the *Maydenhead*
in the occ. of Thomas Sleigh, late servant of the
woodyard, abutting on the highway north and
Arundel Place south
vi) messuages in the separate occs. of Robert
Wilson, sadler and Thomas Saunders, chandler,
and Elizabeth Wall, widow, abutting the highway
north and Arundel Place south
vii) messuage called *Le Blew Anker* in the occ.
of Henry Starkey, blacksmith, abutting on the
highway or street north and Arundel Place and
its grounds south
viii) messuage in the occ. of Richard Fidling
abutting on the common street there to the
north
ix) messuage called *Le Redd Crosse* in the occ. of
Richard Beadowe, and another called *Le Raven*,

with its garden, in the occ. of Anthony Millington, both abutting on the high street from Temple Barre towards Charing Crosse north and Le Bowling Alley of Arundel Place south

x) messuage called *Le Pye* in the occ. of Thomas Ellis, cordwayner, another in the occ. of John White, painter stainer, and another in the occ. of Leonard Forman, haberdasher, each abutting on the common street north

xi) messuage called *Le Axe* in the occ. of Robert Seale abutting to the highway north and the aforesaid lane lying next to the wall of the Bowling Alley and the orchard of Arundel Place, leading to Strondlane there to the south; and all the garden there in the occ. of Thomas Ellis abutting on the said Bowling Alley south

xii) messuage called le *Spred Eagle* in the occ. of Nicholas Wright, sadler abutting on the lane leading to Strondlane south, the highway or street called Strond to the north

– with all the channels called conduyt pipes and the edifice called Conduyt Head and the water duct taking water to the said mansion called Arundel Place which lawfully belong to Arundel Place alone and to no other building

All of which premises yield an annual rent of £65 8s. 4d. and were lately parcel of the possessions of Philip, Earl of Arundel who was lately attainted for High Treason;

with all buildings, barns, gardens, orchards, shops, cellars, solars, ways, water courses, rents and profits etc. to hold to the Earl and Cansfield and their heir in free and common socage as of the manor of East Greenwich co. Kent.

Great Seal slightly worn but entire

MXD8   Quitclaim   **1 Apr. 1624**

Robert Cansfield to the Right Hon. Thomas, Earl of Arundel and Surrey

> Capital messuage or mansion place and all the messuages, lands, tenements, rents, reversions, services and hereditaments in the parish of St Clement Danes without the Temple Bar

Signature and armorial seal of Cansfield, slightly damaged

ii. 'Arundel rents': Earls' leases

The term *Arundel rents* was used by the earls and their successors to refer to the huddle of Londoners' houses, taverns and shops that stood along the Strand in front of Arundel House and in the lanes and back alleys on the east and west of the House. The approach into the house from the Strand ran through these premises. As the Arundel House deeds **MXD1-8** above show, most of them were part and parcel of the estate as it was granted out of the King's hands in 1545. However, there seem to be a few others which were subsequently acquired. Together they provided a rent income as well as the convenience for the earls of having near neighbours who were under their control.

This section contains those of the earls' leases that survive; while the following section 1(iii) contains such title deeds and leases as have survived for *Arundel rents* before the estate was redeveloped in 1672. The premises in the Strand remained as part of the estate throughout its subsequent history. During the first phase of redevelopment they were distinguished from the newly built houses by this term *Arundel rents*. The new houses and streets were *Arundel buildings*. The old houses were gradually brought into line with the rest of the estate from the 1680s by lease renewals which insisted on a substantial or a total rebuild (see Strand Estate Development 1672-1701 below).

An important deed in this section is **MXD14**, in which an annuity is granted to Daniel Nys in part payment for his collection of gems. Nys was an art dealer in Venice, with close contacts to the Dukes of Mantua, whose collection he brokered for Charles I. He sold his cabinet of gems to the Earl of Arundel.

MXD9	Lease	**24 Feb. 1567**

The Rt Hon. John Lumley, knight to Joseph Elferack alias Helper

> Messuage in St Clement Danes Place in the occ. of Elizabeth Harding, widow of John Harding deceased; between Robert Reade, sadler on the east, the King's Highway on the north and the capital messuage of Lord Lumley on the east called Arundell House

The premises are leased for 21 years at 40 shillings annual rent

Signature: Lumley; copy enrolled before John Hill, auditor, 20 Jan. 1589.
Seal: absent

MXD10   Lease   **20 Apr. 1583**

The Rt Hon. Philip, Earl of Arundel to John Keper, of
St Clement Danes, gentleman, servant to the said Earl

> Two messuages in St Clement Danes, one called
> the *Raven*, in the occ. of Edward Robinson, lying
> between the messuage of Richard Bedoo on the
> west and the messuage wherein Garret Dewes
> dwells on the east; the other called the *Pie*, in
> the occ. of Thomas Ellis lying between tenements
> of Tadie Domus [*sic*] on the west and of Richard
> Bedoo on the east

Leased for 21 years at 40 and 15 shillings rent respectively

Witnesses: George Harrys, John Whyte, ?Luke Barman
Seal: very indistinct; decorative **signature** of John
            Keper [whose wonderful art work decorates the
            Earl's accounts of this period]

MXD11   Assignment of lease   **10 Aug. 1597**

Richard Bedoe, yeoman to Susan Saunders, lately wife of
Thomas Saunders, chandler, deceased

> Messuage called *The Tower and The Sonne*, lately
> in the tenure of Marie Towerson and now in the
> tenure of said Susan Saunders; lying between
> tenements in occ. of Henry Sterckie, west, and
> Thomas Wilson, east; with all houses, edifices,
> cellars, solars, garrets, shops, chambers, gardens,
> yards, ways and passages leading to the River
> Thames

Recites lease 28 March 1586 by Philip. late Earl of Arundel
and Countess Anne his wife to Bedoe for 21 years at 26s. 8d.
annual rent. Now, in return for a single payment of £50,
Bedoe assigns the remainder of the term to Saunders. 26s. 8d.
payable to the Earl and Lady Arundel.

MXD12   Lease for 80 years   **26 May 1609**

Anne, Countess Dowager of Arundel, Thomas, Earl of
Arundel and Surrey, and Robert Cansfield of London, esq.
to Francis Shukburgh of Lincolns Inn, gentleman

messuages as described in **MXD7** i) – xii) above. Same occupiers given

The lease is made in return for a payment by Shukburgh of £400, without any further annual rent liability.

MXD13	Assignment of lease	5 Jul. 1623

Sir Thomas Trevor of the Inner Temple, London, knight, solicitor general to *the Prince his highnes* to Nicholas Dawson, citizen and haberdasher of London

> messuage with appurts. abutting north on the high street (Strand) formerly in the occ. of Richard Ball, tailor but now of the lessee

Recites lease for 21 years at 42 shillings annual rent by the Hon. Charles, Earl of Nottingham to the lessor; who now, for a payment of £120, assigns it to Dawson for the remainder of the term.

Armorial seal (image faint) and signature of the lessor.

MXD14	Lease for 99 years	31 Jul. 1642

Right Hon. Thomas, Earl of Arundel and Surrey, Countess Alatheia his wife and the Right Hon. Henry Lord Mowbray and Matravers, their son and heir apparent, to Daniel Nys of London, merchant

> Messuage and buildings with appurts. in the occ. of John Standish abutting east on a messuage in the occ. of [blank] Middlehurst, tailor, west on the mansion house of Lord Viscount Stafford, south on the mansion house of the Earl of Arundel called Arundel House and north on the King's high street from the Temple Barrs to the City of Westminster; containing in the part which fronts the street two cellars, one shop and room adjoining, six chambers above stairs and two cocklofts or garrets over the chambers; and one little yard adjoining the messuage with all the little rooms adjoining the south side of it, viz. a hall, a kitchen, four chambers over them and two cocklofts or garrets over the chambers

The Earl and Countess and Lord Maltravers lease the premises to Nys for 20 shillings a year, in return for an undertaking to repair *their greate decays and defaults of reparacions*; and also in consideration of articles of agreement between them made at Ratisbone in Germany 15 Nov. 1636 whereby Nys would transfer to the Earl *a certaine cabinett wherein were diverse rarities as drawings, paintings, Medalls, Agatts cutt and cornelians anticke cutt, cristalls, jewells and many other rare curiosities which were particularly named in a book of octavo in writing and every leafe subscribed by the said Daniel Nys as an Inventory of all things contained in the said cabinett.* Following the agreement at Ratisbone the cabinet and its contents has since been sold to the Earl together with *several other rarities*, which Nys had also inserted into the cabinet [no details]. Nys and his wife Cecilia are to have an annuity of £150 out of the premises for life, payable until 10 years after the death of the longest liver out of the two of them.

MXD15   Draft bill of complaint   **undated, ?c.1655**

William Wall, gentleman against John Shelbury *in the custody of the Marshall et al.*, relating to:

> a messuage called the *Axe* divided into several dwelling houses, with their gardens, yards, ways, and passages, formerly leased to Thomas Seale

Recites that the premises were formerly in possession of Thomas Seal, gentleman. The Earl of Arundel and Countess Alatheia had leased the property to Wall on 10 Jan. 1642 and that it included several subdivided lettings giving him an annual rental of £105. All residents enjoyed the use of a common passage way out of the Strand, into the Axe yard and out of that into Strand Lane and so down to the River Thames *for to fetch water, coles, wood and other* necessaries. Now Shelbury, a neighbour in possession of *a messuage nexte adjoining to the Blacke Spread Eagle Alley and upon the messuages and tenements of the said William*, has stopped the path up by erecting a brick wall, preventing Wall's tenants from getting down to the River. As a result, his properties are empty and unlet and he has lost a great deal of rent money.

For the earlier lease of the Axe *to Robert Seale, see* **MXD26** *below*

iii Arundel Rents: Ducal leases (and their agents)

MXD16   **Lease** for 7 years at £52 annual rent   **21 Mar. 1667**

The Hon. Henry Howard of Norfolk to Thomas Stagg as above

> i) premises as above, the shop being in the occ. of William Synth, goldsmith
> ii) another messuage with a yard, part of which is paved with freestone, all in the occ. of Walter Chadley, tailor, lying backwards from the street, behind i), abutting north on the same, west on stables of the *Talbot Inn*
> ii) plot of land 140 feet north to south and 24 feet east to west lying behind ii), inclosed with pales and having a house of office in the north east corner; with a door in the pales at the south end and steps leading down into a passage way into Strandbridge Lane

Flourishing signature of Henry Howard

MXD17   **Assignment of rents**   **15 Dec. 1668**

The Hon. Henry Howard, second son of the Right Hon. Henry, Earl of Arundel to Richard Slowe, gentleman

> Messuage known as the *Lion and the Lamb* standing next to Arundel House and abutting north onto The Strand, in the occ. of John Spence, upholsterer

In return for a payment of £50, Howard assigns the £10 annual rent from the premises to Slowe for 7 years
Seal with a squashed impression of Slowe's crest

iv Londoners' deeds and leases of premises in 'Arundel rents'

House in the Strand, 1280-1357

MXD18   Gift (undated)   *c.*1280

a) Brice Gerveys and Serena his wife to b) Adam of Warrewic

> One messuage with all appurts. in the par. of St Clement Danes without the Bar of the New Temple of London; lying between the tenement of Thomas le Lyndraper (linen draper) on the east and the tenement once of Walter Wolleward on the west, its south head abutting on the garden of the Noble man, Lord Edmund Earl of Leycestre, the north head on the highstreet

a) grant to b) and his heirs to hold of a) and their heirs by hereditary right for ever, paying to a) on rose at Midsummer in lieu of all dues, rendering on a)'s behalf the usual dues to the chief lords of the fee.

Witnesses: Hamon of the Barre, William of the Well [or Fountain, *de fonte*], Robert of Bergholt, Thomas le Lyndraper, Robert of the Barre, Thomas le Charrun, Roger of Arderne, Edward the carpenter, Hugh le Roer, Peter the clerk

Seal: formerly two seals of which one remains, with a shield impression, and legend, severed in two

MXD19   Gift (undated)   *c.*1285

a) Adam of Warewyke   b) William of Alderwiche   c) Christine, daughter of a)   d) Thomas le Lyndraper

> Property as in **MXD18** above, with same abuttals

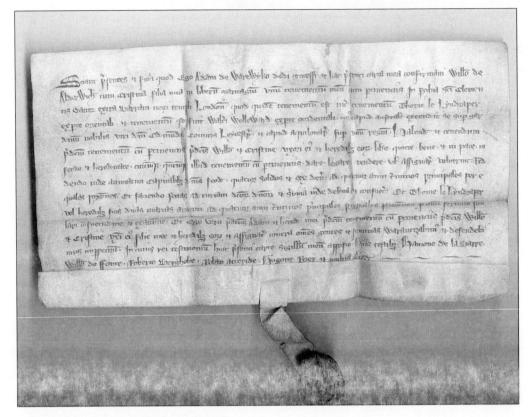

Fig. 3 An early house in the Strand, _c._1285.

This is one of only a handful of early deeds in this collection relating to the houses lying between Arundel House and the Strand. It demonstrates that 'suburban' development outside London's City walls has a long pedigree. Precise identification of the plot may be difficult, but the existence of the deed in the Duke of Norfolk's archives indicates that it later became one of the rental properties of his Arundel House estate. The name of one of the witnesses, Hamon of _La Barre_ [Temple Bar], illustrates the prevalent practice of inviting near neighbours to witness property transactions. (Ref. **MXD19**.)

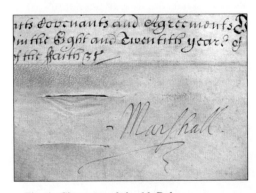
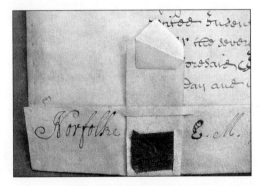

Fig. 4 Signatures of the 6th Duke.

It was Henry Howard, second son Henry Frederick, 15th Earl of Arundel (d. 1652), who first developed the Strand Estate. The first signature is from a deed of 1676 when he was Earl Marshal, but not yet Duke; and the second is from 1684 after his older brother had died and he had gained the Dukedom. (Refs. **MXD86, MXD89**.)

14

As a gift to their marriage a) grants to b) and c) and their heirs for them to hold in fee and by hereditary right; they paying 4s. 6d. a year to the chief lords of the fee, suit of court and the usual services due. They shall also pay d) 2 marks of silver annually in lieu of all secular dues and taxes

Witnesses: Hamon of the Barre, William of the Welle (or Fountain), Robert Bergholte, Robert Atteride, Hugh Roer

Seal: fragment of impression and legend

MXD20   Grant and quitclaim: at London, Thurs., All Saints day,   **1 Nov. 1357** 31 Ed. III

a) John son and heir of John of Alderwyche   b) Alice, former wife of Henry of Hakeneye

Tenement which b) holds in St Clement Danes

a) grants and releases to b) all his rights in the property.

Witnesses: Thomas Bryx, John Wygan, John Sadeler, John Rote, John Barneville, John Wantyng, William atte Celer

Seal: absent

House in the Strand, 1479-1505

This may well be the same property as above if Alice Mone, formerly Craven, was a descendant of Alice Hakeneye. The southern abuttal is to a garden in both cases.

MXD21   Gift   **15 Apr. 1479**

a) John Mone, son and heir of Geoffrey Mone   b) Alice, now deceased, former wife of John, who was herself the daughter of John Cravene and Margaret his wife   c)William Worme, John Burgeys, chaplain and John Horsley   d) John Worme

All that tenement with the appurts. in the parish of St Clement Danes without the Bar of the New Temple of London, between the tenement once of Thomas Lovell on the east a, the tenement of the Abbot of Combe on the west, the highway north and the garden of the Bishop of ?Llandaff [*Landavius*] south.

Recites that b) inherited the property from Margaret Cravene who had lived there for 16 years; b) had lived in it for 22 years and after her death it was inherited by a) who has now occupied it for eight years. He now grants it to the parties of f) to hold of the chief lords of by the usual services. He appoints f) as his attorney to enter and deliver seisin to f).

Witnesses: Thomas Stokes, William Lynley, John Porter, Richard Hill, John Burley, Richard Wodeward, Michael Moland

MXD22   Grant   **13 Dec. 1495**

a) Robert Blackwall, John Swafeld and William Thornhill
b) Agnes Russell, widow

Property as in **MXD21** above, with the same abuttals

a) grant to b) and her assigns for the term of her life and for six years following her death, to hold of the chief lords by the usual services.

Witnesses: Richard Wodeward, Nicholas Clyff, Rowland Skynner, Robert Bewykke.
Seal: two of three remain, neither with impressions

MXD23   Gift 'in the parish of St Clements'   **20 Oct. 1504**

a) Robert Blackwall and John Swafeld to   b) William Worme of St Clements without the Bar of the New Temple, London, tailor   d) Nicholas Clyff

Property as in 21 above, with the same abuttals

Recites that a), together with William Thornhill now deceased, got the property from b) as son of William Worme, deceased. They appoint d) as their attorney to deliver seisin.

Witnesses: none
Seal: one of two remains, with faint impression

Memorandum – of livery of seisin on 3 February is endorsed witnessed by William Toft, a clerk in the King's chapel, Humphrey Adam, a chancery clerk, Richard Strode and Edward Bury of the Hospice of the Lions, William Bokyngham and John Graye

MXD24   Gift 'in the parish of St Clements', 10 April 20 Henry VII   **10 Apr. 1505**

William Worme gives the above premises to further trustees William Toft of the King's chapel, chaplain, William Bokingham of St Clements, Robert Wootton of the parish of the Blessed Mary of the Strond, John Shorting of the same, John Hawkesby of St Clements, George Pecock and Laurence Long of the town of Westminster co. Middx No witnesses

MX25   Gift and appointment of attorney   **8 Jun. 1505**

The trustees of the above deed assign the premises to Hugh Dobenet and Henry Reye; and appoint John Orwell to deliver seisin.

Messuage called the *Axe* off Strand Lane, 1591

MXD26   Lease   **8 May 1591**

The Queen to Robert Seale, one of her yeoman ushers

> Messuage called the *Axe*, with free access by a passage way leading south towards the River Thames lately belonging to Philip the former Earl of Arundel, between a tenement of the former Earl, in the occ. of Leonard Forman and Thomas Ellis, on the east and one of Nicholas Wright, sadler on the west, abutting north on the highway; and the said passage way which lies alongside the wall of the Bowling Alley and the orchard of Arundel Place, on its south and west side, and which leads to Straundelane; and garden lying next to and abutting east on the garden of the former Earl in the occ. of Thomas Ellis, and abutting west on a garden of the said former Earl in the occ. of Nicholas Wright and his assign Robert Cooke; abutting north on the tenement in the occ. of Leonard Forman and John Wright and on the house of Robert Seale; and south on the said bowling alley

Acting on the advice of her counsellors, William, Baron of Burghley, Treasurer and John Fortescue, esq., Deputy Treasurer, the Queen grants the premises to Seale on a 50-year lease at £4 annual rent

Good sample of Great Seal

Re the Axe, *see also* **MXD15** *above. For an abstract of title dated 1717, reciting from 1659, see Strand Estate Development 1701-1777 below.*

The *Talbot Inn* (formerly *Queens Head*), 1611-66

MXD27   Lease   **7 Nov. 1611**

George Sympson, lately citizen and vintner of the city of London to Edmond Jacome of Colleshull co. Warwick, yeoman

> Messuage or inn with its appurts., lately divided into two, in the occs. of David Boulton and John Phillippes; formerly known as the *Talbott* or sign of the *Talbott* and now known as the *Queen's Arms*; with all ways, easements and commodities, etc., in the par. of St Clement Danes

The premises are leased for 21 years at £40 annual rent

Witnesses: John Bevan, John Todd, Abraham Eyre

MXD28   Assignment of mortgage (lease for 500 years)   **30 Nov. 1666**

a) John Hawkins of Kingston upon Thames, barber chirurgeon, b) the Hon. Henry Howard of Norfolk c) Arthur Onslow of West Clandon, Surrey, son and heir of Sir Richard Onslow lately styled as Lord Onslowe c) Jeffrey Howland of Streatham in Surrey, esq.

> Four messuages with appurts. formerly known as the *Queen's Head* but now as the *Talbot* late in possession of John Hawkins, joiner and in the several tenancies of Anthony Bartley, William Newton, Thomas Palfrey and George Bedbury

Recites previous mortgages on the premises in 1659 and 1661 whereby c) and Richard Onslowe; his father, owed £1,030 to John Hawkins, father of a); now a) as his father's heir, and with the consent of b) and c) assigns the remainder of the term to d) for £1,000

Schedule of previous deeds from 1564.

London and Middlesex, 1154-1917: *Londoners' deeds*, MXD27-30

Re. abstract of title dated 1717, reciting the above deed and an earlier one of 1659, see Strand Estate Development, 1701-1777, *Legal papers.*

Roper family houses in the Strand, 1576-1625

George Farrewell's house:

MXD29 Declaration and release   1 Jun. 1576

Charles Broughton of St Clement Danes, gentleman to George Farrewell of Hilbishops [Bishops Hull], co. Somerset, esq.

> A house in the parish of St Clement Danes [no details]

Broughton had leased the premises to Farrewell the previous February. He now itemises its contents and releases the same, together with the house, to Farrewell.

Witnesses: Richard Farrewell and William Walton; seal absent

MXD30 Assignment of lease   12 Feb. 1583

George Farewell of Maydon Bradley, co. Wilts, gentleman to John Rooper of Lynstead, co. Kent., esq.

> One tenement and one garden 32 feet towards the Queen's highway and 26 feet in breadth *at the nether ende of the seide garden*, lately in occ. of Robert Skantt, locksmith and since of Charles Broughton; abutting east on the messuage in the occ. of Tyderuke Domoys, servant to the Earl of Pembroke and of John Rawlyns alias Yonge, south on the garden of the Earl of Arundel *being parcel of the garden belonging to the late Strond Inn*, west on the tenement *lately called the Three Crownes wherein one Rauffe Sympson lately dwelt ... commonly called The Talbott*, and north on the Queen's highway

The premises were leased in 1573 for 5 years by Agnes Cawood and John Kene to Charles Broughton; renewed for 21 years in 1579 and assigned the same year by Broughton to Farewell. Now, for a payment of £250 Farewell assigns to Rooper the remainder of a 21-year term until Michaelmas 1598

Signature and seal showing Farewell's arms

Three houses in the Strand

MXD31   Lease   **29 Feb. 1559**[1]

William Roper, esq. to John Keyme of St Clement Danes without the Bars of the New Temple, smith, of:

> Three tenements in the parish of St Clement Danes, lying between the tenement belonging to the late Bishop of Bath and Wells on the east, the tenements of Robert James, grocer and of John Studde, gentleman on the west, the Queen's highway on the north and the garden belonging to the late Strond Inne on the south; the three tenements and alley having previously been five tenements, five gardens and an alley

The premises are leased for 60 years from Lady Day next at £14 annual rent

Witnesses: Alexander Wylgose and Thomas Parrys
Seal: fragment with stag's head impression

MXD32   Bargain and sale for £300   **15 Feb. 1585**

Anthony Roper of Farningham, co. Kent, esq. and John Gawber of the City of London, gentleman to Christopher Rooper, son and heir apparent of John Rooper of Lynsted, co. Kent, esq.

> Three messuages, three gardens and appurts. Lying between the lands and tenements of the Earl of Arundel on the east, a tenement of the heirs of Ralph Sympson called the *Talbot* and tenements of [blank] Plather and of Edmond Yonge on the west, the street leading from the Temple Bar towards Westminster on the north and lands and tenements of the Earl of Arundel on the south

Witnesses names are endorsed; signatures and seals, with impressions, of the vendors.

MXD33   Contemporary copy of **MXD32** above

---

1   Not a leap year; ? clerical error for 1 March.

MXD34   Surrender of lease   **9 Jun. 1590**

John Keyme of St Saviour, Southwark, blacksmith to Sir John
Rooper (no details)

Premises as in **MXD31** above

Recites various subleases on the premises since 1559 which
Keyme has inherited from John his father and Agnes his
mother; whereby a tenement, garden and great chamber
occupied by Charles Broughton is parcel of premises leased
to John Gardyner and now occupied by said John Rooper;
and whereby other premises have been sublet to Richard
Lyne, Richard Cuxsone, Henry Drake, Henry Starkey and
Humphrey Armitage. Now, in return for a payment of £40,
Keyme surrenders the remainder to run on the above lease
to Rooper.

MXD35   Lease   **25 Mar. 1619**

The Rt Hon. Christopher, Lord Teyneham, Baron of Teyneham,
to William Rooper, esq., his second son

> Messuage in St Clement Danes now in occ. of the
> said Lord Teyneham, having 20 rooms, with all
> cellars, sollers, ways, backsides [etc.]; and *one privye
> howse standing at the lower end of the yarde*, and
> one garden plot adjoining the privye howse on the
> sowth side thereof; *together with a pumpe standing
> in the said yarde and together also with a pipe and
> cocke of the newe Ryver water lately brought into the
> said yarde*; abutting north on the King's highway
> called the Strande Streete, east on several tenements
> of said Lord Tyneham in occs. of John Collyer,
> George Nicholls, [blank] Hunte and [blank]; south on
> the garden of the Rt Hon. Philip, Earl of Arundel
> and west on a tenement now called the *Blewe Lyon*
> in the occ. of Henry Batten, esq. and the stables
> belonging to the *Talbott Inn*

The premises are leased together with some contents (schedule
attached signed by Teynham) for 21 years at 6s. 8d. annual
rent

Witnesses: George Lawley, Christopher Hopper, James
          Monington, Richard Hayes

MXD36-38   Bargain and sale, quitclaim and appointment   **26 May 1623**

Christopher Rooper, Lord Teynham (as above), George Lawley of the New Inn, co. Middx, gentleman and William Collyns of Lynsted, co. Kent, gentleman

> Five several messuages in the Strond, with their cellars, sollars, backsides, gardens, yards, passages, ways, lights, easements, profits and commodities, in the respective occs. of Charles Spence, upholsterer, John Collyer, tailor, George Nicholls, John Hunte and John Kempe

Lord Teynham sells to Lawley, for *a certen competent somme of money*, and quitclaims his interest in the premises. Lawley appoints William Collyns as his attorney to accept livery of seisin.

Armorial seals of both parties, but Teynham's is fragmentary. 3 docs.

MXD39   Assignment of lease   **28 Mar. 1625**

Sir Henry Batten and Dame Susan his wife to Charles Spence, 'upholster' [*sic*]

> messuage of 20 rooms as in **MXD35** above with the garden, backside, wainscott and goods

Recites lease for 20 years 11 months and 20 days made on 26 March 1619 by William Roper to Charles Spence. The Battens, who are in possession of the *reversion and inheritance* of the premises, assign to Spence the remainder of the term, at £8 annual rent.

Room by room schedule of fixtures and fittings.
Signature and small seal of Charles Spence.

Roper family properties: Gunstock Alley, Strand, 1623-1657

MXD40   Lease   **16 Aug. 1623**

Reynold Beyneon, bricklayer to George Puckford, cordwainer, both of St Clement Danes

> messuage containing 4 rooms and a yard being one of two new brick tenements lately built *and set up*

backwards in a certain alley called Gunstock Alley;
abutting west on the garden of Charles Spence, east
on the alley or yard called Lynes Alley, north on
the other new tenement, and south on a back lane
leading into Strand Lane; together, in common with
the other 'tenants backwards' of the said Beyneon,
with use *of the house of office there made and built
backward*

Recites that Beyneon holds the premises by virtue of a long
lease granted to him by Lord Teyneham on 20 October 1621.
The new property is now leased to Puckford for 21 years at £8
annual rent with covenants for sharing costs of repairing the
pavement in the street in front of the said alley and of sharing
reponsibility for cleansing, scouring and repairing the 'house
of office' and *the sincke, watercourse or channell made for the
conveing away of the foule water* from the tenements of said
Beyneon.

Witnesses: John Snowe, Charles Spence, John Browne 'scr'
and Thomas Ashby his servant
Seal: impresssion of a ?dolphin

MXD41-42   Bargain and sale   **17 Feb. 1625**

Sir John Roper, knight, Lord Tenham, Baron of Tenham,
William Roper, esq., his brother and William Collins of
Linstead, Kent, gentleman to Sir Henry Batten of St Clement
Danes, knight and Dame Susan his wife

Seven messuages and one alley called Gunstock
Alley with all their appurts. (occs. given); lying in
the Strond, abutting north to the street, west on
the messuage of Sir Henry Batten and the stables
of the *Talbot Inn* now in the occ. of William Blunt;
south upon the wall of the garden of the Earl of
Arundel and east on a messuage now in the occ. of
John Snowe and other tenements behind the same
called Lynes Yard

Sir Henry and Dame Susan Batten purchase the premises for
£1,150. A copy final concord is attached.   2 docs.

MXD43   Lease   **28 Mar. 1625**

Sir Henry Batten of St Clement Danes, knight and Dame Susan
his wife to Charles Spence, upholsterer

messuage of 20 rooms as in **MXD35** above, now in the occ. of the lessee; abuttals as in 35 above, except east now in the several occs. of Anthony Franckford, Thomas Wotton, William Creed, George Nicholls, John Puckford and Thomas Shrubb

Lessee shall keep the messuage in good repair with tiling, glazing and walling, keep the courtyard or backside paved and cleanse, empty and scour the privy house *as need shall require*; licence required to sublet to any smith, pewterer, or *handye tradesman that useth to forge with the hammer or without*. By this deed the premises are let for 15 years at £40 per year, but another lease of same date is cited whereby they are let for £8, total £48 a year.

Witnesses: Lewis Dyne, John Brown, George Johnson
Signature   *Charles Spence*   **Seal**:   absent

MXD44-48   Lease for 99 years and release   **Mar. 1646**

Richard Powell of St James, Clerkenwell, esq., and Dame Susan, late the wife of Sir Henry Batten, deceased (and now wife of said Powell); Henry Batten of St Clement Danes, gentleman and Charles Spence of same parish, upholsterer

seven messuages and an alley called Gunstock Alley abutting west upon the dwelling house of John Gorste, citizen and merchant tailor of London and upon the stables of the *Talbot Inn* in the occ. of Anthony Berkeley, innkeeper; south on the garden wall of the Earl of Arundel and Surrey; east on houses in the occ. of William Raven, sempster and John Baker, tailor and various small tenements and grounds called Lynes Alley

The transaction forms a marriage settlement whereby the premises are granted to Batten and Spence in trust to attend the marriage of Susan Batten and Richard Powell and, after the marriage has taken place, released again to the use of Richard and Susan Powell and the heirs of Richard Powell.

MXD45 has a reasonable example of Powell's seal, with crest.

Includes two final concords and one copy of same. 5 docs.

MXD49   Lease for 15 years at £8 annual rent   **10 Mar. 1657**

Henry Batten, gentleman to Robert Tooms, tailor

> messuage in an alley formerly called Gunstock Alley
> but since Green Dragon Alley and now *The Angell*
> and Sun Alley, containing a cellar and three rooms
> above it, one above another, with a garden and
> backside on the south; formerly in the occ. of John
> Hall, now of the lessee; with free access to and from
> the premises by the said alley but reserving to the
> lessor access with carriages, ladder, timber, bricks
> etc. by and through the common way lying under
> the east side of certain rooms hereby demised and
> through the east side of the yard; and with liberty
> for Batten to enlarge the stoole room or house of
> office, used in common by all the tenants there, by
> 6 inches all round

House in the Strand: the *Golden Lion*, 1667-1672

MXD50   Lease for seven years   **9 Jan. 1667**

Thomas Stagg, distiller to Richard Spence, upholster [*sic*]

> messuage in the Strand called by the sign of the
> *Golden Lion and Lamb*, containing two cellars, one
> shop with a parlour and kitchen behind the same,
> 8 chambers, 5 closetts and 3 garrets, with all ways
> and other easements

Stagg leases to Spence, existing occupier of the premises, for
seven years at £36 annual rent.

MXD51-53   Final concords (two copies) and receipt   **Nov. 1666**
                                                                  -Feb 1667

Concerning the sale of a messuage by Hugh Dalton and
Elizabeth his wife to Thomas Stagg, distiller and Hannah his
wife; and sale by Stagg to the Hon. Henry Howard of Norfolk
for £720.   3 docs.

MXD54   Surrender of lease   **14 Jan. 1672**

Thomas Stagg of St Martins, vintrey, London, distiller to
Thomas West, gentleman [the Duke's agent]

> messuage called the *Lyon and Lamb* in the Strand,
> lately in the occ. of Richard Spence, upholster [*sic*]

and one shop on the east side of the shop belonging to the said messuage; the adjoining shop being in the occ. of William Smith, goldsmith; another messuage, in the occ. of Walter Chadley, with a yard part paved with freestone, lying backwards on the south side of the first messuage and abuts west on stables of the *Talbot Inn*; and a garden plot 24 feet in width east to west by 140 feet in depth north to south, lying at the back of Walter Chadley's house and having a house of office at the NE corner; the garden enclosed with pales at the south end, having a door in the pales from which steps go down to a passage way leading to Strand Bridge Lane

Recites that on 21 March 1667 Henry Howard (later 6th Duke) leased the premises to Stagg for 7 years at £52 annual rent. Stagg now surrenders the lease back to the Duke's agent together with the relevant documents which include a sub-lease [not present] from Lady Day 1667 of the shop, backhouse and garden to William Harwarr, goldsmith.

Unspecified premises, 1637-1639

MXD55	Exemplification of a common recovery by	17 Feb. 1637

Sir Thomas Penruddock, knight *v.* Thomas Manning, gentleman; Edward Howse as vouchee

    messuage, garden and 5½ perches of land in St Clement Danes

Great seal absent

MXD56	Final concord	Nov. 1639

Nicholas Crowne and Edward Jones, plaintiffs, *v.* John Hawkins and Rachel his wife, defendants, re

    three messuages and appurts. in St Clement Danes

Houses in Milford Lane, 1630-1688

MXD57-59	Bargain and sale and final concord	4 Nov. 1630

William Kinge, citizen and merchant tailor of London and Judith his wife to John Blitheman of Chawton in co. Hants., Bachelor of Divinity and Mary his wife three messuages in Milford Lane with all their shops, cellars, gardens, etc.; in the respective occs. of William Bridge, salter, William Ball, waterman and Martha Beck, widow, all abutting east on the said lane and their gardens and backsides abut west onto Arundel House; north on the dwelling house of Doctor Bates and south on the dwelling house of Margery Michell

The Kinges sell to the Blithemans and their heirs for £484. Two copies of final concords in Martinmas fortnight (November), 1630 are attached.   3 docs.

MXD60-61   Lease for 31 years at £11 annual rent   **6 Nov. 1639**

Mathias Bennett of St Saviours, Southwark, gentleman to Thomas Knowlis, citizen and linen draper of London

two messuages formerly erected by one Alphonsus Fowle, deceased, in Milford Lane, abutting south on the parsonage garden and yard, an alley leading into a court or yard on the north, east on Milford Lane and west on the said yard and on messuages formerly belonging to one Mr Bobbett

For a down payment of £200, Bennett leases to Knowlis. Signature of Bennett and seal with small impression; and receipt by Reginald Morgan for £105 of this purchase money paid to him by Knowlis to clear a former debt on Mathias Bennett's account.   2 docs.

MXD62-63   Lease and counterpart   **7 Apr. 1653**

William Pease, citizen and merchant tailor of London to Elizabeth Uryn, widow

messuage containing six rooms and three other little rooms or closets, with a yard and house of office, fenced in with pales on the south side and a brick wall on the north side; being on the south side of an alley called Balls Alley in Milford Lane, formerly in the occ. of Edward Mathews, waterman and now of Kathryn Wallupe. widow and said Elizabeth Uryn

In return for a single payment of £8, Pease leases to Uryn for 21 years at £7 annual rent.   2 docs.

MXD64 Lease for 21 years at £13 annual rent **3 Jan. 1654**

William Pease, as above, to Stephen Baker, tailor

> messuage with one stone yard behind the same and
> a low room or kitchen at the end of the yard and one
> piece of ground or garden plot behind the kitchen,
> as the same is now fenced about, and one house of
> office at the end of the garden; with all appurts.,
> ways and easements (etc.)

Additional undertaking by the lessee is endorsed, that he will
deliver to William Pease at his house at Long Acre in St Martin
in the Fields ... *on* [one] *fatt and seasonable Turkey bird at the
feast of Christmas* ...

MXD65-67 Leases of the *Greyhound* **Apr.-Jul. 1667**

Lease, 2 April 1667, by Thomas Hollier of St Giles in the Fields,
surgeon to John Mills, victualler

> messuage known by the sign of the *Grayhound* in
> Milford lane abutting north on a tenement of John
> Henslar, south on a tenement of Edward [*sic*, see
> below] Girling, west on premises of [blank] Morting
> and east on Milford Lane; having one cellar, one
> shop and kitchen behind the same; four chambers,
> two garrets above the shop and kitchen, one yard
> behind the kitchen; and the Drinking Room and
> house of office therein built; with all lights, ways,
> easements, etc.

For a payment of £15 Hollier leases to Mills for 11 years at
£22 a year. On 13 April Mills sublets to John Burgesse, coal
merchant for 10½ years at the same rent; and in July of the same
year Hollier, in return for a payment of £10, leases directly to
Burgesse as from Lady Day 1678 at the same rent for a further
11 years.
Flourishing scriveners' signatures endorsed as witnesses,
Stanislaus Bowes and John Ramsey. 3 docs.

MXD68 Lease for 21 years **24 Jun. 1671**

Thomas Hollier, as in **MXD65-67** above, to Edmund Girling,
merchant

> messuage in Milford Lane, with the little court or
> passage way leading into the same out of Milford

Lane, and all outhousing and garden plot on the west and south, and with all ways, watercourses, easements (etc.)

In return for interior decorating (no details) done by Girling, Hollier leases to him at £20 annual rent for the first three years and £30 for the remainder of the term.
The name of Edward Meakins, a witness, is endorsed with a print stamp.

MXD69 Lease for seven years at £25 annual rent **17 Sep. 1688**

Charles Prior of Highgate, Middlesex, esq. and Mary his wife to Thomas Harding, joiner

messuage with appurts. in Millford Lane in the occ. of Edward Mason and Mary Girling, abutting north on Mrs King and south on Mr Darnell

Properties of Nevinson Fox in Strand and Milford Lane, 1662-1672
NB: *Nevinson Fox's properties continue after 1680 as* **MXD156-171** *below.*

MXD70 Assignment of remainder of 99-year lease **6 Nov. 1662**

Joshua Collin, citizen and grocer of London, administrator of the goods of Mary Younge, late of the Covent Garden, widow, deceased to Henry Dickon of St Martin in the Fields, cordwainer and William Pease, citizen and merchant tailor of London

Messuage with the appurts. in Milford Lane in the occ. (in 1647) of Tobias Urin

Recites mortgage for £30, 25 June 1647, by Mary Blithman of Covent Garden, widow and Robert Blithman of Eversley, co. Hants to Collin on condition that they repaid this sum to Mary Younge. When the sum was not repaid Collin got possession. He now assigns the remainder of the lease to Pease and Dickon for a payment of £47.

MXD71-75 Bargain and sale and conveyance (lease and release) **8-30 Nov. 1669**

Hugh Batten of Bradford, co. Wilts., plumber to Nathaniel Fox, of Stradbrooke, co. Suff., gentleman

messuage in The Strand near Arundell Howse, in the occ. of William Brooks; and five messuages abutting north upon it, lying backwards from the street, within an alley called Gunstock Alley, on the east side thereof, in the several occs. of Robert Tombes, William Smyth, Elizabeth Hill, Thomas Whitehurst and Mary Johnson; the premises all being under a current lease to Thomas Stagge and were by deed of 17 February 1625 conveyed by Roper to Batten [as above]. Subject to the various leases to the lessee and the under-tenants [details given] the premises are conveyed to Fox for £900

Final concord (two copies) are appended.   5 docs.

MXD76   Declaration (deed poll)   **9 Jun. 1672**

Revocation of the terms of a ducal lease for 59 years, dated 22 June 1669, to Simon Fox of St Clement Danes, esq., relating to the house in which Fox now dwells.

MXD77-79   Conveyance (lease and release) for £400   **10-11 Oct. 1672**

William Pease, as above, to Nevinson Fox, gentleman

messuage and appurts. late in the occ. of John Meecke, gentleman, now of Roger Ives; messuage and appurts. late in the occ. of Elizabeth Euryn, widow, now of John Skynner; messuage and appurts. late in the occ. of Stephen Baker, deceased, now of Stephen Baker his son

With two copies of final concords, morrow of All Saints 1672, to confirm the transaction.

MXD79 has a seal with impression of Pease's arms.
4 docs.

MXD80   Exemplification of a final concord   **28 Nov. 1672**

Thomas Barker, gentleman against Nevinson Foxe, gentleman, as to

3 messuages and appurts. in St Clement Danes

With a note that seisin was granted to Barker 4 Dec. 1672

2. STRAND ESTATE
THE FIRST PHASE OF DEVELOPMENT, 1672-1701

i. Introduction

The creation of an estate of rental properties from the site and grounds of the former residence of the Fitzalan and Howard families was made possible in the first instance by Act of Parliament of 22-23 Charles II (1670-71). Entitled *An Act for Building Arundell House and tenements thereunto belonging ...*, it first removed the restraints of the 1627 Settlement (relating to the lordships and baronies of Arundel, Fitzalan, Clun and Oswestry which prevented any of the premises annexed to the Earldom of Arundel (including the London property Arundel House) from being leased or sold. The preamble of the 1671 Act acknowledged that the Duke of Norfolk had urgent need to improve his revenues, while observing that Arundel House itself was *now in decay and very ruinous.* The prospective development of the grounds would enable the Duke either to restore the old house itself or to build it anew to a standard suitable to the dignity of his status. The Right Hon. Henry Marquis of Worcester and Arthur Onslow of West Clandon, Surrey, esq., the Guardians of the 5th Duke of Norfolk, were appointed as two of the trustees, with Henry Howard as a third party, all jointly responsible for putting the plans into effect.

The petition for the Act was not submitted by Thomas, 5th Duke of Norfolk, for he was living in Padua and of uncertain mental state. Instead it was his younger brother Henry Howard who had applied, the burden of restoring the family fortunes being on his shoulders. His position was acknowledged by the King who in 1669 had created him Baron of Castle Rising and, in 1672, Earl of Norwich. Barring periods of attainder, the office of Earl Marshal had been held by earlier members of his family. In 1672 the King confirmed this to Henry and to his heirs as an hereditary right. These various titles are referred to in the first phase of development of the estate. Under their new powers, on 18 March 1672, the trustees Worcester and Onslow conveyed to him Arundel House and its grounds for a term of 60 years from the passing of the Act, for the purpose of making leases within that term. The old houses in the Strand, known as 'Arundel Rents', were to be leased for terms of up to 21 years from 1665.

The building contracts in subsection iv below, as well as the earliest leases themselves, show that the new plots had been measured out by 1676 and that construction work was then beginning. The potential of the site had been enhanced by the acquisition of a run of newly reclaimed river frontage, which was immediately incorporated into the overall scheme. With the benefit of river views, it later accommodated some of the best properties on the entire estate.

Henry succeeded to the dukedom on the death of his elder brother in 1677 and he held it until his death in 1684. His son and heir, also Henry, continued to develop the estate until his own death in 1701. He achieved this mainly by obtaining a new Act of Parliament in 1689-90 (1 William and Mary). The new Act aimed to extend the rental premises over *the remaining part of Arundel Ground* which the text stated, *lyeth in wast*. £480 a year had been reserved from the new rents, in order to rebuild a new residence, fitting for the status of the family. However, much of this sum had unfortunately been *swallowed up*, as the preamble graphically affirmed, in the construction of Surrey Street. New powers were thus needed, and were duly obtained; and the core of the estate was subsequently developed as Norfolk Street and Howard Street, on the footprint of the formerly intended mansion.

In Section 9 below there is a large copy deed (**MXD1344**) containing 17 folios relating to the development of the Essex House site (adjacent to Arundel House) and other premises in the city of London and Middlesex 1683-1700. It was perhaps acquired by the Duke's agents during this period for comparative purposes.

Sections 2-8 of this catalogue follow the estate development from the 1670s to the early 20th century. Readers are referred to the Contents page of this catalogue to see the overall scheme of organisation of the material. The earliest phase of new building was under way by the late 1670s as shown, for instance, by **MXD205-231** and the building contracts in subsection iv. The lion's share is occupied by the leases themselves, with a small amount at the beginning of each section representing acquisitions and appointments made by the various dukes; and at the end of each section, tenants' purchases and sublets, and agents' papers where they have survived alongside the leases.

The leases themselves are organised in the same order in each section throughout this catalogue starting with Strand, then west to east – Surrey Street and Strand Lane, Norfolk Street with Howard Street, Arundel Street and finally Water Street and Milford Lane.

ii. Acquisition

MXD81   Lease for 30 years   **16 Aug. 1687**

Anthony Plomer of Parsons Green, co. Middx, merchant
tailor to Henry, 6th Duke of Norfolk

> two small parcels of ground now taken in and made
> into a shed (6ft 3in east/west x 4ft 11in north/south)
> and a yard (6ft 4in east/west x 2ft 8in north/south),
> between two messuages, one called the *Maidenhead*,
> in possession of Thomas Potter, periwig maker and
> the other being a coffee house in the possession
> of Henry Clinch

For a down payment of 5 shillings Plomer leases to the Duke
at a peppercorn rent; with covenants to protect the signage
of the coffee house, its ancient lights and its water supply.

iii. Trusts and appointments

MXD82-83   Assignments by trustees to trustee   **18 Mar. 1672**

The Right Hon. Henry, Lord Marquis of Worcester and
Arthur Onslow of West Clandon, Surrey, esq., guardians of
the body and the estate of the Most Noble Thomas, Duke of
Norfolk to Henry, Lord Howard, Baron Howard of Castle
Rising

> i) capital messuage called Arundell House and all
> the ground it stands on and all buildings, gardens,
> backsides, wharves, ways and easements (except one
> parcel of ground now staked out and delineated
> for erecting a capital messuage and a garden) the
> west side of which (which is about 193 feet from
> Somerset House garden wall) is 151 feet in length
> and the east side, towards Milford Lane, is also
> 151 feet; the south side towards the River Thames
> is 171 feet and the north side towards The Strand
> is also 171 feet

ii) all the messuages, tenements and their grounds commonly known as Arundel Rents

Reciting the Act of Parliament of 22-23 Charles II authorising the redevelopment of the site, Arundel House and grounds are assigned to Howard as trustee at a nominal £5 rent; Arundel rents (presumably from the other pre-existing buildings along the Strand) are also assigned (by a separate deed) to Howard as trustee who is to render £400 in rental value each year to the Duke's trustees.

2 docs., each with signatures of Worcester and Onslow

MXD84   Contemporary copy of the above deed on 4 paper folios.

MXD85   Assignment to trustees   **18 Apr. 1673**

The Rt Hon. Henry, Earl of Norwich, Earl Marshal of England to Thomas Dalmahoy of Guildford, esq. and Thomas West of St Clement Danes, Middx, gentleman

> The capital messuage called Arundell House with all its grounds, gardens, buildings, wharves, etc., together with the messuages, tenements, courtyards, gardens, etc. known as Arundel rents

Recites deed of 18 March 1672 in which the Marquis of Worcester and the other trustees of **MXD82-83** above assigned the premises to the Earl of Norwich for 60 years. The Earl now assigns the remainder of that term to Messrs. Dalmahoy and West to the use of himself.

MXD86   Appointment of attorneys   **20 Sep. 1676**

Henry, Earl of Norwich, Earl Marshal appoints Francis Burghill, William Wind, John Wright and Richard Marriott, esqs., and Jonathan Wilcox, gentleman as his agents in the development of

> a piece of land 40 feet in depth north to south, taken from the soil of the River Thames next adjoining the wall of Arundel House, extending in breadth all along the wall east to west from Milford Lane to Strand Bridge

Recites the Parliamentary Act and that His Majesty *hath since been gratiously pleased* to grant the Earl this extra piece of land which the Earl wishes to include in the developments. The Earl now empowers his attorneys to draw up leases of not more than 40 years duration.
Signed 'Marshall'.

MXD87   Agreement   **1 Jun. 1678**

The Right Noble Henry, Duke of Norfolk, with his agents Messrs. Dalmahoy and West, and Henry Hall of Harding Court, co. Oxon.

> i) a parcel of garden ground, south of the messuage in occ. of John Barton, in which there is *a lyne now digged and stakt out extending from north to south 52ft 6 inches in length and then turning east to west and extending 27ft 8 inches in breadth*
> ii) messuages in occs. of James Swan, William Henshaw, George Jenkins, Henry Brockwen, Walter Challoner and John Burton, parcel of Angel Court

Reciting a dispute between Hall and the Duke as to the boundaries of their gardens the parties agree that the line as staked out in i) will be the agreed boundary and that the Duke will build a brick wall on within 20 days; that he will maintain it and that Hall may *have liberty to plant wall fruit trees...and to naile and penn the same upp against the said wall*. The Duke also releases to Hall any claim he might have had to any ground within the new wall or to any part of ii). **Plan** showing Hall's garden north and west of the Duke's land.

MXD88   Appointment by deed poll   **25 Feb. 1679**

Henry, Duke of Norfolk and Earl Marshal appoints his servant Charles Mawson as agent in the drawing up of leases in Norfolk Buildings or in Arundel Rents.
Signed, 'Norfolke and Marshall'

MXD89-90   Assignment to trustees and quitclaim   **1680, 1683**

The Most Noble Henry, Duke of Norfolk, Earl Marshal, Henry, Earl of Arundel, Lord Mowbray, eldest son of the Duke, Thomas Dalmahoy of Guildford, esq. and Thomas West of St Clement Danes, gentleman, Francis Howard of Bookham, Surrey, esq., Paul Ricout of St Martin in the Fields, esq., and Cuthbert Browne of Hansworth, co. Yorks., clerk

> Various premises in Arundel Buildings (see schedules below)

On 24 Nov. 1680 (**MXD89**), pursuant to an agreement of 20 November, the Duke and his agents, Messrs Dalmahoy and West, assign to the other parties £508 3s. in Arundel rents, for the remainder of the original 60-year term of the development: in trust for the Duke for life, with remainder to the Earl and to their succession; without prejudice to pre-existing tenancy agreements; and specifically in trust for a new capital messuage to be built for the Duke.

3 schedules, marked A, B and C are appended on five membranes:

A, leases to attend the Duke's inheritance (houses fronting the Strand); B, in trust for the building of Norfolk House (houses in all streets of the development); C, ground rents sold for the term by the Duke during the builders' leases; and annuity to John Forshee, gentleman for life.
On 5 Nov. 1683 (**MXD90**) Francis Howard, described as Lord Howard, Baron of Effingham, quitclaims his interest in the premises to the other two trustees.   2 docs.

MXD91   Appointment of attorney   **25 Apr. 1684**

Paul Rycaut of St Martin in the Fields, esq., and Cuthbert Browne of Handsworth, co. York, the 6th Duke's trustees, appoint Charles Mawson of St Clement Danes, gentleman, as their attorney for rent collection on the Duke's behalf in both the Arundel Buildings and the Arundel Rents sections of the Strand Estate.

MXD92   Articles of agreement   **31 May 1688**

Simon and Nevinson Fox, esqs. agree with Lord Thomas Howard of Worksop as trustee for Henry, Duke of Norfolk, that they will open and widen:

the street called Surrey Street at the upper end by
The Strand by running a straight line from the
upper end of a house already built or being built
by Messrs. Fox on the east side of the street to the
upper corner of a house belonging to Henry Hall
*next the greate street commonly called The Strand
... and thereby to make the streete as large as the
Ground Unbuilt or the Ground of a place commonly
called Green Dragon Alley*

In return for a payment of £1,000 Messrs Fox agree to do
this work and to finish off with a brick wall opposite Daniel
Sunderland's house and to pave the area.

MXD93   Bond in £10 for return of livery   **3 May 1690**

John Howard, recently appointed waterman, agrees with the
Duke to return, upon request, his livery coat with the silver
plate buttons and a badge of silver on the sleeve *of considerable
value,* displaying *a horse passant with an oake branch in his mouth
and other ensignes of his Graces armes.*

MXD94-95   Unexecuted assignment to new trustee   **1 Oct. 1696**

The intention was to assign Sir Paul Rycaut's trusteeship to
the Rt Hon. Henry Howard, commonly called Lord Walden,
eldest son and heir of the Rt Hon. Henry, Earl of Suffolk; but
only the Duke signed; and a note says that the deed was not
executed by Sir Paul Rycaut *by reason that alteration was therein
made as to that trust by His Grace the Duke of Norfolk.*

MXD96-97   Assignment (2 copies) to new trustees   **4 Aug. 1697**

Henry, Duke of Norfolk, Earl Marshal, Knight of the Garter,
one of the lords of His Majesty's Privy Council and Sir Paul
Rycaut, Knight Resident for His Majesty *at Hamborough*
[Hamburg], The Rt Hon. Charles, Earl of Carlisle, the Rt Hon.
Henry, Lord Walden, William Longueville of the Inner Temple,
esq. and Miles Philipson of the Inner Temple, gentleman

Citing previous trusts, the Duke and Rycaut assign the
trusteeship to the other parties for the remainder of the several
60-year terms.   2 docs.

iv. Norfolk Buildings: building contracts and papers

NB: For further contracts 1689, see ACA MD2580 (23 docs.)

The building contracts of 26 October 1676 relate to the buildings that were to be erected on new measured plots, to be known as 'Norfolk Buildings' (as opposed to 'Arundel Rents' which were the pre-existing houses on the estate). They were all drawn up between Henry, Earl of Norwich, the head of the family, and the lessees of individual plots. All contracts except **MXD129** below were negotiated directly with the Earl of Norwich.

The Earl agreed to clear away all remaining buildings of old Arundel House by 1 March next. The contractors agreed to erect brick-built houses which conform to the requirements of the recent Act for the Rebuilding of the City of London. Architectural style and/or dimensions are specified as to balconies, cornices, windows, joists, party walls, etc. For example, ...*That all Mantle Trees* [mantelpieces] *shalbe of good oake and not lesse than seven and nine inches.* Shop fronts were not allowed. The lessee was to contribute to the costs of the common sewer and was to pay for all drains connecting into it and then to level and pave outside with good Purbeck or Swindon stone. There was also provision for kennels outside and a covenant as to removal of household rubbish.

The Earl undertook to pave all parts of Arundel Ground that are still in his ownership, and to set out the new streets by 1 March next except the cross street, Howard Street, which he will set out by 26 March 1679. He was also to take in the reclaimed land by the river which he recently obtained by grant of the King, and to make *commodious and good staires* down to the River at the end of Arundel Street and Surrey Street. The contractors were to be completely finished by Lady Day 1678, after which the Earl would grant them each a proper lease for 41 years.

As from 1689 a new clause was added to some of the contracts preventing the contractors from providing a coach house or stabling to any house they build. Presumably the Duke wanted to retain the monopoly on coach house leases in the estate after he had developed part of Water Street for that purpose.

Many of these contracts are in a tatty condition, being on paper rather than parchment. Except where indicated these are the contractors' counterparts, containing their signatures. As elsewhere in this catalogue, parties' parish of residence is only stated if it is not St Clement Danes.

MXD101-129   Contracts for the development of new house plots, viz: **1676-1681**

Surrey Street west

MXD101-102   The Hon. Charles Howard, esquire: 60 x 40ft plot   **26 Oct. 1676**
newly reclaimed from the River Thames

MXD103   – another copy of the same

MXD104   Cornelius Lilley, victualler : 20 x 60ft plot

MXD105   John Toomes, gentleman: 20 x 40ft plot

MXD106   John Wright, esq.: 24 x 70ft plot

Arundel Street, east   **26 Oct. 1676**

MXD107   William Blackwell, carpenter: 20 x 55ft plot.

Earl's signature and seal. Endorsed with Blackwell's assignment
to John Christmas of Southfleete, Kent, gent.,   **27 Nov. 1677**

MXD108   William Blackwell, carpenter: 32 x 50ft plot

MXD109   Cornelius Lilly, coachman: 30 x [blank] ft plot stretching
east to Water Street. Seal with impression.

MXD110   Edward Pearce: frontage of 20ft plus 40ft taken
out of the Thames, extending east to Water Street

MXD111   Jonathan Wilcox, carpenter: north end of Arundel
Street, 20ft frontage to the Strand x 60ft in depth

MXD112   Jonathan Wilcox, carpenter: 48ft frontage x 30ft in depth

Arundel Street, west   **26 Oct. 1676**

MXD113   John Gumley, citizen and haberdasher of London:
14 x 32ft plot. Endorsed with permission for the Earl to make
a drain through the premises.

Water Street, east   **26 Oct. 1676**

MXD114   John Sims of London, joiner: plot with 60ft frontage plus
a further 40 feet taken out of the River Thames, extending
eastwards to the limits of the Earl's property; reserving to
the Earl a passage way for carting dung from the stables to
the River Thames

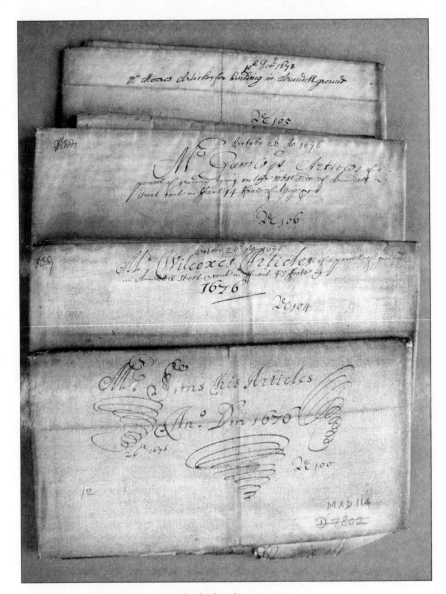

Fig. 4   Articles of agreement for developing the new estate.
Contracts to build the new estate were granted to those individuals whose financial backing or professional craftsmanship would ensure that the new houses conformed to the high standards laid down by Parliament in the aftermath of the Great Fire of London. It is noticeable how many citizens and guild members of the city of London invested in the new development. (Ref. **MXD112-115.**)

Norfolk Street, east   **20 Feb.-10 Dec. 1678**

MXD115   George Moore, gentleman: 20 x 50ft plot

MXD116   George Moore of Albury, Surrey, gentleman:
            37 x 70ft plot

Surrey Street, east   **7 Aug. 1679**

MXD117   William Blackwell, carpenter: plot 97 feet (frontage) x 50 feet
            in depth: to include the construction of a passage 6 feet wide
            by 10 feet in height giving access from Surrey Street into the
            Duke's intended new mansion. Agreement signed by Jonathan
            Wilcox of St Martin in the Fields, carpenter, an attorney for
            the Duke in the letting of Arundel Ground

Norfolk Street, east   **9 Aug. 1689**

MXD118   Robert Powell, plasterer: 20 x 70ft plot

MXD119   John Green of Newington Green, Middx, carpenter:
            20 x 70ft plot

MXD120   John Cheshire, locksmith: 20 x 70ft plot

MXD121   John Tompson of St James, Westminster, mason:
            40 x 70ft plot

Norfolk Street, west   **9 Aug. 1689**

MXD122   Humphrey Bradshaw, gentleman: 60 feet (frontage)
            x 70 feet in depth

MXD123   Charles Johnson, bricklayer: 20 x 70ft plot

MXD124   Charles Beasly, bricklayer: 20 x 70ft plot

MXD125   John Shorter, esq.: 20 x 70ft plot

MXD126   James Brown, tailor: 20 x 70ft plot

MXD127   John Thompson of St James, Westminster, mason:
               46 x 70ft plot

MXD128   Richard Biddle, bricklayer: 22 x 70ft plot

Arundel Street, west   **24 Mar. 1681**

MXD129   Francis Howard of Bookham, Surrey, esq., Paul Rycaut of
               St Martin in the Fields, Middx, esq., and Cuthbert Browne
               of York, clerk, the Duke's trustees, with Edward Bird, citizen
               and painter stainer of London

                              plot at the south end of the street with a 21ft frontage,
                              together with a plot of 40ft depth lately taken out
                              of the River Thames; the two having a combined
                              frontage of 53 feet and extending in depth to the
                              wall of the Duke's ground for his intended capital
                              messuage

MXD130   Draft articles of agreement (unexecuted) to set up a lime kiln   **24 Aug. 1691**

               Charles Howard, esq. and Robert Cable of Penrice in Cornwall,
               mariner

               Howard agrees to set up and equip a *kiln and limehouse* on
               some suitable wharf near the City of London in which Cable
               should produce lime and render to Howard due account of
               his produce, sales and dealings. Interesting details despite
               rough text.

v. *Block leases to agents*

Various agents and contractors were used to get the new building under way. In 1673, Henry Howard assigned the Arundel House estate to Thomas Dalmahoy of Guildford, Surrey, esq., and Thomas West of St Clement Danes, gentleman, as the first step towards putting the project into effect (**MXD85**). They were to hold it for 60 years, to the sole use of the Earl, in effect, to do the routine work of negotiating leases. Developers were attracted by peppercorn rents for the first year of building, followed by very reasonable rents for the remainder of the 60-year term. This enabled them, on completion of the work, to sell the lease on for a capital sum, plus the ongoing annual ground rent. Section 3 below, *Londoners' tenancies*, contains further details as to how things proceeded.

An important element in the scheme seems to be the 'Arundel rents' – the rental income from the pre-existing properties along the Strand. These were able to accrue for a few years before building started. They perhaps financed the purchase of the reclaimed river frontage, about which there are no details in this archive. It appears as a 'fait accompli' in 1676 when its development was put in the hands of Francis Burghill, William Wind, John Wright and Richard Marriott (later the Duke's surveyor and accountant), esqs. (**MXD86**).

Some of the 'Arundel rents' were later sold 'en bloc' to Nevinson Fox (**MXD157-161** below). Other persons, such as John East in 1679, a City of London goldsmith (**MXD131**) might fund the development with a large cash sum, and receive a block of leaseholds for their pains. In the later years of this first phase of building, there seems to have been no shortage of rich citizens of London coming forward with their money. In the wake of the Great Fire, the interest in this project must have been considerable. The contractors themselves were mainly skilled craftsmen, the majority being carpenters and joiners. The 6th Duke's younger brother Charles gained a raft of properties in three of the new streets, retaining one, in Surrey Street as a family residence. Charles Mawson, a ducal agent, had a similar package together with further premises in the old 'Arundel rents'.

There is much repetitive verbiage in the leases including lengthy recitals of the terms of the 1627 and the 1672 Acts. None of this has been reproduced in this catalogue. In the subsection that follows and in all subsequent sections merely the essence of each transaction is noted. The property descriptions are, however, as full and accurate as possible, barring, again, repetitive phrases and outdated language; and, as before, a person's parish of residence is only cited if it is NOT St Clement Danes.

Agents Messrs. Dalmahoy and West

MXD131   Assignments of rents   **15 Apr. 1679**

a) Henry, Duke of Norfolk and   b) Messrs. Dalmahoy and
West to   c) John East, citizen and goldsmith of London
rents on:

> i) parcel of ground begun to be built by Jeremy
> Coney, citizen and plumber of London lying on
> the east side of Arundell Street having a frontage
> of 17 feet 17 inches; with a depth of 43 feet east
> to west, abutting north on Water Street
> ii) parcel of ground on the west of Surrey Street
> in Arundel Buildings lying on the west of Surrey
> Street having a frontage of 38 feet, abutting west
> on Strand Bridge Lane
> iii) parcel of ground begun to be built on the back
> side (west) of Surrey Street, 18 feet in depth, with
> a frontage of 20 feet to Strand Bridge Lane
> iv) messuage lately erected by John Prince, and
> ground on the west of Norfolk Street in Norfolk
> Buildings, having a frontage of 20 feet, a depth
> of 36 feet and a yard of 11 feet long containing
> a house of office at the west end of the yard and
> *one stacke of closetts over the said yarde* 8½ feet
> long by 7 feet wide, abutting west on Norfolk
> Street. Names of occupants and adjoining owners
> are given

Recites an assignment by the Duke to b) of the rents issuing
from the above premises on 18 April 1673 for a 60-year term.
Now for a single payment of £762 by East, the Duke assigns
to him the same rents, for the residue of the term.

MXD132   Confirmation   **16 Dec. 1680**

The 6th Duke and Henry his son, Earl of Arundel, to
John Stone of New Inn, Middx, gentleman, Charles Daw
of Langley Marsh, co. Bucks., gentleman, John East and
John Coggs, citizens and goldsmiths of London and William
Melmoth of St Sepulchres, London, apothecary

Reciting the original assignment to Messrs Dalmahoy
and West on 18 April 1673 and a subsequent agreement
on 20 November 1680, the Earl of Arundel now ratifies
the original assignment and confirms to the other parties

full possession of specific rents (as set out in an attached schedule) that they have been assigned by Messrs Dalmahoy and West.

Agent Charles Howard, esquire

MXD133-134 Assignment of remainder of lease term   **18 Jan. 1678**

The 6th Duke of Norfolk and his agents, Messrs Dalmahoy and West, to the Hon. Charles Howard, his brother

> Parcel of ground begun to be built on by the lessee, on the west side of Surrey Street in Norfolk Buildings, and parcel of land on the south side of this, newly taken out of the River Thames (abuttals given).   2 docs.

MXD135-136 Lease for 41 years, and counterpart   **11 Aug. 1679**

The 6th Duke and his agents to his brother, the Hon. Charles Howard

> Parcel of ground in Surrey Street begun to be built on by the lessee, 20 feet (frontage) x 45 feet in depth; north John Toombs, west Cornelius Lilley and south other ground of the lessee

Annual rent: a peppercorn, first year, and £10 after. 2 docs.

MXD137-138 Lease for 41 years, and counterpart   **11 Aug. 1679**

– Messrs. Dalmahoy and West to Joseph Hickes, joiner

> parcel of ground begun to be built by Joseph Hickes 20 feet (frontage) x 45 feet; abutting north on ground leased to John Toombes, west on ground of Cornelius Lilley, and south on land leased to Charles Howard, esq.

A peppercorn rent for the first year of the term, then at rent of £10 a year.   2 docs.

This lease was found with those of Charles Howard perhaps because Hickes was Howard's subcontractor.

MXD139   Assignment of mortgage   **5 Mar. 1680**

Edward Proby, citizen and grocer of London and the Hon. Charles Howard to Thomas Elliott of St Martin in the Fields, esq.

> Premises as in **MXD133-134** above described as, parcel of ground begun to be built by the Hon. Charles Howard on the west side of Surrey Street in Norfolk Buildings, with a 60ft frontage to Surrey Street; and parcel of ground newly taken out of the River Thames; all bounded east by Surrey Street, west by Strandbridge Lane, south by the River and north by land of the Duke of Norfolk leased to Cornelius Lilley

Recites original 60-year lease by the Duke of Norfolk to Messrs Dalmahoy and West (date not given), followed by a mortgage for £850 made by Charles Howard in 1678 by assigning the remainder of a 41-year lease to Proby. He has now been paid off by Elliott, to whom he and Howard assign the remainder of the term

MXD140   Mortgage (by assignment of residue of 41-year term)   **20 Mar. 1683**

The Hon. Charles Howard of St Clement Danes, esq. to Thomas Elliott of St Martin in the Field, esq.

> parcel of ground on which Howard has built a messuage, coach house and stables; with a 22 feet frontage to Surrey Street, and depth of 45 feet; abutting east on Surrey Street, north on ground leased to John Toombes, west on land of Cornelius Lilley and south on other land leased to Howard.

Recites original lease 11 August 1679 (to run from Michaelmas 1677) by the Duke, Dalmahoy and West to Charles Howard; who now assigns the remainder of the term to Elliott a security for a £500 loan repayable with interest (specified)

MXD141   Mortgage by assignment of rents   **25 May 1693**

Henry (7th) Duke of Norfolk, The Hon. Charles Howard, esq. (the Duke's uncle), John Coggs of St Clement Danes, goldsmith

> Two separate rents on premises in Arundel Buildings

The rents are payable to the Duke for life out of premises leased to the Hon. Charles Howard; with whose agreement the Duke now assigns them to Coggs to hold during the Duke's life or until the Duke repays him £500 in a single sum.

MXD142-144   Mortgage (lease and release)   **25-26 May 1693**

Henry, 7th Duke of Norfolk, and his uncle, the Hon. Charles Howard, esq., to John Coggs, goldsmith

> All the messuages, dwelling houses and appurts. in which the Duke has an interest *in Surry Street, Arundell Street and Norfolke Street* or in any other part of Arundell Buildings or Arundell Rents in or near The Strand

The Duke and Charles Howard mortgage the premises for £2,000 repayable over four years at £500 a year, or, in default of repayment, Coggs may take profits from the premises for a term of 51 years.

Includes an additional unexecuted release.   3 docs.

MXD145   Lease for 9 years   **27 Apr. 1696**

The Hon. Charles Howard, esq. to the Hon. Thomas Newport of St Clement Danes, esq.

> Messuage and garden, together with such cellars and vaults and other commodities as are today agreed between the parties to pertain to it; lying at the lower end of Surrey Street on that side of it which is next to Somerset House Garden; lately in the occupation of Robert Pierpoint, esq. and the Hon. Countess Dowager of Kingston, his wife; except a passage lately taken out of the house through the great kitchen and yard into the vault under the garden there

The annual rent of £80 is payable in the common dining hall of the Inner Temple
Charles Howard's properties continue in section 4.iii. below.

Agent Charles Mawson, gentleman
See also his appointment, **MXD88** *above.*

MXD146   Assignment of rents   **17 June 1678**

Henry, Duke of Norfolk and   b) Messrs Dalmahoy and West [the Duke's agents] to   c) Charles Mawson of St Clement Danes, gentleman;   rents on:

i) four separate parcels each 20 x 70 feet leased to Thomas Gamon, carpenter, on west side of Norfolk Street

ii) parcel 15 x 34 feet leased to Cornelius Lilley, coachman, on east side of Arundel Street

iii) parcel 16 x 70 feet on the east side of Norfolk Street, with a passageway 3½ x 36 feet to and from Howard Street, leased to Joseph Hicks, joiner

iv) parcel 22 x 38 feet on the east side of Surrey Street, leased to Richard Atkinson, bricklayer

v) parcel 21 x 26 feet on east side of Surrey Street, leased to John Weble, blacksmith

vi) parcel 20 x 70 feet on the east side of Norfolk Street, leased to John Prince

vii) two parcels 14 x 26 feet and 20 x 30 feet respectively on the east side of Surrey Street, leased to William Blackwell

viii) parcel 22 x 40 feet on the east side of Arundel Street, leased to George Stoakes, bricklayer

ix) parcel 24 x 70 feet in Surrey Street, with a passage 10 feet wide by 10 feet high into Strand Bridge Lane, leased to George Moore.

Abuttals given for each parcel. In return for a payment of £2,500, the Duke and Messrs. Dalmahoy and West assign the rents from the premises to Mawson for a term of 39 years.

MXD147	Assignment of residue of term	**4 Jun. 1679**

Charles Mawson of St Clement Danes, gentleman to John Syms of the City of London, joiner

> Messuage known by the sign of the *Stirrop* on the south side of the Strand in Arundell Rents, in occ. of widow Roberts, with 15ft frontage to the Strand, 60 feet in depth; abutting south on a messuage in occ. of Anthony Plomer, west on the *White Horse Tavern* and east on a messuage called the *Maiden Head* in the occ. of Thomas Potter

Recites lease granted on 6 November last for 40 years by Henry, Duke of Norfolk, Thomas Dalmahoy and Thomas West to Mawson; who himself now assigns the residue of the term to Syms.

See also in 2. Strand Estate development, below

MXD148   Agreement to lease for 8½ years   **25 Jul. 1685**

Charles Mawson, gentleman, executor of the will of Patrick
Buchanan, esq. to John Luke of the Middle Temple, esq.

> brick messuage lately erected and new built by
> Edward Bird, citizen and painter stainer of London
> on the west side of Arundel Street in Norfolk
> Buildings with all its commodities and appurts.

Mawson agrees to lease the premises to Luke at £65 annual
rent. Final clause concerns *the statues and figures now standing
and being in the yard belonging to the said messuage*: they can
stay there till Christmas next, but the Duke in the mean time
shall *have liberty to take away the same*.

MXD149-150 Leases for 11 years   **20 Dec. 1687,**
                                                                    1698

Charles Mawson, gentleman to Charles Beasley, bricklayer

> little backhouse lately taken out of a messuage in
> Strand Lane formerly in occ. of Sir Paul Neile,
> knight, then of the Rt Hon. Lord Witherington, and
> now of Lady Longueville and Lady Clutterbuck;
> together with the yard and house of office
> belonging

As executor of the will of Patrick Buchanan, esq., deceased
Mawson leases the premises in 1687 to Beasley for 11 years at
£11 annual rent; in 1698 a subsequent 11-year term is granted to
Ward Deakes, gentleman at the same annual rent.   2 docs.

MXD151   Lease for 7 years at £22 annual rent   **15 Sep. 1679**

Charles Mawson, gentleman to Edward Hathaway, victualler

> messuage in Milford Lane, adjoining a messuage in
> the occ. of Thomas Biggs, woodmonger, abutting
> east on Milford Lane, north on a passage leading
> from Milford Lane to Water Street in Norfolk
> Buildings and west on other tenements in the said
> passage

This was found with documents relating to the *Greyhound*.

MXD152   Memorandum of agreement to execute a lease   **10 Feb. 1686**

Charles Mawson agrees with Joseph May, victualler, to lease to him for 5 years from Michaelmas next at £18 annual rent

>   messuage at the lower end of Milford Lane (already in May's occupation)

A scribbled addendum relates to decorating and water supply.

MXD153   Lease for one year at £45 annual rent   **13 Apr. 1688**

Charles Mawson to John Chaplyn, button seller

>   messuage called *The White Horse Tavern* situate in Arundel rents in The Strand, as it is divided out for use as a tavern, excluding the shop and the rooms now leased to Isaac Scriven, fringemaker, lately in the occ. of John Martindale [not clear which bit the latter occupied]

The lease is granted with the option for renewal for two further years, provided that Tobias Humphreys, esq. had not re-entered the premises in 1689.

MXD154   Assignment of lease (mortgage)   **25 Jun. 1697**

Charles Mawson, gentleman, as administrator of the goods of George Moore, decd. in trust for the latter's children (named) to Thomas Mawson of the Middle Temple, gent

>   messuage and appurts. commonly called the *White Horse*, in Arundel Rents lately in the occ. of Thomas Furtheren, now of George Jenkins; messuage ajoining lately in the occ. of John King, now of [blank] Stevens, furrier

Recites original lease, 21 Jan. 1678, by the Duke and his agents Dalmahoy and West to George Moore, for 47 years at £56 annual rent. Now C. Mawson assigns the remainder of the lease term to T. Mawson as security for the repayment of £179 4s. by June 1699.

MXD155   Lease for 3 years at £58 annual rent   **25 May 1696**

Charles Mawson to Henry Box of Inner Temple, London, esq.

Messuage and yard or garden on the east side of
Norfolk Street in Arundel Buildings in a plot 20
x 70 feet, east Mr Eaglesfield, south Mr Pember,
north Mrs. Wixstead, widow; all lately in the occ.
of the Lady Clutterbuck and Mr Derben

A brief schedule of locks and bolts is appended.
Charles Mawson's properties continue in **MXD593-594** *below.*

Agents Simon and Nevinson Fox

See **MXD88** *above for the appointment of S. and N. Fox.
For more on their premises in Arundel rents and in Milford
Lane, see* **MXD571-584** *below. As well as their London work,
they are mentioned as trustees, along with Cuthbert Browne,
Doctor of Divinity as co-trustee, in acting for the Duke in
1683 at Shoreham harbour in Sussex (Arundel Castle Archives
MD1638).*

MXD156 Settlement   **22 Jan. 1674**

Simon Fox of Stradbrook in Suffolk, esq. to the Rt Hon.
Henry, Lord Howard, son and heir apparent of the Hon.
Henry, Earl of Norwich, Earl Marshal and Thomas Barker
of the Middle Temple, gentleman

i) messuages and lands in Stradbroke, Hoxne and
Weybread in Suffolk
ii) messuages and appurts. in Green Dragon Alley
formerly called Sunn Alley near Strand Bridge,
abutting at the lower end upon the garden of
Arundel House
iii) three messuages in Milford Lane

Recites that Fox purchased ii) from Hugh Battin, plumber and
iii) from William Pease, citizen and merchant of London.
Fox conveys the premises to the other parties as trustees for
himself for life then to his son Nevinson Fox alias Bushell,
with contingent remainders to other children (named) and
to his wife Elizabeth

MXD158-161 Lease and mortgage with counterparts   **29 Jan. 1681**

Henry [6th] Duke of Norfolk to Nevinson Fox of St Clement
Danes, esq.

13 messuages with their appurts. in Arundel Rents,
fronting the Strand, now or late in the occs. of John

> Gumley, [blank] Young, Jonathan Wilcox, [blank]
> Merge, William Williams, Ellis Moore, Henry
> Grice, [blank] Perks, Anthony Plomer, Lancelott
> Coppleston, and Edward Richards

For a single payment of £3,500 Fox obtains a 21-year lease
of the premises from the Duke at a peppercorn rent; but he
has to raise the entire sum as a loan from the Duke who
thereby retains right of entry if the sum is not repaid at
6 per cent by 30 July next.
Signature 'Norfolke and Marshall' on two items.   4 docs.

MXD162   Lease for 99 years at £30 annual rent   **14 Aug. 1682**

Nevinson Fox, esq., to Joseph Woollhams, tailor

> all those ancient timber-built houses, with appurts.,
> in Milford Lane, part fronting to Milford Lane
> and part to other ground of Nevinson Fox; in the
> (separate) occs. of John Syms, joiner and formerly,
> Mrs Baker, now, Mrs Jones; and another ancient
> timber-built messuage in Milford Lane, known by
> the sign of the *Sugar Loaf*, late in occ. of Robert
> Launder, now of John Buxtall and ancient timber-
> built backhouse in Milford Lane, late in occ. of
> Mrs Jones now of David Thomas

The lease is granted to Woolhams for a down-payment of £20.
Endorsement, 1727, refers to a dispute between the successor in
title to this lease, one Mrs Loyd, and a neighbour concerning
the obstruction of a passage way by some new building; as a
result of which the rent has been witheld. Mrs Loyd is now
dead and the premises belong to the Duke of Norfolk – who
absolves Mrs Elizabeth Collier, executrix of the deceased,
of liability to pay.

MXD163   Lease for 51 years   **24 Mar. 1685**

Simon Fox and Nevinson Fox alias Bushell, esqs. to Richard
Atkinson, of St Martin in the Fields, brickmaker

> corner plot of ground begun to be built by the
> lessee, 13ft 9ins x 57ft at the upper end of a certain
> new street called Surrey Street; abutting north on
> the Strand, south towards the river, east Surrey
> Street, west Colonel Powell

Annual rent: a peppercorn for the first half-year and £28 thereafter

MXD164   Assignment of lease   **30 Apr. 1686**

Richard Atkinson as above and Robert Stone of Lyons Inn, co. Middx, gentleman to Anthony Dewey, joiner

Premises as in **MXD163** above

Recites **MXD163** above; and assignment by Atkinson 1 May 1685 to Stone. Now the lease is assigned to Dewey for £340, £300 of which is due to Stone for all his expense in building the new messuage on the plot, and £40 to Atkinson.

MXD165-167 Articles of agreement and conveyance as marriage   **14-15 Jul. 1687**
                settlement

Simon Fox, esq. and Nevinson Fox alias Bushell, esq., his son; the Hon. Dame Anne Moore, widow and Mary Moore her daughter, spinster, both of St Martins in the Fields, Abraham Highmore, esq.; George Crompton, citizen and goldsmith of London

> i) mansion house of Simon Fox in Stradbroke, and lands in Hoxne and Weybread, co. Suff. (19 names of occupants and former occupants)
> ii) houses and appurts. in Milford Lane, purchased of William Pease 'a broker' and now in occ. of Joseph Woollams
> iii) alley called Green Dragon Alley or Sun Alley and all the ground thereof and tenements thereon, purchased from Nathaniel Fox who got them from Hugh Battin; and are now in a ruinous condition; on the north end of which, towards The Strand is a booth erected by [blank] Doleman and at the south end, stables and coach house occupied by Simon and Nevinson Fox and William Lenthall, esq.
> iv) mansion house on the west side of Surrey Street in the occ. of Simon and Nevinson Fox and house and vault behind it in Strand Lane in occ. of Thomas Thompson; house south of the Foxes' mansion, in occ. of Benjamin Thomas, next door to William Hicks; and messuage behind it in Strand Lane, in occ. of Nathaniel Tucker
> v) messuage or inn called the *Talbot Inn*, in The Strand, in occ. of Agnes Carre, widow

vi) two messuages in The Strand at the north end of Surrey Street in the occ. of Thomas Taylour, linen draper, with two small tenements and a large vault adjoining currently, cont. untenanted, in Surrey Street

vii) messuage in Water Street in Arundel Buildings in occ. of John Syms

A marriage being intended between Nevinson Fox and Mary Moore, properties i-iii are conveyed by the Foxes to Highmore and Crompton as trustees in trust for Nevinson Fox for life with remainders to the heirs of his body. Properties iv-vii are similarly conveyed in oder to provide Mary, after the marriage, with a personal estate of £1,700 in the case of Nevinson Fox's death.   3 docs.

| **MXD168** | Declaration by Nevinson Fox: | **2 Nov. 1687** |

– concerning lands in Stradbroke, Hoxne and Weybred in Suffolk, settled upon him by his father, Fox releases his right to them back to the use of his father.

| **MXD169** | Lease for 51 years | **9 Jan. 1688** |

Simon Fox to Luke Harrod and John Mines, both of St Mary Savoy, carpenters

> messuage now being erected by the lessees on the west side of the *Talbot Inn* in the Strand, 11ft 2in (frontage) x 33ft 1in in depth, together with the little yard behind, 11ft wide x 3ft 2in deep, as it is now separated off from the *Talbot Inn*; east on a house in occ. of Simon and Nevinson Fox, west John Brook and south on the *Talbot Inn*

Liberty is granted for the lessees to build over the gateway leading to the *Talbot Inn* but the gateway and passage itself is reserved to the lessor; liberty also to the lessees to affix their own sign or signs to the existing oak sign and iron fittings on the front of the building over the gateway.

Annual rent: a peppercorn for the first year and £44 thereafter

| **MXD170** | Alteration of trusts | **5 Aug. 1697** |

Further to the marriage settlement above, the Hon. William Moore of St Ann, Westminster, esq., Henry Cope of Icomb co. Glos., esq. and Lawrence Holker of Gravesend, co. Kent, gentleman are made trustees in place of Messrs. Highmore and Crompton, who have died. And on payment of *a necklace of pearl and a parcel of diamonds* by Dame Anne Moore to Nevinson Fox, the marriage trusts are revoked and altered (details given) concerning Mary Fox in respect of:

> i) premises in St Clement Danes (?as in **MXD171** below)
> ii) two messuages and two coach houses in Weld Street, St Giles in the Fields in occ. of Samuel Nelson, apothecary and two messuages in Red Lyon Street in Holborn in occ. of William Paine and John Doogood

MXD171 Alteration of trusts **21 Apr. 1698**

Nevinson Fox, Dame Anne Moore, Mary Moore her daughter, (wife of Nevinson Fox); the Hon. William Moore and Messrs Cope and Holker as above (trustees)

> i) mansion house on the west side of Surrey Street in the occ. of Simon and Nevinson Fox
> ii) house on south side of i), in the occ. of Benjamin Thomas, flanked on the other side by the house of William Hicks
> iii) messuage in Strand Lane at the back of i) and ii)
> iv) messuage called the *Talbot Inn* in the Strand, in the occ. of Agnes Carr, widow
> v) two messuages, each side of a gateway leading out of the Strand into the *Talbot Inn*, in the respective occs. of Samuel Buckle and Joseph Jett
> vi) new-built messuage in the Strand at the north end of Surrey Street, in the occ. of Thomas Taylour, linen draper, with two small tenements and a large vault adjoining in Surrey Street, untenanted
> vii) messuage in Water Street in Arundel Buildings in occ. of John Syms

Reciting **MXD170** above and its recital, Nevinson grants the premises to the trustees on various revised trusts in favour of himself and any children of his marriage.

vi. Various papers

MXD172   Bill in Chancery   **undated, ?c. 1675**

Charles Howard, esq. complains against (his brother) Henry, now Duke of Norfolk concerning his liability to uncollected arrears of £373 10s. 4d. in a potential rental of £839 from the properties in 'Arundel rents' (ie. Strand area) which the complainant had put into good repair on the Duke's behalf.
13 folios.

MXD173   Bill in Chancery   **8 Aug. 1679**

Henry, Lord Mowbray against (his father), Henry, Duke of Norfolk and Earl of Arundel and Surrey as to inheritance issues and the legality of developing the Arundel House estate in London when it was an integral part of the settled family estates of the Castle, Honour and Barony of Arundel (in Sussex).
30 folios.

MXD174   Draft response to a bill of complaint   **6 Mar. 1680**

Response by the Most Noble Henry, Duke of Norfolk, Earl Marshal to the complaint of the Hon. Charles Howard, esq. concerning the designation of rents collected by agent Thomas West from the *Talbot Inn* and other messuages

MXD175   The answer of Henry, Duke of Norfolk   **undated, ?c. 1690**

– to the several complaints of George Roberts, esq., John Bellinger, Mary Perkins, widow of Searle Perkins, deceased, Israel Aylett, widow, John Tombes and Charles Howard, esq. Concerns the lay-out of the defendant's new estate and whether or not his intended new residence will be built. Anxieties relate to the width of Surrey Street (some dimensions are given);

which the Duke avows is indeed wide enough for coaches and carts to pass each other during any building process; and issues concerning the ground rents of the complainants if the house is not built

MXD176   Liberty to make a drain   **19 Mar. 1697**

James Lambourne of Merstham, Surrey, clerk, Christopher Davenport of New Inne, co. Middx, gent., Richard Chapman, apothecary, executor of the will of Richard Chapman, skinner, John Shephard, wax chandler and John ?Booby, sword cutler

re houses in Arundel Street

Lambourne and Chapman give permission to the other parties to make a drain to run into the common shore under the houses where Richard Chapman and Eleanor Buxton live.

vii.   Londoners' tenancies

Between 1660 when the Dukedom was restored to the Howard family and 1677, when the mentally infirm 5th Duke died, his younger brother Henry executed business on his behalf including the first stages of the Strand Estate development. Henry was rewarded in 1669 by King Charles II for his work as 'acting Duke' by his creation as 'Lord Howard, Baron Howard of Castle Rising', and as the Earl of Norwich and Earl Marshal of England in 1672. After his brother's death in 1677 he continued running the ducal estates in his own right as 6th Duke, although much was delegated. The main agents for the Strand Estate were Messrs Dalmahoy and West. They clearly had power to execute leases without the Duke's presence. On 16 November 1680, however, a few years before the Duke's death in 1684, new agents were appointed. They were Sir Paul Ricaut of St Martin in the Fields and Sir Cuthbert Browne, clerk, of Treaton, formerly of Hansworth, in Yorkshire and the Right Hon. Francis, Lord Howard, Baron of Bookham (later Baron of Effingham, Governor of Virginia). In 1693 Rycaut is described as 'Envoy Extraordinary to Their Majesties of Great Britain at Hamburg'. The trustees were all Anglicans, chosen as such to protect the property of a Roman Catholic owner from future punitive fines.

After his death in 1684 the succession fell to Henry's son, also Henry. In the years immediately before his father's death the 7th Duke, then styled as 'Henry, Earl of Arundel', had sometimes acted with his father as co-lessor. His titles in the deeds are Earl Marshal of England, one of the Knights Companions of the Most Noble Order of the Garter; and, by 1691, member of their Majesties' Most Honourable Privy Council. The charter of 1672 awarding new titles to his father, had made the Earl Marshal's office hereditary.

Many of the Londoners who took up the first round of leases in the 1670s were themselves undertaking some of the building work. Peppercorn rents were usually requested for the first year or two of a tenancy, as a way of offsetting the lessees' costs. It was also often specified that the new buildings were to conform to the building regulations agreed between the Duke and various of the contractors whose names appear in Section 2.iv., *Building contracts*, above. However, the properties fronting the Strand, below, were somewhat different, because they already existed. They were usually brought into conformity with the main estate as soon as it became convenient. As this series of deeds progresses, we see that the new leases granted by the 7th Duke generally contained strict provisos that old properties were to be pulled down and new ones erected in their place, conforming with the building standards that were being imposed on the main Arundel House development. Forbidden trades of occupiers were typically, brewer, cloth dyer, melting tallow chandler, slaughtering butcher, soap boiler and 'washstiller' of strong waters.

As before, the lessees' parish of residence is NOT cited here if it was St Clement Danes. The term of the lease and amount of annual rent will be stated in the catalogue for each deed. Where a *consideration* was also required as a single lump sum as a purchase price, this is expressed throughout the catalogue as a *down payment*. At the start of the Arundel House development such payments were not significant, but in later decades, and especially in the 1725 and later rounds of lease renewals, these payments were clearly a vital and effective way of raising ready money for the estate.

Strand: the 6th Duke's leases

For further leases, 1677-1680, see Appendix I

MXD181-182 Lease and sub-lease   **30 May 1672**
                                                                      20 Mar. 1673

> i) – to George More, gentleman
>
>> messuage known by the sign of the *White Horse* situated near Arundel House in the Strand in the occ. of Thomas Vile; and another messuage adjoining in the occ. of John King
>
> ii) George Moore, to Joseph Peterson, goldsmith
>
>> lately new built messuage known by the sign of the *Wounded Heart* late in occ. of John King; north on the Strand, east on the *White Horse Tavern* and west on a passageway towards Lancelott Copplestone's house, with all shops, cellars, solars, yards, ways, easements, etc.
>
> Premises i) and ii) are leased to Moore in 1672 for 52 years at £90 annual rent; and in 1673 he sublet ii) for 21 years for a down payment of £50 and £50 annual rent. 2 docs. *See also 187 below.*

MXD183-184 Lease for 21 years; and upgrade   **5 Dec. 1671-**
                                                                     24 Apr. 1672

> – to Lancelott Coppleston, citizen and painter stainer of London
>
>> messuage, in the occ. of the lessee, abutting north on the Strand, east on John King, shear grinder, west on Peter Gumley, cabinet maker and south on John Caltropp, bricklayer; with all shops, cellars, ways and easements, etc.
>
> Leased in December 1671 at £63 annual rent, and regranted in April 1672 for the remainder of the term at £83 annual rent. 2 docs.

MXD185   Lease for 7 years at £100 annual rent   **13 Jun. 1672**

– to Peter Gumley, cabinet maker

> messuage known as the *Cabinett*, abutting north
> on the Strand, with another messuage lying behind
> it, abutting east on Lancelot Copplestone, west on
> [blank] Crompton; together with two little yards
> belonging to the premises, which were all in the occ.
> of Sir Arthur Onslow then of Sir William Turner,
> but now of the lessee

MXD186   Lease for 7 years   **29 Apr. 1676**

– to Matthew Scott of St Clement Danes, gentleman, a rent
charge of £20 arising out of:

> messuage known by the sign of the *Cabinett*, abutting
> north on The Strand, formerly in the occ. of Arthur
> Onslow, knight, then of Sir William Turner, knight
> and now of Peter Gumley

Down payment £100.

MXD187   Lease for 47 years   **22 Jan. 1678**

– to Henry Moore, gentleman at £56 annual rent

> The *White Horse* near Arundel House in the Strand,
> now in the occ. of Thomas Furtheren and messuage
> adjoining in the occ. of John King (as in **MXD181-
> 182** above).

This lease is granted without reference to **MXD181-182**
above.

MXD188   Lease for 41 years   **6 May 1678**

– to William Williams, glazier

> parcel of ground begun to be built by the lessee,
> on which [was formerly] the messuage that Lady
> Sidenham used to live in, having a 15ft frontage
> north to the Strand by 56 feet in depth, abutting
> east on Edward Richards, south on other ground
> of the lessee, west on John Shelbury

A peppercorn rent for the first year and then £30 annual rent

MXD189   Lease for 21 years at £67 annual rent   **26 May 1678**

– to Ellice Moore, goldsmith

> two messuages on the south side of the Strand,
> one in the occ. of the lessee, the other of Edward
> Richards, haberdasher and a yard 20 x 22 feet
> behind them, with all their rooms, cellars, ways,
> easements etc.

MXD190   Lease for 40¼ years and building agreement   **1 Oct. 1678**

– to John Syms of London, joiner

> messuage known by the sign of the *Stirrop* having
> a 15ft frontage to the Strand x 60 feet in depth,
> late in the occ. of widow Roberts; abutting south
> on Anthony Plummer, west on the *White Horse
> Tavern* and east on the *Mayden Head* in the occ.
> of Thomas Potter

A peppercorn rent for the first year and a quarter, and 5s. a
year for the rest of the term; with an undertaking to demolish
and rebuild a new house or houses within the first five years
of the term.

MXD191   Lease for 21 years   **10 Dec. 1678**

– to Henry Grice, citizen and haberdasher of London

> messuage known by the sign of the *Blew Boare* on
> the south side of the Strand in Arundel Rents, in
> the occ. of the lessee; abutting east on a messuage
> called the *Blew Ball* in the occ. of John Chaplin,
> west on a messuage called the *Ball* in the occ. of
> John Perkes; and all that adjacent entry passage
> 3 feet x 42 feet late in the occ. of Simon Fox; and
> little plot of land at the south end of the passage
> **(with plan)**

The premises are leased at the annual rent of £50 for the
messuage *if the said messuage called the Blew Ball be not
taken down and rebuilt* before the end of the term; and £4
for the passage way and plot.

MXD192   Lease for 7 years at £50 annual rent   **21 Jul. 1679**

– to Edward Richards, haberdasher

> messuage in Arundel Rents known by the sign of the *Black Spread Eagle*, formerly in the occ. of John Shelbery, apothecary; as the same is set out and divided by the order and direction of Simon Fox, esq.; together with a yard as it is set out, or will be set out. [Location not given but Edward Richards and John Shelbury are cited as adjacent occupiers in the Strand in some of the above deeds of 1678.]

MXD193   Lease for 21 years at £44 annual rent   **5 Jun. 1680**

– to John Chaplin, haberdasher

> messuage in Arundel rents, in the occ. of the lessee, with the entry next to the adjoining; and the other ground, and materials on the same, which is all that is left of the house in which Simon Fox, esq. lately dwelt

Strand: the 7th Duke's leases

MXD194-195   Lease, and counterpart, for 21 years at £30 annual rent   **8 Aug. 1687**

– to Thomas Harris, blacksmith

> messuage in Arundel Rents in the occ. of the lessee, abutting north on the Strond, south on a messuage in the occ. of Mr Swift, east on a messuage in the occ. of Thomas Solsbury, *fringmaker* [i.e. fringe maker] and west on a messuage in the occ. of Mr Swan haberdasher of hats

Impressed seals on paper of all parties

MXD196   Lease for 7 years at £42 annual rent   **17 Aug. 1687**

– to Thomas Potter, periwig maker

> messuage in Arundel Rents in the Strand, in the occ. of the lessee, and two small parcels of ground,

one used for a shed (6ft 3in x 4ft 11in) and the other as a yard (6ft 4in x 2ft 8in), adjoining a messuage used as a coffee house in the occ. of Henry ?Chuch

MXD197-198 Lease, and counterpart, for 7 years at £50 annual rent   **25 May 1688**

– to Thomas Salusbury, silkman

messuage in Arundel Rents, in the occ. of the lessee

MXD199   Lease for 41 years at £30 annual rent   **29 May 1688**

– to John Coggs, citizen and goldsmith of London

mesuage in Arundel rents, called the *Blew Boare* 12ft 3in (north) x 60ft (west) x 13ft (south) x 62ft (east); lately in occ. of Henry Price, haberdasher; east John Chaplin, south the *Kinges Armes Cavern* [*sic*], west John Hodge, carpenter

The premises are leased to Coggs on condition that he will pull down the existing buildings and rebuild on the site.

MXD200   Lease and building covenant   **10 Feb. 1691**

– to John Hodge, carpenter

old messuage and ground belonging in Arundel rents in a plot 13 feet 4 inches (frontage to the Strand) by 55 feet 6 inches, abutting south on Mr Smith, east on Mr Templeman, pewterer and west on Thomas Harris, clockmaker

The lease is granted for 40 years 6 months at a peppercorn rent for the first year and £10 a year thereafter; with covenant that the lessee will pull down the old house and will erect one or more new houses by Lady Day 1692, reusing or disposing of the materials as he wishes.

MXD201   Lease of ground rent for 37¾ years   **17 Oct. 1691**

– to John Hickman of St Martin in the Fields, gentleman

messuage in Arundel Rents formerly leased to John Hodge, carpenter, known by the sign of the *Golden Ball*, now in the occ. of Henry Godfrey, watchmaker; being 12 feet 3 inches wide in a 13ft 6in frontage to the Strand; the plot 60 feet in depth north to south and 61 feet in breadth at its south end; abutting north on the Strand, west on a house lately of Thomas Marshall, apothecary, south on the *Kings Arms Tavern* and east on a piece of ground leased to John Coggs, goldsmith

Down payment £180. Little impressed seal on paper (Hickman)

MXD202	Lease for 40 years and building covenant	**10 Sep. 1692**

– to Richard Lamborne, skinner

old messuage late in the occ. of Thomas Potter, periwig maker, in the Strand in Arundel Rents with a frontage of 12 feet to the Strand, by 34 feet in depth, abutting west on Mrs Cherrey, south on ground belonging to the coffee house, east on Nat Worley and John Tiping, woollen drapers, with liberty to build under and over the passage which leads to the coffee house; and two pieces of ground (as in 196 above); except and reserving to Messrs Rycaut and Brown the ancient passage way 34 feet in length leading from the Strand to the said coffee house

A peppercorn rent for the first year and £20 a year thereafter; with the proviso that the lessee pulls down the old house by Christmas and erects one or more new houses on the site by Michaelmas 1693.

MXD203	Lease for 38 years and building covenant	**16 Nov. 1693**

– to Philip Surman, woollen draper

old messuage in the Strand in Arundel Rents known by the sign of the *Indian Gown*, in the occ. of Lancelot Coppleston, Indian Gownman, in a plot 16ft 6in (frontage) by 43 feet in depth, abutting south on a yard of Peter Gumley, west on the messuage of the same and east on Mr Wellitt, mercer

A peppercorn rent for the first year, then £30 a year for the next two years and £40 a year for the remainder of the term. The lessee agrees to pull down the old house before Lady Day (25 March) next and to erect in its place one or more complete houses according to an agreement of 23 October last, the new house(s) to be finished by Lady Day 1695.

MXD204   Lease for 35 years 3 months, and building covenant   **10 Aug. 1696**

– to Richard Chapman, citizen and apothecary of London

> old messuage and ground in Arundel Rents known by the sign of the *Blew Ball*, late in the occ. of John Chaplin, deceased, having a 13½ft frontage to the Strand by 62 feet in depth; abutting south on a yard of Mr Richmond, east on Philip Pinkney and west on John Beby, sword cutler; with all ways, easements and the use of the common sewer

The lessee agrees to pull down the old messuage and to erect a new one at his own cost but to the Duke's specification and in return the lease is granted at the full rent of £35 for the first 3 years 9 months, then a peppercorn for the next three years and finally £25 a year for the remainder of the term.

For further leases re the Strand, 1699, see Appendix I.

Surrey Street: 6th Duke's leases

Several of these leases refer to the recent building covenants agreed between the Duke, Cornelius Lilley, Francis Burghill and Jonathan Wilcox, carpenter as in **MXD101-129** *above. Strand Lane is referred to as 'Strandbridge Lane' in these leases. For Surrey Street, see also* **MXD276** *below.*

East side of Surrey Street

MXD205   Lease for 40 years   **13 Jun. 1679**

– to William Blackwell, carpenter

> Parcel of ground begun to be built by Blackwell 27 feet (frontage) x 16 feet; east to other land leased to Blackwell, south Howard Street and north to land leased to Simon Fox

A peppercorn rent for the first year and at £5 a year thereafter

MXD206   Lease for 40 years to John Weble, blacksmith   **17 Jun. 1679**

> Parcel of ground begun to be built 21 x 26 feet; west on ground leased to William Blackwell, east and north on ground leased to Joseph Hickes, south Howard Street; leaving a passage 3½ feet out of Angell Court into Howard Street

A peppercorn rent for the first year and £4 10s. thereafter

MXD207-212   Lease for 39 years, and mortgage papers   **5 Jun. 1680-**
12 May 1681

– to William Blackwell as above

> Parcel of ground on the east side of Surrey Street 22 x 50 feet; east on the outwall of the Duke's intended mansion, south on other land of the Duke and north on land leased to William Wickens

A peppercorn rent for the first year and £11 a year thereafter.
Includes loose papers concerning Blackwell's mortgage, and redemption, to William Ball, coachman.   6 docs.

MXD213-215   Leases for 41 years   **20 May 1679-**
10 Nov. 1680

– to Richard Atkinson of St Martin in the Fields, brick-maker*

> i) parcel of ground 20 feet (frontage) x 38 feet, begun to be built by Atkinson; east on John Webley, locksmith, north on Howard Street and south on Richard Inwood
> ii) parcel of ground 21 x 37 feet, having a 21ft frontage on the street, abutting east on William Blackwell, north on Richard Inwood and south on William Wickens
> iii) parcel of ground 18 feet (frontage) x 37 feet; south on John Prince, bricklayer, north on other ground of the lessee and east *on the fence or wall belonging to ground whereon is intended to be built a Capitall messuage or Palace for the said Duke*

The Duke and his agents now lease to Atkinson for terms of 41 years on i) and 39½ years on ii) and iii); at a peppercorn

rent for the first year and thereafter at £7 14s. for i), £7 10s. for ii); and at £5 each year for iii).
* In one of the deeds he is described as labourer, but his (adept) signature proves it is the same man   3 docs.

MXD216   Unexecuted lease for 39¾ years   **2 Sep. 1679**

– to Joseph Hicks, joiner

Parcel of ground designed for a yard, between Norfolk Street and Surrey Street, 30 feet 6 inches east to west by 17 feet north to south

A peppercorn rent for the first year and 40s. thereafter

MXD217   Lease for 39½ years   **4 Sep. 1679**

– to John Prince, bricklayer

Parcel of ground 14 x 37 feet, begun to be built by the lessee; north and east on William Blackwell and south on a passage way leading from Surrey Street to the mansion house of the Duke; with liberty for Prince to build over and under the said passage way all along the depth (37 feet) of the leased premises

A peppercorn rent for the first year and at £5 a year thereafter.

MXD218   Lease for 39½ years   **4 Jun. 1680**

– to William Blackwell, carpenter

Parcel of ground in Surrey Street in Norfolk Buildings 52 feet north to south x 17 feet east to west, on the east side of the street between the outwall of the Duke's intended mansion house in Surrey Street and ground leased to Richard Atkinson and John Prince; north on ground leased to Richard Inwood, decd., south upon the passage leading out of Surrey Street into the Duke's intended mansion house, west on Atkinson and Prince (as above) and east on the said outwall

A peppercorn rent for the first year and £6 a year thereafter

MXD219   Lease for 41 years   **7 Jul. 1681**

– to John Hodge, carpenter

> parcel begun to be built by the lessee, 22 feet
> (frontage) together with 40 feet out of the soil of
> the River Thames, both pieces being 54 feet in
> depth, extending from the Duke's wall belonging
> to ground (on which there is to be built a capital
> messuage) to the street; east on the said wall,
> south the River Thames and north William
> Blackwell

A peppercorn rent for the first year and £25 a year
thereafter.

Surrey Street, west side

MXD220-222 Lease for 41 years and assignment of rents   **2 Feb. 1677-**
                                                                       23 Feb. 1680

– to John Wright of Grays Inn, esq.

> parcel of building ground in Norfolk Buildings,
> 24 feet (frontage) x 70 feet in depth; abutting
> west on Strand Bridge Lane; with a 10ft wide
> and 10ft high passage way from Surrey Street to
> Strand Bridge Lane

A peppercorn rent for the first year and an annual rent of
£15 12s. thereafter; in 1680 the rents are assigned to Patrick
Buchanan of St Clement Danes, esq.; with counterpart, and
a receipt by Wright to Jane Parker (see below)

Signature of the Earl and seal bearing his arms on 222.
4 docs.

MXD223-225 Assignment of remainders of lease term   **27 Dec. 1677-**
                                                                       19 Jun. 1678

a) John Wright of Grays Inn, esq., b) Jane Parker of
London, widow c) Richard Hudson, citizen and merchant
taylor of London and Samuel Spilsworth, citizen and joiner
of London, d) Thomas Miller of London, bricklayer &
George Moore of St Clement Danes, gent.

Premises 24 x 70 feet as in 220 above

Recites 220 above. Now Wright and his original backer, Jane Parker, transfer their interest in the premises to new backers, c) who in turn assign to d) as each are paid off.

Counterpart signed by George Moore re the above, 8 Mar. 1678

MXD226   Assignment of rents   **23 Feb. 1680**

The annual rent of £15 12s. on the above premises had been assigned by George Moor, above, to Patrick Buchanan, formerly of St Clement Danes, esq. [present residence not given]. Now, for a down payment of £187, the Duke and his agents ratify this arrangement.

Strand Lane: the 6th Duke's leases

MXD227-228 Lease for 41 years and assignment   **8 Mar. 1678-**
                                                               25 Feb. 1679

– to Joseph Hickes of London, citizen and joiner

> Parcel of ground begun to be built by said Joseph Hickes, 22 feet (frontage), abutting west on Strand Bridge Lane, south on a passage way out of Surrey Street to Strand Bridge Lane

Recites lease in 1678 by the Duke and his agents to Hickes, for 41 years at a peppercorn rent for the first year, then at £14 6s. annual rent; and in 1679 Hickes paid £190 for an assignment of the annual rents, absolving him of any further liability to pay rents.   2 docs.

MXD229-232 Lease for 41 years and assignments   **1 Feb. 1678-**
                                                               2 Jul. 1688

i) Cornelius Lilley of St Clement Danes, yeoman to Thomas Heacock of St Martin in the Fields, yeoman; ii) Edmund Price, husband of Anne, *née* Heacock, and executor of Thomas Heacock deceased to Thomas Harding, joiner; iii) Harding and others to Humphrey Hutchins the elder of 'St Katherine precincts' [*sic*] near the Tower of London, waterman

> Building land 20 x 18 feet on the backside of Surrey Street, fronting Strandbridge Lane. **Plan.**

On 1 Feb. 1678 the Duke and his agents leased to Lilley for 41 years
to hold at £3 rent a year on condition that Lilley built a house on
the plot; the latter subsequently built *a substantiall dwelling house*
on it, to specifications drawn up by the Duke on 26 October 1676.
In 1680 Lilley assigned the remainder of the term to Heacock
for £100; in 1687 Price assigned to Harding for £50 and in 1688
Harding assigned to Hutchins for £49.   4 docs.

Norfolk Street: the 6th Duke's leases
See also **MXD272** *below*

East side of Norfolk Street

MXD233-235 – to Peter Gumley of St Clement Danes, cabinet maker   **2 Feb. 1677-**
18 Mar. 1679

> i) parcel of ground begun to be built 25 feet (frontage)
> to the street by 50 feet in depth; north on a messuage
> newly built by the lessee and east and south by other
> ground of the Earl.
> ii) parcel of ground in Norfolk buildings begun to be
> built by the lessee 25ft (frontage) x 50 feet in depth;
> north on iii) and east and south on other ground of
> the Duke of Norfolk
> iii) parcel of ground on the east corner of Norfolk
> Street, 16 feet 8 inches (frontage) x 45 feet in depth;
> north on the Strand, south on other ground leased to
> Gumley and east on Lancelott Copplestone
> iv) parcel of ground near the Strand, 20 x 20 feet,
> with a yard 16 feet northward by 22 feet east to
> west; east Lancelott Copplestone, north and south
> the lessee

Peppercorn rents for the first year or year and a half, and full
annual rents thereafter, i) for 41½ years, £15; ii) 41 years, £15
iii) 41 years, £30 and iv) 40 years, £10.   3 docs.

MXD236   Lease and agreement   **1 May 1678**

The 6th Duke and John Prince, bricklayer

> Parcel of building land 22 feet (frontage) by 70 feet
> in depth, on the east side of Norfolk Street; east
> Mr Pearson, carpenter, south Mr Greene and north
> William Blackwell

The Duke leases the plot to Prince on condition that he builds
a house to certain specifications (details given) by Lady Day

1679; and that once the first floor is built the Duke will make Prince a proper lease for 41 years at a peppercorn rent for the first year followed by an annual rent of £16 15s.

MXD237-238 Lease with building covenant; and counterpart   **10 Jan. 1679**

– to George Moore of Albury, Surrey, gentleman

> parcel of ground on the east side of Norfolk Street, partly 37 feet (frontage) by 70 feet in depth, the remainder 25 feet frontage by 50 feet in depth; north Peter Gumley, south John Angier, east to the back part of Arundel Street

The lease is granted for 40¼ years at a peppercorn rent for the first year and at £22 annual rent thereafter; on condition that Moore has one or more houses built on the site to specifications agreed on 10 December last, by Lady Day 1780.   2 docs.

Norfolk Street, east side: the 7th Duke's leases

MXD239   Extension of lease term   **10 Oct. 1689**

– to John Thompson of St James, Westminster, mason

> parcel of ground in Arundel Buildings 40 x 70 feet; abutting east on ground in possession of John Luke, north on ground intended to be leased to Charles Mawson, gent. and south on the River Thames

Recites that the premises were leased to Thompson on 30 September last for 42 years at a peppercorn rent for the first two years and £30 annual rent thereafter, in trust for him to build a new house there at his own cost. Thompson, however, needs a longer lease in order to recoup his costs. He is now granted a five-year extension after the end of the original 42 years, at the full £30 annual rent.

Norfolk Street, west side: the 6th Duke's leases

MXD240 Lease for 41½ years at £64 annual rent **2 Feb. 1677**

– to Jonathan Wilcox of St Martin in the Fields, carpenter
parcel of ground begun to be built by the lessee
on the west side and at the north end of Norfolk
Street, having a 32ft frontage to the street x 60 feet
in depth; abutting west on a messuage in occ. of
[blank] Moore, goldsmith, north on the Strand and
south on a messuage leased to William Williams,
glazier

A peppercorn rent for 1½ years and full rent thereafter.

MXD241 Lease for 40 years at £12 annual rent **18 Feb. 1679**

– to Joseph Hickes, citizen and joiner of London

Parcel of ground on the west side of Norfolk Street,
begun to be built by the lessee, 16 feet (frontage) x
70 feet in depth, together with a passage 3½ feet wide
x 36 feet in length running from the said ground to
Howard Street; west on other ground of the Duke,
north Josiah Smith, south Peter Rich

A peppercorn rent for the first year and the full rent
thereafter
Seal with imprint of initials

MXD242 Assignment of ground rents **26 Feb. 1679**

– to Peter Rich of Lambeth, esq.

i) £32 from ground leased to Jonathan Wilcox at the
north end of Norfolk Street, having a 16ft frontage
to the Strand, by 45 feet north to south; south
Jonathan Wilcox, west Ellis Moore, goldsmith, east
Jonathan Wilcox
ii) £32 from ground leased to same Jonathan Wilcox
at the north end of Norfolk Street, having a 16ft
frontage to the Strand by 43½ feet; north, south and
west Jonathan Wilcox and east Norfolk Street

For a down payment of £832 both rent incomes are assigned
to Rich for 40 years from Lady Day 1676

MXD243   Lease for 41½ years   **5 Jun. 1680**

– to William Williams, glazier

> messuage lately erected by the lessee in a plot on the west side of Norfolk Street 24 feet (frontage) x 70 feet; north Jonathan Wilcox, south Thomas Gamon and west the Duke

The lease is granted as from Michaelmas 1676 at a peppercorn rent only for the full term.

MXD244   Assignment of rents   **5 Jun. 1680**

– to John Angier of St Margaret, Westminster, gentleman

> Four parcels of ground in Norfolk Street each 20 feet in front x 97 feet in depth; abutting west on a ground of the Duke, south on ground demised to John Prince and north on ground demised to William Williams

Recites that the premises were leased on 25 Feb. 1678/9 by the Duke and his agents to Thomas Gamon, citizen and carpenter of London for 41 years at a peppercorn rent for the first year and thereafter at £11 5s. per plot on the agreement that Gamon would erect forthwith a house on each plot. Now, notwithstanding the lease to and agreement with Gamon, which are still in force, in return for a payment of £500 by Angier, they assign to Angier the £45 total rent income for the remainder of the lease term.

Norfolk Street: the 7th Duke's leases

MXD245   Assignments of rents   **7 Oct. 1689**

The 7th Duke to John Stone of New Inn, gentleman

> i) plot 20 x 70 feet on east side of and fronting to Norfolk Street in Arundel Buildings; east John Luke, esq., south John Thompson and north John Green
> ii) plot 20 x 70 feet on east side of and fronting to Norfolk Street; east towards Arundel Street, south John Greene, north John Hodge
> iii) plot 20 x 70 feet on east side of and fronting to Norfolk Street; east towards Arundel Street, south John Hodge and north Henry Peirson

iv) plot 20 x 70 feet on the west side of and fronting to Norfolk Street; west towards Surrey Street, south Charles Johnson, north Richard Biddle

v) plot 20 x 70 feet on west side of and fronting to Norfolk Street; west towards Surrey street, south Richard Biddle, north Charles Beasley

The premises were all leased, for 42 years each, by the Duke on 30 September last: i) to Charles Mawson, ii) to William Cooke, tailor, iii) to Robert Powell, plasterer, iv) to James Browne, tailor and v) to John Shorter, esq., all of St Clement Danes; each lease for 42 years, the lessees each paying a peppercorn rent for the first two years and then the full rent of £20 a year. Now, for a down payment of £1,173 10s, all the rent incomes throughout the several terms are assigned to Stone in return for a peppercorn rent each year.

| MXD246 | Extension of leases | 7 Oct. 1689 |

The 7th Duke to John Milbourne of St Giles in the Fields, gentleman

i) plot on the east side of Norfolk Street 40 feet (frontage) by 70 feet in depth; east John Luke., esq., south the river of Thames, north Charles Mawson

ii) plot on the west side of Norfolk Street 20 feet (frontage) by 70 feet in depth; west towards Surrey Street, south John Shorter, north John Thompson

The original 42-year leases on 30 September last i) to John Thompson and ii) to Charles Beasley for a peppercorn rent for the first year, then £30 and £20 respectively. Now, for a down payment of £586 15s. these terms and their rents are assigned to Milbourne.

| MXD247 | Assignments of rents | 7 Oct. 1689 |

The 7th Duke to John East, citizen and goldsmith of London

i) plot 20 x 70 feet on the east side of Norfolk Street; west towards Arundel Street, south Charles Mawson, north William Cooke

ii) plot 20 x 70 feet on the east side of and fronting Norfolk Street; east towards Arundel Street, south on Robert Powell, north on Butler Buggin, esq.

iii) plot 22 x 70 feet on the east side of and fronting
Norfolk Street; west towards Arundel Street, south
on William Cooke and north on Robert Powell
iv) plot 22 x 70 feet on the west side of and fronting
Norfolk Street; west towards Surrey Street, south
James Browne and north John Shorter, esq.

The premises were all leased for 42 years each by the Duke
on 30 September last: i) to John Greene of Newington Green,
co. Middx, carpenter ii) to Henry Peirson, carpenter iii) to
John Hodge, carpenter and iv) to Richard Biddle, bricklayer,
each at a peppercorn rent for the first two years and £20 for
the rest of the term (except iii) at £18), Now, for a payment
of £1,173 10s., all the rent incomes are assigned to East for
the remainder of their respective terms, for a peppercorn rent
each year

MXD248-249 Extension of lease terms   **7 Oct. 1689**

The 7th Duke to John Coggs, citizen and goldsmith of
London

i) plot 40 x 70 feet on the west side and fronting
Norfolk Street; west towards Surrey Street, south the
river of Thames, north Humphrey Bradshaw
ii) plot 20 x 70 feet on the west side of and fronting
Norfolk Street, south Humphrey Bradshaw, north
Charles Johnson
iii) plot 25 x 70 feet on the east side and fronting to
Norfolk Street; east towards Arundel Street, south
Henry Pearson and north Leonard Hancock
iv) plot on the west side of Norfolk Street, having a
46ft frontage but only 22 feet at the back; by 40 feet
on the north side and 70 feet on the south side; south
Charles Beasley, brickmaker, west towards Surrey
Street, north on Howard Street
v) plot 30 feet east to west and 24 feet north to south;
north on Howard Street, south John Thompson,
west [blank]
vi) plot on the east side of Norfolk Street 21 feet to the
street but only 10 feet at the back, 58 feet on the north
side next to Howard Street and 70 feet at the south;
east towards Arundel Street and Leonard Hancock,
south Henry Pierson, north Howard Street
vii) plot on the south side of Howard Street, 12 feet
(frontage) by 11 feet north to south; east towards
Arundel Street, south and west Leonard Hancock

Recites that the Duke made separate leases of each property on 30 September last: i) and ii) to Humphrey Bradshaw, iii) to Butler Buggin, iv) and v) to John Thompson and vi) and vii) to Leonard Hancock; all for 42 years at peppercorn rents for the first two years then £30, £20, £25, £32, £14, £16 and £5 annual rents respectively. Now, for a down payment of £1,666 5s. all the leases and their rents are assigned to Coggs for the remainder of their terms.
With a schedule of locks fitted 'at the house Mr Box lived in'.
2 docs.

MXD250-253   Extension of lease terms by the 7th Duke   **10 Oct. 1689**

Regarding the leases to William Cooke, Robert Powell, James Browne and John Shorter (**MXD245**, ii), iii), iv) and v) above), the Duke grants a five-year extension on each original 42-year lease in acknowledgement of the great costs and charges the lessees have faced in building on their plots.   4 docs.

MXD254-255   Extension of lease terms   **10 Oct. 1689**

The 7th Duke to Henry Pearson, carpenter

> i) plot on the east side of Norfolk Street 20 feet (frontage) by 70 feet in depth; east towards Arundel Street, south Robert Powell and north Leonard Hancock
> ii) plot on the west side of Norfolk Street 20 feet (frontage) by 70 feet in depth; south Humphrey Bradshaw, west towards Surrey Street and north Charles Johnson, victualler

The premises were leased on 30 September last for 42 years at a peppercorn rent for the first two years and at £20 annual rent thereafter, i) to Henry Pearson, carpenter and ii) to Humphrey Bradshaw, gentleman. The Duke now grants 5-year extensions at the same £20 rent, in consideration of the great costs the lessees have incurred in building.
2 docs.

MXD256   Extension of lease term   **10 Oct. 1689**

– to Humphrey Bradshaw, gentleman

house plot 40 feet (frontage) x 70 feet abutting south on the River Thames and north on other premises in the occ. of the lessee

Leased to Bradshaw on 30th September last for 42 years at £30 annual rent, the term now extended for 5 years, as above.

MXD257   Extension of lease term   **10 Oct. 1689**

– to John Greene as in **MXD247**, property i) above.

The Duke grants a five-year extension for the same reasons as above.

MXD258-260 Extension of lease terms   **10 Oct. 1689**

i) plot 25 x 70 feet on the east side of and fronting to Norfolk Street; south on Henry Pearson, carpenter, east towards Arundel Street and north on Leonard Hancock
ii) plot on the east side of Norfolk Street 21 x 10 feet north to south and 58 x 70 feet east to west; the 21ft width abutting west on Norfolk Street, the 58ft length north on Howard Street; the 10ft east to Howard Street and other ground of the lessee; and the 70ft south on Henry Pearson
iii) plot 12 x 11 feet on the south side of Howard Street; north on Howard Street, east on houses in Arundel Street and south and west on other ground of Leonard Hancock

Recites previous leases of property i) at £25 to Butler Buggin of New Inn, esq., of property ii) at £16 annual rent to Leonard Hancock of St Clement Danes, woodmonger, and property iii) to same Leonard Hancock at £5 annual rent. Now the Duke grants five-year extensions on each original 42-year lease in acknowledgement of building costs, as above.   3 docs.

MXD261-264 Extensions of lease terms   **10 Oct. 1689**

i) plot 20 x 70 on the west side of and fronting to Norfolk Street, south Humphrey Bradshaw, gentleman, west towards Surrey Street and north James Browne, tailor

ii) plot 20 x 70 feet on the west side of and fronting to Norfolk Street, south John Shorter, west towards Surrey Street and north John Thompson, mason

iii) plot on west side of Norfolk Street; 46 feet to the street, 22 feet at the west end, 40 feet on the north side and 70 feet on the south side; south Charles Beesley, bricklayer, west towards the back of Surrey Street and north on Howard Street

iv) plot in Norfolk Street on south side of Howard Street, 30 feet east to west and 24 feet north to south; north Howard Street, east and south John Thompson (other land of) west on a house in Howard Street

Recites previous leases 30 September last for 42 years of i) to Charles Johnson, victualler, at £20 annual rent ii) to Charles Beesley, bricklayer at £20 annual rent iii) to John Thompson of St James, Westminster, mason at £20 annual rent and iv) to same John Thompson at £14 annual rent. Now the Duke grants five-year extensions to each lease in acknowledgement of building costs, as above.   4 docs.

Howard Street: The 6th Duke's leases

MXD265   Lease for 40 years   **13 Jun. 1679**

– to William Blackwell, carpenter

> Parcel of ground 16 x 26 feet begun to be built by the lessee on the north side of Howard Street; north on Joseph Hickes, east John Webley and west William Blackwell

A peppercorn rent for the first year and 40s. thereafter.

Arundel Street, east side: The 6th Duke's leases

MXD266   Lease for 40½ years   **12 Feb. 1677**

– to Charles Stoakes of St Martin in the Fields, bricklayer

> parcel of ground to be built on by the lessee having a 20ft frontage x 40 feet in depth, abutting west on Arundel Street, east on a new street to be built

by the Earl called Water Street, south [blank] and
north on other land of the Earl

A peppercorn rent for the first 1½ years, then £9 a year

MXD267-270 Leases for 41 years   **1-8 Mar. 1678**

– to Jonathan Wilcox of St Martin in the Fields, carpenter

> i) parcel of ground having a 40ft frontage to the
> street x 79½ feet in depth; abutting north on other
> ground leased to Wilcox, east on the back of houses
> in Milford Lane and south on ground leased to
> John Prince, bricklayer
> ii) parcel of ground begun to be built by the lessee,
> lying at the north end of Arundel Street in Norfolk
> Buildings, having a 12ft frontage north to the Strand
> by 60 feet in depth, abutting west and south by
> ground leased to Wilcox and east to a messuage
> in the occ. of John Pearkes
> iii) parcel of ground begun to be built by the lessee
> having a 15ft frontage north to the Strand by 60 feet
> in depth, abutting west on Arundel Street, east
> on ii) above and south on other ground leased
> to Wilcox

A peppercorn annual rent for the first year and £24, £24 and
£30 respectively thereafter.   3 docs.

MXD271   Assignment of rents   **20 Nov. 1678**

– to Edward Pearce of the City of London, carver
ground rents of £25, £11, £10 and £10 respectively, issuing from
premises on the east of a new street called Arundel Street:

> i) parcel 20 feet (frontage) x 40 feet in depth and
> another parcel 40 x 40 feet, taken out of the soil of
> the River Thames; east on a new street called Water
> Street, south on the river and north on ground
> leased to Charles Stoakes, bricklayer
> ii) parcel 20 x 60 feet leased to Charles Stoakes,
> with liberty to build under and over a passage
> 4 feet wide x 10 feet high, leading from Arundel
> Street to Water Street; east Water Street, south
> Charles Stoakes, north William Blackwell
> iii) parcel leased to John Christmas 20 feet

(frontage) x 50 feet in depth; south Charles Stoakes, north John Walmesley

v) parcel 20 x 58 feet leased to John Walmesley; south William Blackwell, north George Mann, esq.

For a down payment of £784, the Duke assigns the rent receipts to Pearce for 41 years.

MXD272	Assignment of ground rents	**15 Apr. 1679**

– to John Coggs, citizen and goldsmith of London

> i) parcel of ground 18 feet 2 inches x 41½ feet, in occ. of Thomas Gamon, citizen and carpenter of London; east Water Street, south and north Thomas Gamon
> ii) 17 feet 10 inches x 44 feet 6 inches, south Robert Winter, east Water Street, north Thomas Gamon
> iii) in Norfolk Street, next Howard Street: parcel of ground 30 x 70 feet begun to be built by Peter Rich of Lambeth, co. Surrey, Esq; east Norfolk Street, south Howard Street, west and north, the Duke
> iv) in Howard Street: parcel of ground 16 x 22 feet begun to be built by John Weobly, locksmith; north Howard Street, south Richard Linwood, east Arundel House and west Cornelius Lilley

For a down payment of £495 12s., the respective rents of £7 4s., £7 4s., £22 10s. and £4 8s. are assigned to Coggs for the remainder of their terms (terms not stated)

Arundel Street, west side: the 6th Duke's leases

MXD273-275	Leases for 41½ years	**2 Feb. 1677**

– to Anthony Plomer, citizen and merchant tailor of London

> i) messuage in which the lessee dwells, formerly two tenements, lying at the back of certain houses leased to Plomer; with three separate yards on the east, west and north sides of the messuage; the plot totalling 28 feet x 65 feet; north on ground leased to John Gumley and west and south on other land leased to Plomer
> ii) parcel of ground begun to be built by the lessee, 22 feet (frontage) by 29 feet in depth; north, west

and south on other premises leased to Plomer
iii) parcel of ground begun to be built by Plomer
18 x 29 feet; south Thomas Underwood, west and
north on other ground leased to Plomer

A peppercorn rent for the first 1½ years and £9, £8 and £7
annual rent thereafter for i), ii) and iii) respectively.   3 docs.

MXD276   Lease of ground rents   **15 Apr. 1679**

– to Charles Dawe of Langley Marsh, co. Bucks., gent.

i) parcel of ground 20 x 51 feet, begun to be built
by John Longland; west on premises of the Duke,
north Henry Peirson, carpenter, south William Biggs,
carpenter
ii) parcel of ground 20 x 53 feet, in occ. of John
Angier, carpenter; west on ground on which a capital
messuage for the Duke himself is intended to be
built, north John Angier and south John Prince,
bricklayer
iii) parcel of ground 20 x 53 feet in occ. of John
Angier; west as above, north [blank] Martine and
south John Angier
iv) In Surrey Street parcel of ground 20 x 60 feet on
west side of Surrey Street in occ. of John Tombes;
south Cornelius Lilley, gent, west Strand Bridge
Lane, north George Roberts Esq.

For a down payment of £720, the Duke assigns ground rents
of £10, £11, £11 and £13 on properties i) – iv) respectively
from Lady Day next for the remainder of their respective
terms (terms not stated).

MXD277   Lease for 41½ years   **6 Sep. 1679**

– to Richard Wynn, gentleman

parcel of ground 20 x 51 feet, begun to be built by
Thomas Underwood, glazier; north Anthony Plomer,
west the Duke, south Henry Peirson

Recites that building covenants between the Duke and Thomas
Underwood were agreed on 26 October 1676 and held on a
peppercorn rent. Now the formal lease term is granted to
Wynn for the remainder of a 41½-year term, at £10 annual
rent. Duke's signature.

MXD278   Lease for 39½ years   **8 Sep. 1679**

– to John Greene, carpenter

> parcel of ground 19 x 53 feet begun to be built
> by the lessee; west on a wall belonging to the
> Duke, south the Duke, north Joseph Blowers,
> bricklayer

Pursuant to an agreement 8 August 1679 between Francis
Burghill and Jonathan Wilcox, the Duke's commissioners
for the letting of Arundell Ground and John Greene, the
premises are leased to Greene at a peppercorn rent for the
first 1½ years and £10 9s. annual rent thereafter.

MXD279   Assignment of rent   **14 Oct. 1679**

– to John Angier of St Margaret, Westminster, carpenter

> parcel of ground 11 x 53 feet, begun to be built
> by Jonathan Wilcox

Recites earlier lease to Wilcox 23 August 1679 for 39½ years.
Now, for a down payment of £154, the Duke assigns £6 1s.
annual rent to Angier for the rest of the term

MXD280   Lease for 39½ years   **10 Nov. 1679**

– to Nicholas Lance of St Martin in the Fields, plasterer

> parcel of ground 20 x 26 feet, begun to be built by
> Charles Stoakes, bricklayer; west Charles Stoakes,
> south Jonathan Wilcox, north John Angier

A peppercorn rent for the first 1½ years then £8 a year

MXD281   Lease for 41 years   **10 Apr. 1681**

– to Edward Bird, citizen and painter stainer of London

> parcel of ground begun to be built by the lessee
> on the west side of Arundel Street having a 21½ft
> frontage to the street together with 40 feet taken
> out of the soil of the Thames, which jointly are

53 feet in depth; abutting west on the Duke's wall, belonging to a plot on which a capital messuage is to be built, south on the river Thames and north on John Greene, carpenter

A peppercorn rent for the first year then £25 a year

MXD282   Assignment of lease   **24 Feb. 1683**

The 6th Duke and Daniel Sheldon of the City of London, merchant to Elizabeth Harrison alias Betensonne, spinster

> messuage or dwelling house lately erected on a parcel of ground 22 x 44 feet; east on Water Street, and north and south (in 1677) on other ground of the Duke

Recites that the parcel was originally leased to Charles Stoakes for building on 12 Feb. 1677 for 40½ years at £9 annual rent, who assigned it to John Standbrook for the remainder of the term. They assigned it, once the house was built, to Daniel Sheldon, who now, with the Duke's assent, assigns it to Miss Harrison.

Water Street: the 6th Duke's leases

MXD283   Assignment of ground rents   **1 Nov. 1678**

– to John Syms of the City of London, joiner

> i) parcel of ground leased to Syms having a 40 feet (frontage) x 60 feet in Water Street, lately taken out of the soil of the river Thames: extending *as farre eastwards as the ground of the said Duke goes*; west the street, south the Thames and north on other land leased by the Duke to Syms
> ii) parcel leased to Syms on the east side of Water Street, 115 feet alongside the street by 39 feet in depth (south side) and 34 feet (north side)

For a down payment of £852 the Duke and his agents assign to Syms the annual rents of £26 and £40 respectively on the two premises

MXD284   Assignment of rents   **19 Feb. 1679**

– to Joseph Wells, citizen and butcher of London

> parcels of ground being built on by John
> Prince:
> i) parcel of ground 17 x 16 feet in Water Street,
> with a yard at the north corner 8 x 14 feet; south
> on the street and north and west on other ground
> leased to Prince
> ii) parcel of ground 17 x 16 feet in Water Street
> with a yard at the north corner, also 17 x 16
> feet; south on the street, west on other ground
> leased to Prince, north and east on other ground
> of the Duke
> iii) parcel 16 x 20 feet on the east side of Arundel
> Street, with a yard 8 x 14 feet at the NE corner;
> north on other ground of the Duke, west and
> south on other ground leased to Prince
> iv) parcel of ground 16 x 17 feet on the east side
> of Arundel Street on the north corner of Water
> Street

Recites leases in 1678 to John Prince: i) on 18 March, ii) iii)
and iv) on 8 March; all for a 41-year term at rents of £3, £3,
£5 and £5 respectively, and assigned on 26 August last by
Prince to Joseph Wells, as above, for a down payment of
£502. Now, for a down payment of £208 by Wells, the Duke
assigns him the rents for the remainder of the respective
terms.

MXD285   Lease for 38 years   **27 Nov. 1680**

– to John Hodge, carpenter

> parcel of ground 26 x 30 feet, begun to be built,
> on the west side of Water Street; east on house in
> Milford Lane, north Jonathan Wilcox, carpenter
> and south on the Duke's coach houses

The Duke leases to Hodge from Lady Day 1681 at a pepper
corn rent for the first year and £9 2s. annual rent thereafter;
with access to the river at the lower end of Water Street *and
that the barr goeing down to the said River ... shall be opened
to them upon all occasions for to water their horses ...*
Endorsed *late the* White Lyon, *now the* 3 Rings of Wyre

MXD286   Lease for 38 years at a 6d. rent only (for 'diverse good causes')   **30 Nov. 1681**

The 6th Duke and Henry, Earl of Arundel to Obadiah Browne of Oxford, gentleman

> two upper rooms or chambers being two of three new rooms built on the east side of Water Street in Arundel Buildings adjoining the south end of the Duke's stables; east on buildings in Milford lane, north on the said stables and south on land leased to [illeg.] Fox, esq.

Deed affected by serious water damage.

Water Street: the 7th Duke's leases

MXD287   Lease for 11 years and £20 annual rent   **19 Nov. 1689**

– to Sir Thomas Fowles of the City of London

> i) stable on the east side of Water Street, 19 feet (frontage) x 29 feet in depth; east towards Milford Lane, south a stable to be let to Sir Francis Child, north a coach house in occ. of the lessee ii) coach house on the south side of i) above, 16 x 29 feet; abutting north [*sic*] on coachhouse in occ. of Sir Francis Child iii) a hay loft 12½ x 29 feet lying partly over the lessee's coach house and partly over that of Sir Francis Child; north on chambers let to John Hodge and south on iv) below iv) two chambers lying over part of ii) 23 x 22 feet; east towards Milford Lane, west on a passage to the hayloft; with the use, in common with Sir Francis Child, of the passage and the place to lay dung in; and with liberty for Child to carry his own hay through the hayloft hereby demised.

MXD288-289 Lease and renewal   **19 Nov. 1689,**
                                                                        20 Feb. 1700

– to Sir Francis Child of the City of London

> i) stable in Water Street [next door to the above] 26 x 29 feet; north on i) above and south on the passageway leading to the stable ii) coach house 17 x 29 feet; south on the coach house as in ii)

above, north on a coachhouse let to John Hodge
iii) three chambers and one pair of stairs over the
said stable; west on the passage leading from the
stair-head to Fowles' hayloft south on rooms let to
Obadiah Browne and north on rooms let to Fowle
iv) five chambers and two pair of stairs over the
last and which are also over the two rooms let to
Fowle; with liberty of access etc., in common with
Fowle, as above.

The premises, described as *part of the old coach house and
stables of Arundel House* were leased in 1689 for 11 years at
£21 annual rent; renewed for a further 11 years in 1700 at £21
10s. annual rent. Sir T. Fowle's premises next door were then
let to the Lord Chief Baron Ward. The coach house backs
east on buildings in Greyhound Court and north on premises
let to Mr Davenport.   2 docs.

viii. Private deeds, sublets and assignments

MXD290   Assignment of lease   **28 Aug. 1678**

Joseph Wells of St Andrew's, Holborn, butcher to John Prince, bricklayer

> two messuages in Water Street in Norfolk Buildings lately obtained, among other things, by Wells from Prince; in occ. of said John Prince and William Gilbert

Wells assigns his lease to Prince for 11 years in return for the annual rent of £32, but undertaking himself to pay the £6 annual ground rent to the Duke

Memo of surrender of the lease endorsed   **10 Mar. 1682**

MXD291   Lease for 7 years at £20 annual rent   **27 Sep. 1681**

John Hodge, carpenter, to John King, merchant

> messuage in Water Street 14 feet (frontage) x 29 feet in depth; west on the street, east on ground of the *White Horse* in Milford Lane, north Jonathan Wilcox, south John Hodge; the messuage containing a little cellar, a ground room even with the street, 2 rooms up one pair of stairs, two more rooms above, up two pairs of stairs, and two garrets above, up 3 pairs of stairs

MXD292   Lease for 21 years at £64 annual rent   **23 Dec. 1686,**
                                                1697

Robert Crofts, citizen and merchant tailor of London to William Wade, citizen and leather seller of London

> Messuage and yard behind, on the west side of Norfolk Street, late in the occ. of the Duke of

Norfolk and now of the lessee. [Abuttals not given]

Room by room schedule of fixtures and fittings (attached) shows the house to be on the corner of Norfolk Street and Howard Street.
Endorsement: assignment of the remainder of the lease term by William Wade to Alice Banbury, spinster. 1697

MXD293   Bargain and Sale   **19 Mar. 1690**

a) Simon Fox, esq. and Nevinson Fox, gentleman, both of St Clement Danes, to   b) Henry Hall of Harding Court, co. Oxon., esq.

> Parcel of ground on the east side of Surrey Street, 56 feet in length north to south and in breadth 3 feet one inch at its southern end, tapering north towards the Strand; in the occ. of Richard Stokes, carpenter and Joseph Wing, broker; abutting on premises of b) to the west and of a) to the south.

a) sells to b) for £26 17s. 6d.

3. The Strand Estate, 1701-1777

i. Introduction

This period covers the work of Thomas, 8th Duke of Norfolk (1701-1732) and his successor Edward, 9th Duke (1732-1777). Although the latter had the longer incumbency, it was the former, the 8th Duke, who put into effect the second phase of development of the Strand Estate.

The original leases ran for a term of 42 years or thereabouts from 1676 onwards. This meant they were coming up for renewal in the first decades of the 18th century. An Act of Parliament was obtained (10 Geo. I, 1724) *to enable Thomas Duke of Norfolk to make leases for sixty years.* The recitals emphasised that many of the properties were now in a state of disrepair and that, if left to decay, the Duke's financial interest in the estate would be seriously compromised. Because of the entailments and the conditions placed by previous Acts of Parliament upon the ducal estates, a new Act of Parliament was needed before the desired 'building leases' could be put into effect. While specifying in particular the new buildings in Surrey, Norfolk, Howard and Arundel streets, the Act empowered the Duke to include the old houses in the Strand as well as any new premises, mainly in Milford Lane, that had been bought into the Estate.

The handful of lease renewals that predate the Act generally ran for 13 years as from Lady Day (25 March) 1718 even though they may have been executed a decade or more earlier. The lion's share of new leases were drawn up and signed on the last day of the year, 24 March 1724, or, in modern form, 24 March 1725. The content of the documents themselves shows that many leaseholders were indeed required to pull down the old house and to rebuild anew. In other cases 'substantial repairs' were accepted.

The 8th Duke generally acted in his own name without the use of agents, as previous dukes had done. However, in the first round of leases executed from around 1706 to 1718, the witnesses were often Charles Mawson senior, a former ducal agent, Charles Mawson junior and Richard Mawson. Such a big undertaking as the 1725 renewals would have employed several different firms of lawyers. The different styles of handwriting that occur in the series imply that this is indeed the case. Witnesses to each lease signed their names on the back of the deed, as was usual in the 18th century. The same names occur time and time again, inferring that they are ducal agents, legal clerks and others who had been involved in the drafting of the leases and who were therefore habitually present at the signing. Frequently recurring names are Robert Westby, Cornelius Blackwell and Christopher Parker. Others include Thomas Burrow, Richard Canning, John Clark, William Collett, Richard Cotton, Anthony Nott, William Plant, Benjamin Whiten and S. Rock. These names have not been noted in the catalogue. However, witnesses' names which are obviously exceptions to this rule, have occasionally been noted.

The main phase of rebuilding took place between 1731 and 1760 and formed part of the agreement between the Duke and each lessee, written into each new 60-year lease. A few were drawn up in the ensuing years. However, irrespective of when the lease was drawn, all the lease terms were to run from Lady Day 1731. The rebuilding was to be done during the first 30 years of the lease. Each tenant agreed, at their own costs, to pull down the existing fabric and to replace it with *a good and substantial new Brick Messuage*. The tenant was also liable to keep cleansed and repaired *all sewers, sinkes gutters, widdraughts, and pavements in the street before the doors of* his or her house. For the tenancies themselves, prohibited trades include brewer, working smith, working goldsmith, tripeman, cloth dyer, melting tallow chandler, slaughterman, butcher, soap boiler or distiller of strong waters or other trade judged to be offensive to the neighbours.

Thomas the 8th Duke died in 1732 and it therefore fell on the shoulders of his younger brother and successor, Edward, to oversee the, generally stringent, building terms and conditions laid down. Agents were presumably used although it is not entirely clear who they were. Because the new 60-year leases were not due to expire until 1791, there were very few new leases issued under the 9th Duke's hand. Both he, however, as well as his brother were beneficiaries of the accumulated funds of the 'down payments' of the 1725 renewals. With the onus for rebuilding the Strand Estate houses firmly placed on the lessees' shoulders, both Thomas and Edward were free to spend the profits. It cannot be a coincidence that the long-awaited new ducal residence in London, Norfolk House, was acquired during this period (Section 8 below).

With only a few leases coming up for renewal, where tenants had died or wished to surrender their holdings, the style adopted by the 9th Duke for his own leases is far more relaxed than that of his predecessor. Like the 8th Duke, he executed the leases without the use of any agents as trustees. The premises were generally described in rather vague terms. There were no clauses for rebuilding and the provisos for repairs and maintenance, and against unneighbourly tradesmen as residents, are all standard. Occasionally, perhaps where 60-year leaseholders had not repaired or rebuilt their premises in the first 30 years of the lease, as instructed, the leases were endorsed with a memorandum of a new arrangement agreed with the 9th Duke. These memoranda are detailed in this catalogue.

In this section of the catalogue, as before, parties' parish of residence is only stated where it is not St Clement Danes; and the street by street arrangement is in the same order as before. Estate records already catalogued, or recently box-listed at Arundel include useful supplementary information for this period, as, for example: MD852 – a register of leases and names of tenants, 1732. Appendix I below gives further details.

ii. Appointments [etc.]

MXD301   Waterman's pass   **10 Feb. 1777**

The pass is addressed to the civil and military authorities to enable John Audsley, of Lambeth, water man, to go about his business.

Signed by Lord Effingham

MXD302   Assignment to new trustees   **22 Jul. 1777**

Charles Howard the younger to Robert Gosling and George Clive both of Fleet Street, London, on:

> All the messuages and tenements in Middlesex belonging to Edward [9th] Duke of Norfolk.

Recites a deed of 26 June 1771 whereby Charles Howard the elder of Dorking, esq. and Charles Howard the younger assigned the premises to John White of Arundel Castle, gentleman and Thomas Ryder of Lincoln's Inn, esq. for a term of years in order to raise the sum of £9,000 out of the Middlesex estates for the benefit of the elder Charles Howard if he succeeded to the Dukedom. Now that this indeed seems to be the case, the younger Charles Howard, who has borrowed £1,500 from Gosling and Clive, transfers the term to them [Edward, 9th Duke of Norfolk died in September 1777]

-oOo-

Although no premises were bought into the estate in this period, there are some 18th-century title deeds of premises between Water Street and Milford Lane in a later part of the catalogue.
They were acquired by Henry Charles, 13th Duke in 1852, *see* 6. The Strand Estate 1842-1860, *below*

iii. Legal papers

MXD303   Copy bill of complaint filed in Chancery   **Trinity Term 1707**

The Hon. Thomas Newport, esq. *v.* the Duke of Norfolk
Concerns the complainant's house at the lower end of Surrey
Street, next to Somerset House garden which he held by lease
from the Hon. Charles Howard, esq. dated 27 April 1696.
Subsidence and dilapidations made the house uninhabitable
and disputes have arisen between Charles Howard and his son
Henry Charles Howard on the one part and the complainant
on the other as to compensation, etc. [details] in which the
Duke is now asked, as a higher authority, to award Newport
a new lease term as compensation.   104 folios.

MXD304   Abstract of title   **(1659)-1715**

Relates to a dispute between the Duke and his trustees and
Simon and Nevinson Fox, relating to the site of the *Talbot
Inn* in the Strand, the site of Arundel House itself and the
terms as to its development by Act of Parliament, and to
land in Surrey Street.
A deed of 1659 relating to the *Talbot Inn* is cited in detail,
of which the original is not extant in this collection.   1 doc.
of 14 folios.

MXD305   Attested copy answer to a bill of complaint   **?c.1750**

Richard Anders, defendant, to the complaint of Thomas
Mawson and Thomas Smith
Refers to the defendant's house in Norfolk Street (originally
leased to Benjamin Richardson in 1680) and issues concerning
Mr Mawson's adjoining house in Howard Street and rights
of way attached.
Copy examined by R. Wilbraham (ducal agent)

iv. Londoners' tenancies

Lease renewals 1706-1717: Strand

MXD306   – to Thomas Templeman, pewterer for 13 years   **1 Nov. 1706**

> messuage on the south side of the Strand in Arundel
> Rents 15ft fronting north on the Strand by 56 feet
> in breadth, abutting south on a messuage in occ.
> of Thomas [blank], west on a messuage in the occ.
> of Mr Harrendine and east on a messuage in the
> occ. of Mrs Parsons

Down payment nil; annual rent £30
Small impressed seal on paper (Templeman)

MXD307   – to Thomas Tipping, woollen draper for 13 years   **1 May 1707**

> messuage having 16ft frontage to the Strand by
> 60 feet in depth, abutting east on Mr Ashe, south
> on [blank] and west on Mr Taylor; with free liberty
> to use an alley way leading out of the Strand, by a
> messuage formerly called the *Maidenhead*, to the
> back of the leased premises; all in the occ. of the
> lessee and known by the sign of the *Golden Key*

Down payment nil; annual rent £32

MXD308   – to Agnes Parsons, widow for 21 years   **1 Dec. 1707**

> messuage, with the yard behind it as it is now
> divided and enclosed with a brick wall, formerly in
> the occ. of Edward Richards and of the lessee as
> assignee of Bartholomew Parsons, decd., her late
> husband; with all cellars, solars and appurts., etc.;
> abutting north on the Strand, south on [blank],
> east on Richard Stretch, sword cutler and west
> on Mr Templeman

Down payment nil; annual rent £30

MXD309   – to Benjamin Thornton, gentleman for 13 years   **15 May 1713**

> messuage in the occ. of the lessee on the east side of Angell Court in the Strand, 37 feet in front, north to south; 29 feet from east to west at the north end and 14 feet at the south end; south Mr Witchchurch, north on two messuages in separate occs. of Mr Willett and Mr Williams, west on Angell Court and east on ground leased to Williams and others

Down payment £63; annual rent £10

MXD310   – to John Churchill, citizen and glover of London for 8 years   **1 May 1714**

> messuage in the Strand, formerly known as the *White Horse Tavern* in the occ. of Mrs Charras and the lessee; the next messuage west, in the occ. of Mr Hasslem, hosier; and the next messuage west, known by the sign of the *Beehive*, late in the occ. of Mr Chambers, hatter and now of Nicholas Marquois

– to run from Lady Day 1724 at £56 annual rent; no down payment

MXD311   –to Anne Hungerford of Great Chelsea, co. Middx, spinster for 11 years   **1 Aug. 1717**

> messuage and yard divided with a brick wall, lying at the south end of Angell Court in the Strand, 13 feet in breadth east to west at the north end of the premises and 6 feet at the south end and 68 feet north to south; abutting west on Angell Court and the messuage in the occ. of Anne Hodge, widow; east on the garden ground in occ. of [blank]; north on the messuage in the occ. of Mr Thornton and south upon a yard in the occ. of Mr Ashton

Down payment £36. Annual rent £6.
Small seal impressed on paper (Hungerford)

60-year lease renewals: Strand   **24 Mar. 1725**

MXD312   – to Katherine Abram of Abingdon, Berks., widow

94

messuage in a 15 x 56ft plot fronting the Strand; south premises in Norfolk Street, east [blank] Jaques and south [*sic*] a messuage in occ. of widow Harrendine; now in possession of Fox Kerry, grocer, and formerly let to Thomas Templeman

Down payment £273; annual rent £18

MXD313 – to John Anstis, esq., Garter, Principal King at Arms

messuage in a 13 x 62ft plot fronting the Strand; south a yard of a tenement of Francis Beauchamp, east William Cooper, west John Radford; in occ. of Peter Gleane, formerly leased to John Radford, toyman

Down payment £240; annual rent £15

MXD314 – to William Brind, citizen and painter stainer of London

messuage containing a yard divided off with a brick wall on the south side, in a plot 13 feet on the north by 68 feet x 6 feet at the south; west Angel court and Ann Hodge, widow, east premises in Norfolk Street leased to John Bullock and Anthony Smith, north Mr Thornton and south a yard of Thomas Vernon, esq.; now in the occ. of [blank] Brush and was formerly let to Ann Hungerford

Down payment £77; annual rent £5. **Marginal plan**.

MXD315-316 – to Mary Fleetwood of St Margaret, Westminster, spinster

messuage near the NE end of Arundel Street:
i) 12 feet (frontage to Strand) by 60 feet in depth in the occ. of Mr Redmayne Fox, grocer; south the *Crown Tavern*, east Anthony Simpson and west on a passage from the Strand to the *Crown Tavern* and a messuage of Mr Cooper; formerly let for 13 years to [blank] Samvorn
ii) 15 feet frontage to Strand by 45 feet in depth, in the occ. of Mr Cowper, goldsmith; east Redmayne Fox and a passage from Strand to the *Crown Tavern*, south Mrs Arrowsmith; with additionally a little messuage on the east side of Arundel Street, 15 feet x 15 feet, in occ. of Mrs Arrowsmith; north on ii), east on Redmayne Fox

Respective down payments are £224 and £378 and annual rents of £16 and £26. For property i) there is a covenant re common use of a drain together with the occupants of the three houses to the east; and a declaration endorsed by the 9th Duke in 1758 that he accepts the lessee's *substantiall and effectual* repairs in lieu of rebuilding. 2 docs.

MXD318-319 – to Mary Fleetwood as above   (1725–58)

> messuage on the south side of the Strand between Arundel Street and Norfolk Street in a plot 12 feet on the north side x 41ft 7in x 12ft 10in on the south side; south William Collins, east Mr Hicks, druggist and west John Robinson; now in occ. of Richard Taylor and formerly let to Richard Samvorn for 40 years, expiring 1732; reserving to the Duke a passage way 3 x 34 feet leading from the Strand to the house of William Collins.

Down payment £212; annual rent £16. With *An account of repairs Necessary to be done at Mr Vaughan's house in the Strand* ... by John Collins and signed by Mary Fleetwood, 1758. 2 docs.

MXD320-321 – to John Gumley of Isleworth, co. Middx, esq.

> i) two messuages with frontage of 16 feet to the Strand and a depth of 60 feet on the west side of Arundel Street; west Mr Hicks, south Mr Holt; in the occ. of Henry Plaistow and Thomas Atkins and formerly let to the lessee
> ii) messuage at the north east end of Norfolk Street fronting the Strand in a plot 16ft 8in x 40 feet; south Benjamin Luile, east James Willett; in the occ. of Anthony Haslam and was formerly let to the lessee

Down payments £385 and £329 respectively; annual rents £27 and £23; endorsements state that the Duke accepts Gumley's intended repairs in lieu of a rebuild. 2 docs.

MXD322-323 – to Anne Mills, spinster

> messuage in Arundel Rents known by the sign of the *Angell*, in the occ. of Anthony Sympson, 12ft 3in

in front to the Strand, by 60 feet in depth north to south on the west side and 61 feet on the (east) side by 13 feet width at the south end; west on Redmayne Fox, grocer, south on the *Crown and Anchor Tavern* and east on John Radford, toyman

Leased in May 1688 for 41 years to John Hodge and now as from Midsummer 1729 at £15 annual rent. Down payment £280   2 docs.

MX324-327   – to Hugh Mills of New Inn, Middlesex, gentleman

i) messuage in a plot 16 x 60 feet fronting the Strand; east Henry Plaistow, south Richard Holt, west Richard Taylor; now in the occ. of [blank] Hickes, druggist and formerly let to John Tipping

ii) messuage in a plot 13ft 8in at the north end fronting the Strand x 52ft 6in x 13ft at the south end; south [blank] Thornton, east [blank] Harrendine, widow, west Ivory Tarras; in occ. of Thomas Rider and formerly leased to John Hodge in 1690 for 40 years.

iii) messuage in a plot 16 x 44 feet fronting the Strand; south on premises in Norfolk Street, west William Stretch, sword cutler, east [blank] Edwards, widow; in occ. of Thomas Rock and formerly leased to Thomas Sandys. **Plan in margin.**

iv) two messuages, the first 11 x 46 feet, fronting the Strand, with a yard and house of office behind, divided from next door, below, by a brick wall; west Luke Jacques, east Thomas Rock; in occ. of William Stretch, sword cutler; the second (dimensions not given) on the west side of the first, in occ. of Luke Jacques; south on [blank], west Fox Kerry; both having been recently leased on 1 July 1724 to John White for six years (expiring Lady Day 1731)

Down payments £280, £240, £245 and £380 respectively and annual rents of £15 apiece for i) – iii) and £6 for property iv) 4 docs.

MXD328   – to Adrian Moore of New Inn, gentleman

messuage on the east side of Angel Court having a 37ft frontage to the court north to south x 26 feet in depth on the north side and 15 feet on the south side; west on the court, east on premises on Norfolk Street, south Thomas Brush and north on premises in the Strand; in occ. of [blank] and formerly let to Benjamin Thornton

Down payment £126; annual rent £10.
Marginal plan.

MXD329-330 – to John Robinson, linen draper

i) messuage in a plot 15 x 60 feet fronting the Strand; south William Collins, west Jane Syms, widow and east Richard Taylor; in the occ. of the lessee and formerly let to Jane Syms, widow. **Marginal plan**.
ii) messuage in a plot 16 x 49 feet fronting the Strand; south Mary Charras, west Henry Garbrand, east the lessee; in occ. of widow Wheeler

Down payments £238 and £100 respectively; annual rents £16 and £13. Memorandum re property i) that the Duke accepts the repairs that Robinson has done in lieu of a total rebuild. 2 docs.

MXD331-332 – to Mary Scott, widow

i) messuage with a frontage of 13ft 4in at the north end to the Strand x 55ft 6in in depth x 12ft 8in in breadth at the south end; south a messuage in Angel Court, west Mr Ryder, glover and east Mr Fox Kerry, grocer; in the occ. of widow Harrendine and was formerly let to John Hodge, carpenter for 40½ years
ii) messuage with a frontage of 12ft 3in at the north end to the Strand x 60 feet in depth x 13ft 6in at the south end; south the *Crown Tavern*, west Anthony Sympson, haberdasher and east Mr Glean, apothecary; in the occ. of John Radford, toyman and formerly let to John Coggs for 40 years

Down payments £222 and £238; annual rents £18 and £16 respectively. 2 docs.

MXD333-334   – to John Walthoe, citizen and stationer of London   **(1725-61)**

> messuage in a plot 16ft x 43ft 6in fronting the Strand; south widow Smith, west Thomas Rock, east widow Edwards; in the occ. of widow Edwards and formerly let to John Ward, esq.

Down payment £329; annual rent £23
Two copies, both mutilated by removal of seal and signature. One copy endorsed with memorandum of assignment of lease **30 Sep. 1761** by Henrietta Marmillod, daughter of John Walthoe deceased, and John R.F. Marmillod her husband, to Eleanor Walthoe of Kensington, Middlesex, spinster.
2 docs.

MXD335   Lease for 60 years   **22 Mar. 1731**

– to John Bullock, tailor

> messuage in a plot 12 x 67 feet; south John Gumley, east Mary Charry and Widow Wheeler, west John Willett and Benjamin Linle; now in the occ. of Henry Garbrand, formerly let to John Churchill

Down payment £180; annual rent £15

9th Duke's leases, 1742-1767: Strand

MXD336   Lease for 31 years   **27 Mar. 1742**

– to William West, fan painter

> messuage on the west side of the gateway into the *Talbot Inn* in the Strand, now in the occ. of the lessee (no dimensions or abuttals)

Annual rent £30 with no down payment

MXD337   Lease for 21 years   **8 May 1764**

– to James Chauval of St James, Westminster, esq.

> messuage on the east side of Angel Court abutting north on Thomas Edgell, esq.

Annual rent £5 and down payment waived in lieu of the lessee's expenses in doing the repairs.

MXD338   Lease for 21 years   **10 Feb. 1767**

– to John Nott of St Clement Danes, fruiterer

> messuage in the occ. of the lessee, on the south side of the Strand on the west side of the gateway to the *Talbot Inn*, abutting east on [blank] Neilson [no dimensions given]

Annual rent £35 with no down payment

Lease renewals, 1706-1718: Surrey Street and Strand Lane

Surrey Street, east side

MXD339   Lease for 9 years   **8 Feb. 1714**

– to Humphrey Bradshaw, gentleman

> two messuages on the east side of Surrey Street in Arundel Buildings on a plot of ground 64 feet fronting the street by 54 feet in depth, abutting east on Dr Johnson and Mr Arnold, south on the River and north on premises of the commissioners for licensing Hackney coaches

To run from Lady Day 1723; down payment £9; annual rent £25

MXD340   Lease for 13 years   **8 Feb. 1713**

– to James Browne of Chiswick, merchant tailor

> messuage and ground on the east side of Surrey Street in Arundel Buildings, 22 feet fronting west on the street, x 37 feet in depth, abutting east on the premises below, south on the commissioners for Hackney coaches and north on [blank]; and little tenement at the back of the above, and a passage way, in all containing 6 feet under and over the passage; all in the occ. of Browne

To run from Lady Day 1719; down payment £80; annual rent £12

Surrey Street, west side

MXD341-343 Leases   **1 May 1707**

– to Joanna Warner, widow

> i) two messuages with a frontage of 22 feet east to the street, abutting west on Strandbridge Lane, south on a passage way and north on Mr White

– to Amy Blake of St James, Westminster

> ii) messuage 20 feet (frontage) x 68 feet; west on Strandbridge Lane, north Lady Longueville and south, William Draper

– to William Draper, esq.

> iii) messuage 38 feet (frontage) x [depth not given] west on Strandbridge Lane and south and north on Messrs Mills and Nutt

For respective down payments of £69 13s. and £49 10s., the Duke leases i) and ii) for 13 years as from Lady Day 1718 at £14 and £13 respective annual rents; and property iii) for 12 years as from Lady Day 1719 for a down payment of £110 and £24 14s. annual rent.

MXD344 Lease for 13 years   **20 Jun. 1715**

– to George Moore, gentleman

> Premises 24 x 70 feet as in **MXD220-222** above, now in the occ. of Lady Longueville and George Moore

Down payment £170; annual rent £23

Strand Lane

MXD345   – to Jeffery Nash, victualler   [blank] 1719

messuage on the back side of Surrey Street fronting Strandbridge Lane, 20 feet frontage x 18 feet in depth; south and east the Hon. Charles Howard, north Arthur Allibone

– to run for 12 years from Christmas 1781 at £10 annual rent; no down payment

60-year lease renewals: Surrey Street   24 Mar. 1725

Surrey Street, east side

MXD346-350   – to William Ingram of New Inn, gentleman
Plots on the east side of Surrey Street: **Small marginal plans**.

> **MXD346:** 22 (frontage) x 53 feet depth, 20 feet 6in at rear; south Mr Ashton, north James Brown; in occ. of Mr Challoner

> **MXD347:** 17 (frontage) x 54 feet; east on premises in Norfolk Street, south John Farr, north John George; in occ. of Walter Challoner and Ann Sleak

> **MXD348:** 21 (frontage) x 54 feet; east on premises in Norfolk Street, south Walter Chaloner, north Jonathan White and David Hopkins; in occ. of John George

> **MXD349:** 21 (frontage) x 54 feet; east on premises in Norfolk Street, south Mr Bellasise, north Walter Challoner; in the occ. of John Farr and Ann Sleak, formerly Thomas Batt

> **MXD350:** 20 (frontage) x 54 feet; east Mr Jones, south John George, north on premises in Howard Street; in occ. of David Hopkins and Jonathan White

Outbuildings in three of the properties are *commonly called the prison*. Down payments £150, £119, £133, £126, £182 and annual rents: £12, £8, £9, £9, £13 respectively.   5 docs.

MXD351   – to William Ingram as above

> two houses on the corner of Surrey Street and
> Howard Street: 22ft frontage to Surrey Street x
> 38ft frontage to Howard Street; west Surrey Street,
> north Howard Street, south Jonathan White and
> David Hopkins, east Grace Fuller, widow; in occ.
> of [blank] Blackway and [blank] Harding. **Marginal
> plan**. Down payment £175; annual rent £13

MXD352   – to James Browne of Chiswick, tailor

> messuage on the east side of Surrey Street in a plot
> 22 (frontage) x 54 feet; east on premises in Norfolk
> Street, south Mr Ingram, north Mr Ingram; in
> the occ. of George ?Farr [or ? Farrell]. **Marginal
> plan**.

Down payment £221; annual rent £13; renewed from Lady
Day 1732

MXD353   – to Joseph Ashton, gentleman

> Three messuages at the south-east end of Surrey
> Street and a vault at the south-west end of Norfolk
> Street jointly containing a 64ft frontage x 54 feet
> in depth (south side) x 69 feet (north side) in the
> several occs. of Joseph Hayne, esq., Mary Kemp,
> widow, and the lessee and were formerly let to
> Humphrey Bradshaw; east on premises in Norfolk
> Street, south the River Thames, north on premises
> of the commissioners for licensing Hackney coaches
> and of Mr Broadbelt. **Marginal plan**.

Down payment £400; annual rent £30

MXD354   – to John Bentley, victualler

> Messuage having a 27ft frontage to Surrey Street x
> 16 feet in depth in the occ. of the lessee, formerly
> let to William ?Clind; west Richard Rawlingson,
> south Howard Street, north on stables of Thomas
> Vernon, esq.

Down payment £130; annual rent £9. Damaged document

Surrey Street, west side   24 Mar. 2725 (cont)

MXD355   – to William Congreve, esquire

> plot 24 (frontage) x 70 feet; abutting west on Strandbridge Lane, south Mr Guest, north on a passage of 10 feet wide x 10 feet high leading from Surrey Street to Strandbridge Lane

Down payment £450; annual rent £25

MXD356   – to William Draper of Adgcombe Place, co. Surrey

> plot 38 feet (frontage) x 69 feet; west Strandbridge Lane, north Richard Guest, south Doctor Peters; now in the occ. of Thomas Ward, esq. and Thomas Martin, esq.

Down payment £448; annual rent £32

MXD357   – to Richard Guest, tailor

> Messuage in a plot 20 x ?68 [illegible] feet, in the occ. of the lessee, formerly of Amy Blake, widow; west Strandbridge Lane, north William Congreve, south Mr Ward

Down payment £210; annual rent £15

MXD358   – to George James Guidot of the Inner Temple, London, gent.

> Messuage in a plot 14 feet (frontage) x 52 feet in depth x 8 feet at the west end, in the occ. of [blank] Webster; south Mr Warner, north and west Thomas Vernon, esq.

Down payment £180; annual rent £10

MXD359   – to Richard Millan of Guildhall, London, gent.

> Messuage in a plot 19 x 47 feet in the occ. of Mrs Rowe; west Strand lane, south Sir Clement Wearge, north Arthur Allibone. **Marginal plan**.

Down payment £216; annual rent £13

MXD360   – to Hugh Mills of New Inn, London, gentleman

> Messuage in a plot of 20ft frontage x 65 feet in depth and 27 feet wide at the west end, in the occ. of M. Peters and formerly leased to Arthur Allibone. Abuttals not given, **Marginal plan**.

Down payment £280; annual rent £10

MXD361   – to Lydia Warner, spinster

> Messuage in a plot 22 x 72 feet, in the occ. of the lessee and was formerly let to Joanna Warner; west Strandbridge Lane, south Edward Porter, esq., north Mrs Webbster

Down payment £238; annual rent £16

Strand Lane

MXD362   – to Richard Millan of Guildhall, London, gentleman

> Messuage in a plot 13ft 3in x 19ft 6in on the ground floor and on the second floor 19ft 6in x 19ft, in the occ. of Widow Nash and formerly let to [illegible]; west on premises in Surrey Street, south Sir Clement Wearge, north Arthur Allibone. **Marginal plan**.

Down payment £54; annual rent £3
Memorandum of agreement endorsed, 7 Mar. 1729: permitting the lessee to pull the house down and replace it with a brick-built one.

The 9th Duke's leases, 1762-1775: Surrey Street

For further leases, 1762-1764, see Appendix I

Surrey Street, east side

MXD363-364 Lease renewals   **10 May 1762**

– to Elizabeth Flinn, widow

> i) messuage and yard in a plot 21ft 6in (frontage) x 54 feet, being the 5th house from the corner of

Howard Street, except a 5ft-wide passage running from Surrey Street by the side of this messuage and its yard whose use is reserved for the occupiers of a house in Norfolk Street leased to William Davis, esq. **Marginal plan**.

– to Edward Salkeld of St George the Martyr, bricklayer

ii) messuage and yard in a plot 20ft 6in (frontage) x 54 feet, being the 2nd house from the corner of Howard Street. **Marginal plan**.

Renewed for 21 years, at respective rents of £12 and £10 only and their expenses on repairs in lieu of down payments. 2 docs. *For further leases 1762-1764, see Appendix I.*

Surrey Street, west side

MXD365   Lease for 21 years to James Theobald, esq.   **31 Jan. 1758**

Messuage in the occ. of the lessee; west Strand Lane, south John Locks, north [blank] Moore

No down payment; annual rent £38

MXD366-372   Lease for 21 years   **19-22 Jun. 1773**

– to Hans Winthrop Mortimer of Caldwell, co. Derby, esq. Thomas Griffin of Lincolns Inn, his attorney

i) messuage in a plot 30ft 7in x 58 feet; south the River Thames, north ground formerly in the occ. of Mrs Bolt and lately of the Commissioners for licensing Hackney Coaches, on which a former messuage had since burnt down. **Marginal plan**.

ii) messuage in a plot 20ft 6in x 60 feet; south on part of the above-mentioned plot in occ. of the Hackney Coaches, north on premises formerly of Lady Wearge, since of Robert Smith Esq. **Marginal plan**.

iii) messuage in a plot 21ft 6in x 59 feet; south on ground on which a former messuage burnt down, since in the occ. of Joseph Ashton and lately of [blank] Cumming, gentleman, north on another messuage which has burnt down, since in the occ. of Mr Nicholls and lately of [blank] Neal. **Marginal plan**.

The leases are granted in consideration of the covenants undertaken by the lessee before he built his present houses, upon surrender of the previous leases by the persons whose premises had burnt down. Three copies of the lease relate to property ii) and two to property iii). There is also a draft surrender of the previous lease of the premises to Joseph Ashton.
Annual rents £10, £20 and £35 respectively.   7 docs.
Further deeds relating to Hans Winthrop Mortimer, 1795 and 1833, occur later in the catalogue.

MXD373-374   Lease and counterpart for 16 years   **14 Jun. 1775**

– to John Troughton of Surrey Street, mathematical instrument maker

> messuage in a plot 14 feet (frontage) x 52 feet x 8 feet at the rear, in the occ. of the lessee, formerly leased to George James Guidott; south Elizabeth Jewell, north and west James Smith

No down payment; annual rent £10. Both leases mutilated by removal of signatures.

Lease renewals, 1706-1714: Norfolk Street

Norfolk Street, east side

MXD375-376   – to John Gumley, looking glass maker   **1 Nov. 1706**

> i) messuage on the east corner of Norfolk Street with a 16ft 18inch frontage to the Strand, depth 40 feet; south John Gumley, west Norfolk Street, east Mr Willet, mercer
> ii) messuage with 25ft frontage on east side of Norfolk Street, depth 50 feet; north Dr Dawes, south Mr Emerton an apothecary, west the street and east Mr Willet, mercer
> iii) messuage with 25ft frontage on east side of Norfolk Street, depth 50 feet; north John Gumley, south Mr Smith, west the street and east Mr Willett
> iv) messuage with 20ft frontage on the east side of Norfolk Street, 16ft width at the back, the north side 20 feet 8 inches, the south side 22 feet; east Mr Willett, south Dr Dawes, west Norfolk Street and north John Gumley

Terms due to expire in 1718 or 1719 are renewed to 1731.
Down payments £95, £83 2s. 6d., £83 2s. 6d., £47 and annual
rents £30, £15, £15 and £10 respectively.   4 docs.

MXD377   – to John Green, citizen and carpenter of London

> messuage in occ. of Mrs Sneaton, with 22ft frontage
> on east side of Norfolk Street, depth 70 feet; north
> Mr Body, south Mr Devonport, west the street,
> east [blank]

Terms as above. Down payment £67 13s. 9d.; annual rent
£16.

MXD378-379 – to George Jenkins, vintner   **1 May 1707**

> i) messuage in occ. of Mr Gifford, surgeon, with
> a frontage of 19 feet on the east side of Norfolk
> Street, depth 70 feet; west on the street, south on
> William Longueville, esq., east [blank] and north
> on Mr Emerson, apothecary
> ii) messuage in occ. of Mr Emerson with a frontage
> on the east side of Norfolk Street, depth 50 feet;
> west on the street, south Mr Gifford, east [blank]
> and north on Mr Smith

Renewed for 12 years from 1718. Down payments £40 10s. and
£44 11s. and annual rents £12 and 4 shillings respectively.
2 docs.

MXD380   – to Sarah Harrison of St Andrew Holborn, spinster   **May 1713**

> i) messuage in the occ. of the Earl of Stamford,
> in a plot 22 x 70 feet on the east side and fronting
> Norfolk Street, east Mr World, south John Green,
> north William Longueville, esq.

MXD381   – to Edward Porter of St Clement Danes, gentleman   **May 1714**

> ii) messuage in the occ. of William Longueville,
> esq. (no dimensions or abuttals)

For separate payments of £160 each, the Duke leases i) and ii)
above for 13 years as from 1718, each at £20 annual rent.
2 docs.

Norfolk Street, west side

MXD382   – to Christopher Broughton, upholsterer   **1 Nov. 1706**

> messuage in occ. of Mr Turner, surgeon, with 12ft 6inch frontage on west side of Norfolk Street, depth 30 feet 6 inches; north Christopher Broughton, south Mrs Fane, east the street and west a yard belonging to [blank]

Renewed for 14 years from 1718. Down payment £45 13s. 4d., annual rent £6.

MXD383-384   – to Robert Croft, citizen and merchant tailor of London   **1 Nov. 1706**

> messuage in occ. of Mrs Bandburg, with a 30ft frontage on the west side of Norfolk Street, depth 52 feet; north Mrs Turgis, south a house in Howard Street, west Mrs Diplow and east the street

Renewed for 14 years from 1717. Down payment £104; annual rent £16; with copy of Robert Croft's renewal.   3 docs.

MXD385-387   Lease renewal and assignment   **1 Nov. 1706-**
                                                                 27 May 1712

– to Christopher Broughton, upholsterer

> messuage on the north west end of Norfolk Street having a 16ft frontage to the Strand and a depth north to south of 43 feet 6 inches; north the Strand, south Mr Turner, surgeon, west Mr Sands and east Norfolk Street

For a down payment of £100 the Duke leases for 14 years from Lady Day 1714 at £36 13s. 4d. annual rent; an assignment was made on 27 May 1712 to John Ward of the City of London, esq., for 14 years from Lady Day 1717 at the same rent; and a corroborative endorsement by Ward, 26 May 1712.   3 docs.

MXD388-389   Lease renewals, and counterparts   **1 May 1707**

– to Christopher Broughton, upholsterer

> i) two messuages in occ. of Mrs Charnock and a tenant of Mr Batt's, in a plot 40 x 70 feet on the west side of Norfolk Street; east on the street, south on an entry leading from a house of Mr Mawson

to Norfolk Street, west on houses in Angell Court and north on Mr Batt

ii) two messuages in occ. of Mr Batt and Mrs Batt, in a plot 40 x 70 feet on the west side of Norfolk Street; east on the street, south on a tenant of Mr Batt, north on Mrs Fane and west on houses in Angell court

For two down payments of £275, the Duke renews the two leases for 13 years as from 1718, each at a peppercorn rent.

Endorsements by Broughton surrendering the leases 26 May 1712. 4 docs.

MXD391-393   – to Thomas Batt, tailor   **27 May 1712**

i) two messuages together in a plot 40 feet (frontage) by 70 feet in depth; south ii) below, north Mrs Fane, west towards Angel Court

ii) two messuages together in a plot 40 x 70 feet as above; north i) above, south an entry to a messuage of Mr Mawson, west towards Angel Court

Recites that premises are in the occ. of Batt and they were formerly leased to Christopher Broughton and assigned to John Ward. For a token down payment, the premises are each leased for 13 years from 1718 at a peppercorn rent only.   3 docs.

MXD394   – to Richard Whitchurch, tailor   **1 May 1714**

messuage in a plot 25 x 61 feet together with the building 17 x 8 feet standing on the back part of the plot, and its yards; north Mrs Bartlet, east the street, south [not given] and west Mr Thornton

– for 13 years from 1718. Down payment £148; annual rent £18

MXD395   – to George Fuller, chandler   **1 May 1714**

messuage in the occ. of Mr Clark, west on a back-house of George Woolley, tailor, north Mr Bullock, tailor and south Mr Mackworth

– for 13 years from 1718. Down payment £87; annual rent £15

MXD396   – to Mary Warter of East Barnet, Hertford, widow   **Aug. 1715**

Messuage in the occ. of Mr Mackworth; south Mr Conyers, west Mr Russell, north Mr Clark

– for 13 years from 1718. Down payment £80 10s; annual rent £12.

60-year lease renewals: Norfolk Street   24 Mar. 1725

Norfolk Street, east side

MXD397   – to Ann Carter, spinster

House plot 22 x 70 feet in the occ. of the lessee, formerly let to John Hodge; east to premises in Arundel Street, south Robert Weston, esq., north Doctor Robinson

Down payment £468; annual rent £18

MXD398   – to Elizabeth Cockaine, widow

House plot 22 x 70 feet in the occ. of Benjamin Sweet, esq., formerly leased to John Green; east to premises in Arundel Street, south William Shippen, esq., north Robert Weston, esq.

Down payment £288; annual rent £20

MXD399   – to Edward des Fontaines, gentleman

House plot 22 x 70 feet in the occ. of the lessee, formerly leased to John Green; north Widow Body, south John Taylor, esq. **Marginal plan.**

Down payment £238; annual rent £16 10s.

MXD400   – to John Gascoigne of St Martin in the Fields, esq.

i) House plot at the south east end of Norfolk Street 41 feet (frontage to the south) x 41 feet in depth south to north, in the occ. of Mr Balam, formerly leased to John Thompson; south on the River Thames, north William Shippen, esq., west

Mr Allen, east James Pearse ii) passage leading from the premises to Norfolk Street 33 feet in length x 7 feet in width

Down payment £450; annual rent £15

Witnesses: Joseph Stanion and Robert Johnson

MXD401-402 – to John Gumley of Isleworth, Middx, esq.

i) House plot 25 x 50 feet in the occ. of Mrs Grayham and formerly leased to John Gumley; east John Churchill, south Mrs Glanville, north Benjamin ?Levile
ii) House plot 20 x 37 feet in the occ. of Benjamin ?Levile and formerly leased to John Gumley; east Henry Garbrand, south Mrs Greyham, north Anthony ?Haslum. **Marginal plan**, which also refers to a Mr Willit's house on the north side of Mr Haslum's yard

Down payments £238 and £189; annual rents £16 and £13 respectively. Endorsement of the Duke's acceptance of the intended repairs in lieu of a total rebuild.

MXD403 – to John Gumley of Isleworth, Middx, esq.

House plot 25 x 50 feet lately in the occ. of Mrs Glanville and formerly leased to said John Gumley; east Mr Churchill, south William Matthews, north Mrs Graham

Down payment £238; annual rent £16; endorsement of the Duke's acceptance of the intended repairs in lieu of a total rebuild

MXD404 – to Sarah Harrison of St Paul, Covent Garden, Westminster

House plot 22 x 70 feet in the occ. of Widow Body and formerly leased to Sarah Harrison; east on a yard in occ. of Andrew Richmond, north Charles Longueville, south Mr Fountain, occulist

Down payment £260; annual rent £20

Endorsement 22 May 1760: unexecuted acceptance by the 9th Duke of repairs done by Elias White of Great Kirby Street, St Andrew's Holborn, to whom the lease has been assigned.

MXD405-406 – to Charles Longueville, esq.

i) House plot 20 x 70 feet in the occ. of the lessee, formerly leased to Edward Porter, gentleman; north Mr Giffard, south Widow Body. **Marginal plan.**
ii) House plot 18 x 70 feet in the occ. of Mr Gifford, chirugeon and formerly leased to George Jenkins; south Charles Longueville, north William Mathews

Down payments £285 and £196; annual rents £15 and £12 respectively

MXD407 – to William Matthews, apothecary

House plot 19 x 50 feet (the width including under and over a passage leading from Norfolk Street to the house of John Gumley) in the occ. of the lessee and formerly leased to George Jenkins; east John Gumley, south Mr Gifford, north Mrs Glanville. **Marginal plan.**

Down payment £168; annual rent £12

MXD408 – to Hugh Mills of New Inn, gentleman

House plot 24ft 6in x 35ft with a back yard and a necessary house in the occ. of John Tayler, esq. and formerly leased to John Green. Abuttals not given. **Marginal plan.**

Down payment £231; annual rent £12

MXD409 – to Edmund Probyn, serjeant at law

House plot 20 x 70 feet in the occ. of the lessee and formerly leased to Henry Pearson; south Dr Robinson, north Sir Peter King

Down payment £330; annual rent £20

MXD410   – to William Shippen, esq.

> House plot 20 x 70 feet in the occ. of the lessee and formerly let to Charles Mawson; south Mr Allen, esq., north Benjamin Sweet, esq.

Down payment £342; annual rent £20

MXD411   – to Robert Weston, esq.

> House plot 20 x 70 feet in the occ. of the lessee, formerly let to William Cooke; south Benjamin Sweet, esq., north Mrs Ann Carter

Down payment £288; annual rent £20

MXD412   – to the Rt Hon. Peter, lord King, Baron of Ockham   **1 Oct. 1725**

> House plot 25 x 70 feet in the occ. of the lessee and formerly leased to Butler Buggin, esq.; south Mr Serjeant Probyn, north Thomas Hancock, esq.

Down payment £337; annual rent £25

Between Norfolk Street and Arundel Street

MXD413-414 – to John Gumley of Isleworth, co. Middx, esq.   **24 Mar. 1725**

> i) messuage in a plot 14 feet (frontage) x 34 feet, in occ. of Mary Charas and formerly let to John Churchill; north widow Wheeler, south the lessee, west Henry Garbrand and premises in Norfolk Street, east John Robinson and premises in Arundel Street
> ii) messuage in a plot 20 feet at the south end x 63 feet x 16 feet at the north end in the occ. of the lessee and formerly let to Mr Chirchill; west premises in Norfolk Street, east premises in Arundel Street, south Mrs Gifford, north Mrs Charrows; with the passage 5 feet wide x 50 feet in length x 10 feet in height, leading out into Norfolk Street;

Down payments £80 and a nominal 5 shillings respectively; annual rents £7 and £8. Each lease with the Duke's acceptance of the intended repairs in lieu of a total rebuild.

Norfolk Street, west side   **24 Mar. 1725**

MXD415   – to Edward Barker of the Inner Temple, esq.,

> House plot 20 x 70 feet in the occ. of Mrs Shelley and
> formerly leased to Henry Box, esq.; north Mr French,
> south John Drummond, esq.

Down payment £360; annual rent £20

MXD416   – to James Browne of Chiswick, tailor

> House plot 20 x 70 feet in the occ. of Joseph
> Pennington, esq. and formerly leased to the lessee;
> south Mr Broadbelt, north Sir John Williams

Down payment £270; annual rent £20. Witnesses Edward Erlin
and R. Hawkins, both of Chiswick

MXD417   – to John Bullock, tailor

> House plot 21 x 70 feet in the occ. of Thomas
> Batt and formerly leased to Thomas Batt; north
> Mr Morgan, south on a passage leading from a
> messuage in possession of Mr Mawson, west on a
> house in Angel Court

Down payment £252; annual rent £16

MXD418   – to Grace Fuller, widow

> House plot 23 x 52 feet in the occ. of Mrs Swift,
> formerly leased to George Fuller; west Mr Mawson,
> north John Bullock and south Peter Stour,
> gentleman

Down payment £259; annual rent £17

MXD419   – to the Rt Hon. Simon, Lord Viscount Harcourt

> House plot 30 x 52 feet formerly leased to Robert
> Crofts, citizen and merchant tailor of London
> [present occupation of the house not given]; west
> Mrs Marsh, north Mr Storer, south on Howard
> Street

Down payment *a competent sum*; annual rent £16

MXD420   – to Samuel Hilliard, rector of Stifford, co. Essex, and
                                              Lettice his wife

Houses in a plot 40 x 70 feet in the occ. of Thomas Jobber, esq., Thomas Beesley, gentleman, [blank] Shortis, gentleman and Ann Holman, and were formerly leased to Humphrey Bradshaw; south on the river Thames, north Henry Jones, gentleman

Down payment £770; annual rent £45

Witnesses: Elizabeth Fidell and Gabriel Leaver

MXD421   – to Charles Johnson of Mortlake, co. Surrey, gentleman

House plot 20 x 70 feet in the occ. of Mr Broadbelt and formerly leased to the present lessee; south Mr Gold, north [blank] Pennington, esq.

Down payment £360; annual rent £20.
Witnesses: Henry Overton, James Breach, Charles Kinsey

MXD422   – to Henry Jones, gentleman

House plot 20 x 55 feet now in the occ. of Mr Gold and was formerly leased to Captain Bradshaw; south Mr Beesley, north Mr Broadbelt

Down payment £270; annual rent £20

MXD423-425 – to Anthony Smith, perriwigmaker   **(1725-1755)**

i) House plot 20 x 70 feet in the occ. of the present lessee and formerly leased to Thomas Batt; north Mr Bartlett, south Mr Morgan and west on a tenement in Angell Court
ii) House plot 20 x 70 feet in the occ. of [blank] Morgan, esq. and was formerly leased to Thomas Batt; south John Bullock, north Anthony Smith and west on premises in Angel Court
iii) House plot 20 x 70 feet in the occ. of Widow Bartlett and formerly leased to Thomas Batt; west on premises in Angell Court, north [blank] Shatlock and south Anthony Smith

Down payments £252, £238 and £170 respectively; annual rents £16 for each property
Endorsement on **MXD425**, 2 Apr. 1755, records acceptance by the 9th Duke of the repairs done by incoming lessee Thomas Tomkyns, surgeon, as sufficient in lieu of a complete rebuild.   3 docs.

MXD426   – to Thomas Smith of New Inn, gentleman

> House plot 22 x 30 feet in the occ. of Thomas Mawson to whom it was formerly leased; east Grace Fuller, west on a coach yard of Thomas Vernon, esq., north John Bullock, south Mary Warter

Down payment £112; annual rent £6

MXD427-428 – to Margaret Thompson, widow

> i) House plot 24 x 40 feet, together with a yard 30 x 12 feet, in the occ. of Richard Cannin and formerly leased to John Thompson; west Margaret Thompson, south Mr French, north on Howard Street
> ii) House plot 22 x 70 feet in the occ. of Mr French and formerly leased to John Thompson; south Mrs Shelley, north the present lessee

Down payments £360 for each property; annual rents £16 apiece

MXD429-430 – to John Walthoe, citizen and stationer of London   **(1725-1761)**

> House plot 12ft 6in x 30ft 6in in the occ. of Widow Smith and formerly leased to Christopher Broughton; north Widow Edwards, south Mr Shatlock and west on a yard of Fox Kerry, grocer

Down payment £161; annual rent £10
2 copies, the signature cut out of each. Endorsement on **MXD430**, 30 Sep. 1761 whereby Eleanor Walthoe, daughter and heir of Thomas Walthoe, deceased, assigned to Thomas Waller, citizen and stationer of London, the residue of the lease term

MXD431   – to Mary Warter of East Barnet, co. Herts., widow

House plot 15 x 70 feet in the occ. of Peter Storeer, gentleman and formerly leased to the present lessee; west Widow Smalewood, south John Conyers, esq., north Mrs Swift

Down payment £170; annual rent £13

MXD432   – to Susannah Whitchurch of Walton on Thames, widow

House plot 25 x 61 feet in the occ. of [blank] Shatlock and was formerly leased to Richard Whitchurch; west on premises in Angell Court, north Widow Smith, south Widow Bartlett

Down payment £266; annual rent £18
Endorsement 22 April 1755 whereby the 9th Duke acknowledges that the repairs done by incoming lessee, Henry Plant, esq., are sufficient and that a complete rebuild is not necessary.

MXD433   – to John Williams, knight and alderman of the city of London

House plot 20 x 70 feet in the occ. of John Drummond, esq., formerly let to Henry Box, esq.; south Sir John Williams, north Mrs Shelley

Down payment £360; annual rent £20

The 9th Duke's leases
There are no surviving leases executed by the 9th Duke for Norfolk Street properties, but it will be seen from the above section that he often verified the building terms of his predecessor's leases.

Lease renewals 1701-1718: Howard Street
As before, the leases were all to run from 1718 for 13 years (or slight variations of that formula)

Howard Street, north side

MXD434   – to Robert Crofts, citizen and merchant tailor of London   **1 Nov. 1706**

House plot 17 x 30 feet in the occ. of Mr Diplow; east Mrs Banbury [north and west blank]

Down payment £32 1s. 3d.; annual rent £6 10s.

MXD435   – to John Greene, citizen and carpenter of London   **1 Nov. 1706**

House plot 34 feet (frontage) x 16 feet in the occ. of Mr Langley; north [blank], west Mr Davenport, east Mrs Bracegirdle; together with all that ancient vault under the premises 60ft north to south x 17 feet east to west

Down payment £57; annual rent £6

MXD436   – to Ann Bracegirdle, spinster   **1 May 1707**

House plot 17 x 25 feet in the occ. of the present lessee; west Mrs Langley, north [blank], east Mr Hugh Mills junior

Down payment £38; annual rent £3

MXD437   – to William Child, citizen and haberdasher   **1 May 1710**

House plot 27 feet (frontage onto Surrey Street) x 16 feet, commonly known as the *White Lyon*, in the occ. of John Warrington; north on stables of Nevinson Fox, esq., west on Surrey Street, east Mr Sills and south on Howard Street

Down payment £33 15s.; annual rent £5

MXD438   – to Thomas Batt of St Pancras, tailor   **1 Aug. 1716**

Back house [dimensions not given] with the passage pertaining, 33 x 3½ feet leading into Howard Street, in the occ. of Mr Russell; north on stables of Mr Vernon, south Mr Rawlins, east Mr Stretton

Down payment £24; annual rent £4

MXD439   – to George Fuller, chandler   **1 May 1714**

Messuage 15 x 28 feet in the occ. of Mr Nixon, tailor; north on the coach house and stables of Thomas Vernon, esq., west John Bentley, east Mr Stretton

Down payment £40; annual rent £6

Howard Street, south side

MXD440   – to Edmund Ebbutt, citizen and vintner of London   **1 May 1707**

> House plot 23½ x 33½ft in the occ. of the present lessee; east Mr Biggs, south Mr Loggins, west Thomas Jackson

Down payment £56 5s.; annual rent £5

MXD441   – to George Fuller, chandler   **8 Feb. 1713**

> House plot 16 x 22 feet in the occ. of the present lessee; east Mrs Temple, west Thomas Harding, south on a yard of Samuel Ashbrook

Down payment £30; annual rent £5

60-year lease renewals: Howard Street
See also **MXD351** *above*

Howard Street, north side   24 Mar. 1725

MXD442   – to Thomas Batt, of Highgate, co. Middx, gentleman

> Back messuage behind Howard Street, 18 x 25 feet in the occ. of Widow Smallwood and formerly let to the present lessee; east Mr Storrer, west Richard Rawlinson, north on a stable of Thomas Vernon, esq.

Down payment £59; annual rent £4
Acknowledgement by Mr Batt of an (unspecified) sum in compensation for being unable to enter upon this lease nor on the lease of a house in Surrey Street, in the occ. of Mr Farr, for the space of 9 months, due to an error on the Duke's part.

MXD443   – to Ann Bracegirdle, spinster

> House plot 17 x 25 feet in the occ. of the present lessee and formerly leased to her; north Andrew Richmond, east Hugh Mills, west John World

Down payment £119; annual rent £3

MXD444   – to Grace Fuller, widow

House plot 15 x 23 feet in the occ. of Richard Rawlinson and was formerly leased to George Fuller; north on a coach house and stables of Thomas Vernon, esq., west John Bentley, east Thomas Welford

Down payment £130 10s.; annual rent £9

MXD445   – to the Right Hon. Simon, Lord Viscount Harcourt

House plot 17 x 30 feet (occ. not given); east Edward Conyers, esq. (in Norfolk Street), north Peter Storrer, gentleman, west Thomas Walford

Down payment, 'a competent sum'; annual rent £6

MXD446   – to Reginald Marriott of Parsons Green, co. Middx, esq.

House plot 32 x 22 feet in the occ. of Hugh Mills and was formerly leased to the present lessee; north Andrew Richmond, west Mrs Bracegirdle, east on Arundel Street

Down payment £196; annual rent £14

MXD447   – to Hugh Mills of New Inn, gentleman

House plot 20 x 25 feet in the occ. of Widow Willford and formerly leased to Joseph Whiston; north Mrs Smallwood, west Richard Rawlinson, east Mrs Marsh

Down payment £105; annual rent £5

MXD448   – to John World, tailor

House plot 34 feet (frontage) x 16 feet in depth; north Mr Fountain, east Mrs Bracegirdle, west Mr Taylor; and an ancient vault lying underneath the above, 60 x 17 feet; all in the occ. of the present lessee and Mr Ebbott and all formerly leased to John Green. **Marginal plan** showing a yard 10 x 19 feet with a narrow extension down to a *bog house*.

Down payment £203; annual rent £10

Howard Street, south side   24 Mar. 1725 (cont.)

MXD449   – to George Calvert, tailor

House plot 13 x 25 feet formerly leased, together with the premises in the occ. of Mr Gatterell, to Humphrey Hyde; south Jane Loggan, west Mr Ebbott, east Mr Gatterell. **Marginal plan** shows an additional small yard and indication of a jetty construction to the house.

Down payment £126; annual rent £4

MXD450   – to Elizabeth Ebbutt, widow

House plot 23½ x 33½ feet in the occ. of the present lessee and formerly leased to Edmund Ebbutt; south Jane Loggan, west Mr Hancock, east Mr Calvert

Down payment £140; annual rent £10

MXD451   – to Grace Fuller, widow

House plot 16 x 22 feet in the occ. of the present lessee and formerly leased to George Fuller; south on a yard of [blank], west Thomas Harding and east Henry Jones

Down payment £71 10s.; annual rent £5

MXD452-453 – to Thomas Hancock of Winkfield, Berks., esq.

i) House plot 13 feet (frontage) x 10 feet in depth on the west side and 21 feet on the east side; south Mr Justice Denton and Sir Peter King, west Mr Justice Denton and east Elizabeth Ebbutt; together with the vault 90 feet (east to west) x 20 feet (north to south) abutting south on Thomas Hancock; all now in the occ. of Elizabeth Ebbutt and formerly leased to Leonard Hancock, north Hugh Mills and John World, west Margaret Thompson and east Elizabeth Ebbutt

ii) House plot 57 feet (frontage) x 22 feet in depth in the occ. of Mr Justice Denton and formerly leased to Leonard Hancock; south Sir Peter King, west Norfolk Street, east on the above house

Down payments £131 and £169; annual rents £5 and £16 respectively.
Witnesses: Leonard Hancock and Richard Woodward

MXD454   – to Margaret Thompson, widow

Two house plots jointly containing 32 feet (frontage) x 23 feet in depth on the east side and 35 feet on the west, in the occ. of Margaret Thompson and Mr Jones and formerly leased to John Thompson, stone cutter; south Mr Cannin and Mr French, east Mr Cannin, west Grace Fuller and Jonathan White

Down payment £306; annual rent £14

Lease renewals 1706-1715: Arundel Street

As before, the leases for 13 years, all to run from Lady Day 1718 except where noted otherwise

Arundel Street, east side

MXD461   – to Katherine Bold of St Margaret, Westminster, widow **1 Nov. 1706**

messuage, ground and premises with appurts. commonly called by the sign of the *Crowne Tavern*, now in the occ. of Andrew Richmond, vintner

Down payment £150; annual rent [?]

MXD462   – to Arthur Allibone, baker   **1 Nov. 1707**

ii) messuage known by the sign of the *Red Dragon*, 15 feet (frontage); east on Water Street, south on [blank] and north on a passage from Arundel Street to Water Street

Down payment £49 10s.; annual rent £6

MXD463-466   Leases for 13 years   **1 May 1707**

– to Charles Johnson, victualler

> i) messuage and premises in the occ. of the lessee; 18ft (frontage) by 45ft in depth, abutting south on [blank], east on Water Street and north on [blank]

– to Sarah Cony of Kingston upon Thames, widow

> ii) messuage and premises in the occ. of Mr Parsons, 22 feet (frontage) by 50 feet in depth; south on [blank], east on Water Street and north on [blank]

– to Richard Baynard of St James, Clerkenwell, salesman

> iii) messuage and premises in the occ. of John Gooden, 16 feet 8 inches (frontage) by 51 feet in depth; abutting north on a tavern in the occ. of Mr Richmond, east on [blank] and south on Mrs Clark; and another messuage, in the occ. of Mrs Clark, 16 feet (frontage) by 17 feet 9 inches in depth; north on the previous messuage, east on Mr Martin and south on a passage from Arundel Street to Water Street

– to Richard Doyley of Drayton, Middx, gentleman

> iv) messuage and premises in the occ. of [blank], 24 feet (frontage) by 42 feet in depth; east on Water Street, north on a passage from Arundel Street to Water Street and south on [blank]; together with all the buildings over the passage

Down payments £51 6s., £67 14s., £80 and £90; annual rents £7 4s., £9 18s., £10 and £15 respectively.   4 docs.

MXD467-469 **Lease renewals** for 13 years   **8 Feb. 1714**

> – to Richard Hawkins of St Paul's, Covent Garden, yeoman
>
>> i) messuage with the stable and coach houses and the yard belonging, in a plot 17 feet 7 inches by 43 feet in occ. of Joyce Collings, widow; east Water Street, north Richard Oldner and south Charles Johnson
>
> – to Richard Oldner of St Saviour's, Southwark, co. Surrey, lighterman
>
>> ii) messuage with the stable and coach house and ground belonging, 18 feet 5 inches x 40 feet, in the occ. of the lessee; east Water Street, north Richard Hawkins and south Joyce Collings
>
> – to Anne Christmas of St Andrew, Holborn, spinster
>
>> iii) messuage and ground 20 x 55 feet, in occ. of Henry Baker, esq.; east Water Street, north and south on [blank]
>
> For down payments of £60, £60 and £84 respectively the premises are leased for 13 years from Michaelmas 1718: at annual rents of £10 4s., £9 8s. and £11 respectively.   3 docs.

MXD470   Lease renewal for 13 years (unexecuted)   **1 May 1714**

> – to William Bridges, esq.
>
>> messuage 20 x 58 feet in the occ. of the lessee; south Captain Baker, east Water Street and north Mr Bowtell
>
> Down payment £84; annual rent £12

MXD471-475 Lease; and mortgage by assignment of lease   **17 Dec. 1714**

> James Pearce, gentleman, Elizabeth McCarty of St Giles in the Fields and Anthony Cracherode of the Inner Temple, gentleman
>
>> messuage in Arundell Street late in occ. of Colonel Bond, deceased; 22 x 40 feet; west on the street, east on Water Street, north on a messuage in occ. of Richard Bayley, surgeon and south on a messuage in occ. of [blank]

The Duke leases to James Pearce for 13 years at £15 annual rent, starting in 1718; in trust for McCarty. Pearce now raises £30 by assigning the lease term to Cracherode; the principal and interest repayable by 17 March next. Receipt, 1705, for insurance on the house to sum of £300, Fire Insurance policy, 1715, and abstract of constitution of a local *Amicable Contributors'* insurance company *to be seen at large at Tom's Coffee House in St Martins Lane* Duke's signature on **MXD475**.   5 docs.

MXD476   – to Thomas Dodd, citizen and haberdasher of London   **20 Dec. 1715**

messuage and premises in Arundel Street 'in Arundel Buildings' in a plot 25 x 60 feet, in the occ. of Mr Paris, tailor; with the buildings over and under a passage 4ft wide by 10ft high from Arundel Street to Water Street; south Mr Parks, upholsterer, east Water Street, north Captain Baker

Leased for 13 years: down payment £70; £12 annual rent

MXD477   – to Ann Killingworth, widow   **1 May 1717**

Messuage having a 20ft frontage on east side of Arundel Street together with a parcel of ground formerly taken out of the River Thames; abuts south to the River Thames [the east and north abuttals illegible]

Leased for 13 years: down payment £101; annual rent £25
Much of this lease is too faded to read

MXD478   – to Philip Bowtall, gentleman   **16 Dec. 1717**

i) messuage, yard and premises in a plot 18 x 39 feet in the occ. of the lessee; north on a messuage now known as the *Blew Ball*, south Mr Handshaw, tailor, east a back messuage of Francis Bridge

Leased for 13 years: down payment £65 11s. 8d.: annual rent £9 6s. 8d.

MXD479   – to Thomas Hamerton, gentleman   **16 Dec. 1717**

> Messuage, yard and premises now known by the name of the *Blew Ball*, with the little house on the back side, in Water Street, lately in the occ. of Thomas Abram, [sedan] chairman with the passage leading under the leased messuages out of Arundel Street into Water Street; the combined plots being 14ft 4in x 50ft 8in and in the occ. of the lessee; north Widow Tindsley, south Philip Bowtell

Leased for 13 years; down payment of £70 5s.; annual rent £10

Arundel Street, west side

The leases are all for 13 years except where stated, to run from Lady Day 1718, the approximate termination of the original 40-year leases

MXD480-482   **1 Nov. 1706**

480   – to Bartholomew Dutton of St Mary le Savoy, gentleman

> i) messuage, ground and premises in the occ. of Martin Pickard, 20 feet (frontage) by 51 feet in depth; north on Mr Cambridge, west on [blank] and south Mr Piggott

481   – to Reginald Marryott, esq.

> ii) messuage on the corner of Arundel Street and Howard Street in the occ. of Hugh Mills junior, 22 feet (frontage) by 30 feet in depth; south on Howard Street, west on Mr Bracegirdle and north on Stephen Werd

482   – to John Greene, citizen and carpenter of London

> iii) messuage in a plot 19 x 53 feet, in the occ. of Mr Rhymer; north Mr Playford, south Richard Atkins, west on [blank]

Down payments of £74 5s., £67 10s. and £65 8s. 4d.; annual rents £10, £8 and £10 9s. respectively   3 docs.

MXD483-486 Leases for 13 years   **1 May 1707**

– to William Biggs of St Bennet, Paulswharf

> i) messuage and premises in the occ. of Mr Spadman, apothecary, 20 feet (frontage) by 50 feet in depth; abutting south on Mr Werd, west on [blank] and north on Mr Austin

– to Charles Austin, gentleman

> ii) messuage and premises in the occ. of Charles Austin, 20 feet (frontage) by 50 feet in depth; south on Mr Spadman, west on [blank] and north on Mr Piggott

– to John Loggan, merchant

> iii) two messuages and premises [measurements blank] in the occ. of John Loggan, south on John Loggan, west on premises in Norfolk Street and north on Mr Baynes

– to William Barnsley of Inner Temple, esq.

> iv) messuage and premises in the occ. of Mr Scarborough; 20 feet (frontage) by 26 feet in depth; north on Mr Baxter, west [blank] and south Mr Playford

The lease re iv) is specified as from the end of a 39-year lease (from 1679) between the 6th Duke and Nicholas Lance. Down payments £67 10s. apiece for i) and ii), £146 5s. for iii) and £31 10s. for iv); annual rents £10, £10, £20 and £8 respectively.   4 docs.

MXD487   Lease for 13 years to George Jenkins, vintner   **15 May 1712**

> little back messuage with the passage leading from it into Arundel Street in a plot [blank] x 21 feet, in occ. of Widow New; east Mrs Sowton, west John Carter, esq., north John Loggan and south the said passage

Down payment £15; annual rent £3

MXD488   Lease for 13 years to Tabitha Marshall of Westminster,   **15 May 1713**
widow

> messuage and premises on the west side of Arundel
> Street in the occ. of Mr Lany, 11 feet (frontage) by
> 53 feet in depth; together with the use of a passage
> way [no details]; west on widow New and north
> on Mr Sowton [south not given]

Down payment £92 15s.; annual rent £13 10s.

MXD489-490 Leases for 13 years   **8 Feb. 1714**

– to Basil Fitzherbert, esq.

> i) messuage, 20 x 51 feet, in the occ. of John Angell;
> abutting north, south and west on messuages of
> [all blank]

– to James Pearse, gentleman

> ii) messuage in the occ. of Mr Spavan, clerk, 21½
> x 53 feet, with a piece 40 x 53 feet lately taken out
> of the soil of the Thames; east [blank], south the
> Thames and north John Green, carpenter

Down payments £70 and 5 shillings; annual rent £15 and £25
respectively.   2 docs.

MXD491   Lease for 13 years   **1 Aug. 1716**

– to Thomas Batt of St Pancras, tailor

> south messuage in a plot 20 x 54 feet, in the occ. of
> Mr Rayes; north Mr Poote, Mr Edwards and west
> on a messuage formerly called the *White Horse*

Down payment £81 13s. 4d.; annual rent £11 13s. 4d.

60-year lease renewals: Arundel Street   **24 Mar. 1725**

Arundel Street, east side

MXD492   – to Elizabeth Macartey of St Giles in the Fields, widow

> Messuage in Arundel Street as in **MXD471-475**
> above

Down payment £189; annual rent £13. Two endorsements

record a mortgage for £250 raised by Elizabeth Macartey with Anne Knight of St Ann, Westminster, widow 24 June 1729, transferred to Francis Loggin of the Middle Temple, gentleman on 24 July 1734.

MXD493   – to Arthur Allibone of Mowsford, co. Berks., gentleman

> messuage and plot 15 x 34 feet in occ. of John Harding and previously let to Arthur Allibone: south Mr Robins, east and north on Water Street

Down payment £122; annual rent £7

MXD494   – to Johannah Baker, widow

> i) messuage and plot 16ft 8in x 51 feet in occ. of Thomas Stevens: east and north Mr Beauchamp, south John Siffard
> ii) messuage and plot 16ft x 17ft 9in in occ. of John Siffard: east Mr Bowers, north Thomas Stevens above, south Water Street; both premises formerly let to Richard Baynard

Down payment £238; annual rent £16

MXD495   – to Sarah Bowtell, widow

> messuage and plot 18 x 39 feet in occ. of the lessee and formerly let to Philip Bowtell; east Thomas Hamerton the younger, north Thomas Hamerton the elder, south Joseph Henshaw

Endorsement: 22 Apr. 1755, recording purchase of the premises by John Prince, carpenter, and the [9th] Duke's satisfaction with the substantial repairs he has done.
Down payment £135; annual rent £9 6s. 8d.

MXD496   – to Thomas Hamerton the elder, victualler

> messuage and plot containing a little back messuage in Water Street, 14ft 4in x 50ft 8in; with the passage leading under the premises from Arundel Street to Water Street; in the occ. of the lessee and formerly

let to him: east on Water Street, north Widow
Fielding and south Widow Bowtell

Down payment £140; annual rent £10

MXD497   – to Henry Hankey, citizen and haberdasher of London,
executor of the will of Thomas Dodd

two messuages in a plot 20 x 60 feet, one fronting
Arundel Street and one on Water street (west side)
in the occ. of Mr Morley and formerly let to Thomas
Dodd; south Thomas Arundell, esq., north Peter
Walraven

Down payment £196; annual rent £12

MXD498-499   – to Richard Hawkins of Hamersmith, gent.

i) messuage and plot 7ft 7in x 43 feet in the occ. of Mr
James and was formerly let to the lessee: east on Water
Street, north [blank] Pierce and south James Breach
ii) messuage and plot 18ft 5in x 40 feet in the occ.
of [blank] Pierce and was formerly let to Richard
Oldnar: east on Water Street, south Mr James, north
Mr Culham

Down payments £120 for each property; annual rent £11 apiece
Endorsements: 22 Apr. 1755, recording purchase of both
premises by John Prince, carpenter, and the [9th] Duke's satisfaction with the substantial repairs he has done.   2 docs.

MXD500   – to Charles Johnson of Mortlake, Surrey, gentleman

messuage and plot 18 x 48 feet in the occ. of James
Breach and formerly let to the lessee; east on
Water Street, south Eustace Budgell, north [blank]
James

Down payment £100; annual rent £11

MXD501   – to Elizabeth McCarty of St Giles in the Field, widow

messuage in a plot 22 x 48 feet in the occ. of Mrs
Holton and formerly let to James Pearse, esq.: east

on Water Street, south Sarah Symons and north Eustace Budgell

Down payment £189; annual rent £13

MXD502-505 – to Hugh Mills of New Inn, gentleman

i) messuage and plot 18ft 2in x 41ft 6in in the occ. of [blank] Gullam and Benjamin Sweet and was formerly leased to William Tidmarsh, cardmaker: east on Water Street, north Mrs Robins and south [blank] Pierce

ii) messuage and plot 15 x 31 feet in the occ. of Mrs. Robins and formerly leased to Reginald Marriott, esq.: east on Water Street, south John Culme, apothecary, north John Harding

Down payments £150 and £114 respectively; annual rents £10 and £5; with counterparts containing the Duke's signature. 4 docs.

MXD506 – to James Pearse, esq.

messuage and plot 20 x 58 feet in the occ. of Joseph Henshaw and formerly let to William Bridges, esq.; east on Water Street, north Mrs Bowtell, south Mr Walraven

Down payment £161; annual rent £12

MXD507 – to Sarah Simonds, widow

messuage and plot 22 x 50 feet in the occ. of the lessee, formerly let to Sarah Cony; east Water Street, south Thomas Hamerton the elder, north widow Holton

Down payment £189; annual rent £13

MXD508 – to Peter Walraven, esq.

messuage and plot 18 x 55 feet in the occ. of the lessee and formerly let to Ann Christmas; east Water Street, south George Morley, esq., north Joseph Henshaw

Down payment £162; annual rent £11.

Endorsement: 13 Mar. 1756, recording purchase by James Clutterbuck and George Vaughan, exors. of the will of Abraham Beath, tailor; and the [9th] Duke's satisfaction with the substantial repairs done.

MXD509   – to Francis Willett of St Martins in the Fields, hosier

> messuage and plot 32 x 44 feet in the occ. of Eustace Budgell, esq., formerly let to Richard Doyley; east on Water Street, south widow Holton, north Charles Johnson

Down payment £252; annual rent £17

Endorsement: 22 May 1760, recording that the premises are now in possession of Mary Willet, of St George's, Hanover Square, widow and that the [9th] Duke is satisfied with the substantial repairs done.

MXD510   – to John Bullock, gentleman   **2 Dec. 1728**

> messuage with appurts. known as the *Crown and Anchor Tavern* 45ft (frontage) x 81ft. on the south side and 73ft on the north side; east towards Milford Lane, south Water Lane and north towards premises in the Strand; in the occ. of Francis Beauchamp, vintner and formerly let to Catherine Bold

– as from Lady Day 1731. Down payment £980; annual rent £45

Arundel Street, west side

MXD511-512 – to Charles Austin, gentleman   **24 Mar. 1725**

> messuage and plot 20 x 50 feet in the occ. of the lessee and formerly let to him; west premises in Norfolk Street, north John Angell, south John White

Down payment £210; annual rent £10

Lease and counterpart, each endorsed, 22 May 1772, by the 9th Duke's memorandum that the premises are now occupied

by George Vaughan, laceman who has carried out substantial
repairs with which the Duke is satisfied.   2 docs.

MXD513   – to William Barnesley of the [blank] Temple, esq.

> Messuage in a plot 20 x 26 feet in the occ. of Widow
> Winter and was formerly let to the lessee; west
> Captain George Jenkins, south Mrs Brabant, north
> Mrs Loggan

Down payment £112; annual rent £8

MXD514   – to George James Guidot of the Inner Temple, gentleman

> Messuage in a plot 17 x 53 feet in the occ. of
> Mrs Bridges and was formerly let to Robert
> Fleetwood; west premises in Norfolk Street, south
> Edward Mountney, esq., north Mrs Brabant

Down payment £161; annual rent £11

MXD515   – to George Jenkins, vintner

> Little back messuage with the passage leading into
> Arundel Street, in a plot 21 x 21 feet, now and
> formerly in the occ. of the lessee; east Mrs Winter,
> west premises in Norfolk Street, north Mrs Loggan,
> south the passage way

Down payment £30; annual rent £3

MXD516   – to Jane Loggan, widow

> Two messuages together in a plot 40 x 53 feet in
> the occ. of the lessee, formerly let to John Loggan,
> merchant; west premises in Norfolk Street, north
> Mr Gaterell, south Mrs Winter

Down payment £380; annual rent £30

MXD517   – to Tabitha Marshall of St Margaret's, Westminster

> Messuage in a plot 17 x 53 feet in the occ. of Mrs
> Brabant and formerly let to the lessee; west to

premises in Norfolk Street, south Mrs Bridges, north Mrs Winter

Down payment £175 10s.; annual rent £13

MXD518-520 – to Hugh Mills of New Inn, gentleman

i) messuage in a plot 18 x 29 feet in the occ. of John Toovey and formerly let to Thomas Batt, tailor; west Robert Cotton, north Richard Holt, south Mr Tinsley

ii) messuage in a plot 22 x 29 feet on the west side of Arundel Street in the Strand, in the occ. of Richard Holt; tailor; north on a little back messuage of same Richard Holt, south John Tovey; and the said little back messuage in a plot 61 x 28 feet, with the passage leading into the Strand under the house in the Strand in occ. of Richard Taylor; east on John Tovey and Richard Holt, north on two houses in the Strand in the occs. of John Robinson and said Richard Taylor, south on the yard of John Tinsley. **Marginal plan.**

iii) messuage known by the name of the *Crown and Sceptre* in a plot 20 x 50 feet, in the occ. of Andrew Richmond, vintner and formerly leased to Thomas Batt, tailor; west on [blank], south on said Hugh Mills, north on John White, silversmith

Down payments £140, £210 and £203; annual rents £10, £15 and £11 respectively.   3 docs.

MXD521   – to Edward Mountney, esq.

Messuage in a plot 19 x 53 feet now in the occ. of the lessee and formerly leased to John Green; west on premises in Norfolk Street, north Mrs Bridges, south James Pierce

Down payment £196; annual rent £14

MXD522   – to James Pearse, esq.

Messuage, garden and ground at the south west end of Arundel Street in a plot 61 x 53 feet, in the occ. of the lessee and formerly leased to him; west on premises in Norfolk Street, north Edward Mountney, south the River Thames

Down payment £181; annual rent £18

MXD523   – to John Robinson, linen draper

> Messuage in a plot 34 x 17 feet in the occ. of Mr Catterell, formerly leased to Humphrey Hide; west John Calvert, north on Howard Street, south Jane Loggan, widow. **Marginal plan**, showing position of closets and *bog house*.

Down payment £175; annual rent £10

MXD524   – to John Shaw, tailor

> Messuage in a plot 20 x 51 feet, in the occ. of the lessee and formerly leased to Basil FitzHerbert, esq.; west John Gumley, south Charles Austin, north John Eddows

Down payment £189; annual rent £13

MXD525   – to John White, working silver smith

> Messuage in a plot 20 x 50 feet in the occ. of the lessee and formerly leased to William Biggs; west on premises in Norfolk Street, north Charles Austin, gent, south Andrew Richmond, vintner

Down payment £189; annual rent £13

MXD526   to George Tilsley, chapman   **22 Mar. 1731**

> messuage in a plot 20 x 52 feet at the south west end and 53 feet at the north west end [*sic*] in the occ. of William Tilsley and formerly leased to Thomas Batt; west Mr Churchill, north John Tovey, south John Eddowes

MXD527   to John Bullock, tailor   **22 Mar. 1731**

> messuage in a plot 20 x 51 feet in occ. of John Eddowes, formerly leased to Bartholomew Dutton; west Norfolk Street, north William Tinsley and south John Angell

Terms for both properties as in the 1725 leases; down payments £189 each; annual rents £13 each.   2 docs.

The 9th Duke's leases

Arundel Street, east side

MXD528   – to Edward Hilliard, oilman   **30 Nov. 1763**

> Messuage called the *Griffin* alehouse in a plot 16ft 8in x 35ft 6in, in the occ. of John Luxford, victualler; north on a passage from Arundel Street to Water Street, called little Arundel Street, south on Mr Knott, attorney at law

No down payment; annual rent £12

MXD529   – to John Winterton, victualler   **10 Sep. 1767**

> Messuage in the occ. of [blank] Symmonds, now of the lessee; south [blank] Smith, spinster, north Thomas Williams, tailor

No down payment; annual rent £28

MXD530   – to Thomas Williams, tailor   **10 Sep. 1767**

> Messuage formerly in the occ. of [blank] McCarthy, now of the lessee; south John Winterton, victualler, north blank Combes, tailor

No down payment; annual rent £40

Arundel Street, west side

MXD531   Agreement and lease   **6 Mar. 1734**

The Duke, Richard Anders, executor of the will of Grace Fuller, widow, deceased, and Thomas Mawson, gentleman

Passage way 4 x 52 feet running from Norfolk
Street to the premises of Thomas Mawson through
the north side of the house plot of 23 x 52 feet [in
Norfolk St as in **MXD418** above] leased to Grace
Fuller on 24 March 1725 and formerly leased to
George Fuller.

A dispute has arisen between Anders and Mawson as to the use
of the passage way, which leads into Mawson's premises on the
west, and concerning part of the yard lying between the two
premises and a *stack of closets* in the yard all of which are within
the premises leased to the Fullers. The Duke now agrees that
Anders rent shall be reduced from £17 to £12 for the remainder
of the lease term and in return Mawson shall continue to use the
passage way and the relevant part of the yard.
Witnesses: Bri [*sic*] Smith and Wilkins Marchant

Lease renewals 1706-1719: Water Street

NB: *Some leases in this section contain later endorsements.*

MXD532-535 – to Jane Syms, widow for 13 years   **1 Nov. 1706**

Water Street, east side

i) two messuages lying together, 28ft 6in (frontage)
x 18ft in depth, in the occ. of Mr Ledge and Mr
Goslin; south on a messuage in the occ. of the lessee
and John Syms, joiner, east on other premises of the
lessee in Milford Lane and north on a passage from
Water Street to Milford Lane
ii) two coach houses or stables, 26 feet (frontage) x
33 feet in depth, in the occ. of Robert Minchall and
Richard Hall, farrier; south on other coachhouses
of the lessee, east [blank] and north on a coach
house of Nevinson Fox, esq.
iii) two coach houses, 26 feet (frontage) x 35 feet
in depth; south on a passage leading from Water
Street to Milford Lane, north on other coach houses
of the lessee

Water Street, west side

iv) messuage, yard, wharfe and premises, 132 feet
(frontage) x 40 feet in depth (south side) and 38 feet
(north); with all outhouses, stables, buildings and
passage ways

Down payments £18, £27, £27 and £53 8s. 9d. respectively; annual rents £8, £12, £12 and £26 5s. respectively the Duke leases to Mrs Syms. The 13-year terms all start on Lady Day 1718. Lessee's signatures absent (see **MXD544-546** below).   4 docs.

Water Street, south end

MXD536-537 Lease for 11 years at a peppercorn rent; and renewal   **1 Nov. 1706-**
20 Apr. 1730

– to Bartholomew Dutton of Mary le Savoy, gentleman; renewed in 1725 to Honoria Dutton

Parcel of ground in occ. of Thomas Harrison at the south end of Water Street containing all the ground from the north end of old *Gundelow House* forward to the River Thames; the room over the passage going down from Water Street to the River, and the messuage built with the platform of freestone before the house, and the stone steps leading up from the river to the messuage and the garden behind it; west Mr Samworth, east Mrs Syms (Thomas Syms in 1725), south the river, north Water Street

Renewal in 1725 is for a down payment of £126 and an annual rent of £8 as from Lady Day 1731.
Assignment, 20 April 1730, to John Robinson, linen draper, is endorsed, with the Duke's acknowledgement that the repairs done by the latter are substantial enough for the premises not to need rebuilding during the remainder of the term.
2 docs.

Water street, north

MXD538   – to Richard Baynard of St James, Clerkenwell, salesman   **1 May 1711**

two messuages on the northside of Water Street, each 17 feet (frontage) x 25 feet in depth: the first in the occ. of Mr Martin; west Mrs Clarke, north Mr Gooding and east Mr Nuthall. The second in the occ. of Mr Nuthall; west Mr Martin, north Mr Richmond and east Mr Bonvill

Leased for 13 years as from Lady Day 1718.
Down payment £59 and £6 annual rent

Water Street, east

MXD539-541 Leases for 21 years   **20 Oct. 1712**

– to Thomas Harding, joiner

> i) two coach houses and a stable in Water Street
> in Arundel Buildings, 33 feet 8 inches (frontage) x
> 33 feet in depth in occ. of Mr Newport; south a
> stable of Doctor Robinson, north a stable of chief
> Baron Ward
> ii) coach house and stable in Water Street 13ft 6in
> (frontage) x 33ft 8in in the occ. of Doctor Robinson;
> south Thomas Simms, north Mr Newport
> iii) coach house and stable in Water Street in Arundel
> Buildings, 17ft 4in frontage together with a passage
> way leading from Water lane through Grayhound
> Court to Milford Lane, x 30 feet in depth, in occ.
> of Mr Campion; [south] on coachhouse etc. of
> chief Baron Ward and north on a messuage of
> Henry Allen

The Duke leases to Harding without down payments and
with immediate effect, at peppercorn rents for the first half
year and £10, £6 and £5 respectively. **A plan of each plot** is
appended.   3 docs.

MXD542-543 Leases for 12 years   **3 Jul. 1717**

– to Thomas Hollinhurst, mason

> i) two messuages having a 26ft frontage to the street
> in the occ. of Thomas Harding and the lessee; east
> on houses in Milford Lane, north Mrs Hull, south
> the Duke's stables
> ii) messuage in a plot 37 feet (frontage) x 30 feet in
> depth, in the occ. of Mrs Hull; west on the street
> and on a messuage in the occ. of Mrs Sherrard,
> east on houses in Milford Lane, north on the *Crown
> Tavern* and south on Thomas Harding

Down payments of £66 13s. 4d. and £33 6s. 8d.; annual rents £16
and £7 4s. respectively, as from Lady Day 1719.   2 docs.

MXD544-546 Leases for 13 years   **25 Mar. 1719**

– to Thomas Syms, wharfinger

Premises on east side of Water street as in **MXD532-535** above (ie. properties i), ii) and iii) of that group)

Recites that Thomas is the son of Jane Syms above and that his mother died before the counterparts of her leases could be signed. The Duke now leases to the son without further down payments and for the same rents of £8, £12 and £12 respectively.   3 docs.

Water Street, west

MXD547-549   Lease for 13 years; renewed for 60 years   **16 Dec. 1717**
                                                                    (1725-65)

– to Thomas Hamerton the younger, plasterer

> back messuage in Water Street in a plot 17 x 13 feet, in occ. of Frances Bridge; west Philip Bowtell, gent, (in 1725 widow Boutell) north Thomas Hamerton the elder and south a stable of Mr Hanshaw (in occ. of Hamerton in 1725)

The premises are leased from Lady Day 1718 at £2 annual rent (down payment of £13 3s. 4d.). At renewal in 1725 the down payment was £28 and annual rent still £2. Lease with counterpart at renewal, the former with the signature of the Duke; and endorsement, April 1765, assigning the remainder of the lease term by Hamerton to Anthony Fryer of the Middle Temple, gentleman as a mortgage to secure the repayment of £20 with interest.   3 docs.

60-year lease renewals
See also **MXD497** *above*

Water Street, north

MXD550-551   – to John Sifford, chandler   **24 Mar. 1725**

> i) two messuages at the north end of Water Street in a plot 34 feet (frontage) x 25 feet in depth south to north; north Thomas Stevens, west the lessee, east William Luddington; in the occ. of [blank] Power and John Wiggmore and which were formerly leased to Richard Baynard

Down payment £175; £10 annual rent. 2 identical copies

141

Water Street, east

MXD552-553 – to Thomas Hamerton, plasterer

> i) messuage in a plot 27 (frontage) by 30 feet in depth; west on the street and on Mr Wiggmore, east on premises in Milford Lane, south John Ganderton, barber, north Francis Beauchamp, vintner
> ii) two messuages in a plot 26 x 30 feet in occ. of John Ganderton, barber and Peter How, mason and were formerly leased to Thomas Hollinhurst; east to houses in Milford Lane, north Mrs Loddington, south a stable leased to John Harding

Down payments £90 and £160 respectively; annual rents of £9 and £16. Both leases are endorsed with unexecuted clauses indemnifying the lessee in case of fire before the lease term commences. 2 docs.

MXD554-557 – to Thomas Syms, wharfinger

> i) two messuages in a plot 28ft 6in by 19ft in the occ. of [blank] Heath and [blank] Ashley and were formerly let to the same Thomas Syms; east on premises in Milford Lane leased to said Syms, north on a passage from Water Street to Milford Lane and south on another messuage leased to Syms
> ii) two coach houses or stables 26 feet (frontage) by 35 feet in depth in occ. of Robert Weston and Eustace Budgell, esqs and formerly leased to Syms; east on a brewhouse in Milford Lane, south a passage from Water Street to Milford Lane, north on other premises leased to Syms
> iii) two coach houses or stables in a plot 26 feet (frontage) x 33 feet formerly leased to said Syms; east a brewhouse in Milford Lane, north a stable of Thomas Harding, south a stable of Dr Robinson and Thomas Ward, esqs
> iv) messuage, yard, wharf and premises 132 feet (frontage) by 40 feet in depth; east Milford Lane, north on other premises of Syms and south on the River Thames

Down payments £98, £133, £140 and £336 respectively; annual rents £6, £8, £9 and £22. 4 docs.

MXD558-561 – to William Curryer of London, gentleman

> six coach houses and stables all formerly let to
> Thomas Harding, viz.:
> i) one in a plot 17ft 4in frontage (including the
> passage way through Greyhound Court into
> Milford Lane) x 30 feet in depth; east on premises
> in Grayhound Court, south [John] Ward's coach
> house, north on [blank] How
> ii) one in a plot 13ft 6in x 33ft 8in; east Milford
> Lane, south Thomas Syms' coachhouse, north John
> Ward's coach house
> iii) two in a plot 31ft 6in x 31ft 6in ; east Grayhound
> Court, north John Ward, esq., north a passage from
> Water Street to Grayhound Court
> iv) two in a plot 33ft 8in (including the passage
> way to a back yard) x 45 feet; east on premises
> in Milford Lane and Grayhound Court, south Dr
> Robinson, north [John] Ward, esq.

All leased as from Michaelmas 1733; down payments £30,
£26, £30 and £30 respectively; annual rents £5, £5, £15
and £8   4 docs.

9th Duke's leases: Water Street
See also some of the 1706-1725 leases,
which contain later endorsements

MXD562   Lease for 21 years   **30 May 1767**

– to Sarah Hutchinson, spinster

> stable and the lodging rooms over on the east side
> of Water Street, in the occ. of the lessee; south a
> messuage of John Prince, north the coachhouse of
> the lessee, east a brewhouse

Leased as from Lady Day last for £26 a year (no down
payment).

Lease renewals 1706-1719: Milford Lane

MXD563-564 Lease for 13 years

1 Nov. 1706
25 Mar. 1719

– to Jane Syms, widow

> two messuages on the west side of Milford Lane in occ. of Mrs Keigow and John Chamberlain, having a combined frontage of 28ft 6in by 18ft in depth; south Jane Syms and John Syms, joiner, west premises of said Jane Syms in Water Street, north a passage from Milford Lane to Water Lane

For a down payment of £18 the premises are leased as from Lady Day 1718 at £8 annual rent

Unexecuted. Remainder of lease assigned to her son Thomas Syms on same terms in March 1719, following Jane Syms' death   2 docs.

60-year lease renewals: Milford Lane

MXD565   Lease and covenant to rebuild

24 Mar. 1725

– to Thomas Syms, wharfinger

> premises as in **MXD563-564** above; west on premises in Water Street and south on premises leased to said Thomas Syms

Down payment £77; annual rent £5

v. *Private deeds and sub-lets (to 1782)*

Fox family properties

For earlier deeds, see. section 2.iii. above. For an agreement between the Duke and Thomas Vernon re the Talbot Inn, *1722, see Steer, vol. IV, p. 89 (MD2382)*

MXD571-572 Conveyance and release   **Apr-Jun 1704**

Joseph Fox of Stradbrook, co. Suff., esq. and Mary his wife to Nevinson Fox of St Clement Danes, esq., and Mary his wife

Various London premises of the Fox family as in **MXD165-168** above. Occupiers as in 165-8 above and Thomas Thomson, Robert Bomont, Joseph Kerby, William Hill, George Eve, John Fogerty, Dorothy Mundy, John Lockwood, John Tuttle, William Okely, John Sedley, watchmaker, John Lane, James Medlicott, [blank] Hanbury, esq., Charles Danvers, woollen draper, John Cockshott, John Banks, William Rasteryane and Nicholas Hill

This conveyance follows a Chancery decree on a dispute between the two parties and is accompanied by a release by Joseph to Nevinson Fox of all further actions in the matter. 2 docs.

MXD573 Lease for 13 years at a peppercorn rent   **1 Nov. 1706**

The 8th Duke to Nevinson Fox of St Clement Danes, esq.

messuage on the west side of Surrey Street having a frontage of 15½ feet and a depth of 73 feet to Strandbridge Lane, abutting north on a mansion house of Nevinson Fox; in the occ. of William White

MXD574   Assignment in trust   **14 Jul. 1716**

Timothy Macarty of St Giles in the Fields, perriwig maker
and Elizabeth his wife, formerly Elizabeth Harrison, Ann
Lloyd, of St James, Westminster, widow, sister and executrix
of Nevinson Fox, deceased and Joseph Sherwood of New
Inn, gentleman

> i) messuage known by the sign of the *Lyon and*
> *Lamb* in the Strand and shop on the east side of
> the messuage; both abutting north to the Strand
> ii) messuage in a yard partly paved with freestone,
> behind i), abutting west on the stables of the *Talbot*
> *Inn*
> iii) plot of ground or garden platt 140 feet in length,
> behind ii) with an area enclosed with pales and a
> house of office at the south end and steps going down
> into a passage leading into Strandbridge Lane
> iv) four messuages formerly known as the *Queen's*
> *Head* or the *Queen's Arms* and then as the
> *Talbot*

Recites deed of 18 June 1669 whereby Henry, Lord Howard,
Baron of Castle Rising and others conveyed the premises to
Simon Fox for 1,000 years at a peppercorn rent in trust to
pay £1,000 to Elizabeth Harrison, an infant daughter of Alice
Harrison (now Macarty), payable at her marriage or her 18th
birthday and an annuity of £60 a year to the mother for the
expenses in raising her. Disputes have since arisen between
the parties to this deed concerning the payments. However,
in return for a single payment of £100, the Macarties convey
their interest in the premises to Sherwood in trust for Anne
Lloyd, whom they release from all further obligation in the
matter.

MXD575-576   Release (lease missing) and declaration   **6 Jun. 1721**

Anne Lloyd, widow, executrix of the will of Nevinson Fox,
to Robert Dale, esq., Richmond Herald

> Premises as above

In return for two separate payments of £400 and a further sum
of £400 a year from the rental of the properties, Ann Lloyd
conveys to Robert Dale; who declares in a separate deed that the
£800 purchase money was put up by Thomas, Duke of Norfolk,
for whom Dale holds the premises in trust.   2 docs.

MXD577-578   Release of legacies   **12-13 Jul. 1721**

James Nuthall, citizen and barber surgeon of London, Elizabeth Woolnough, late of St Andrew's Holborn, spinster, Nevinson Baker of the same, stationer and Robert Dale, esq., Richmond Herald

The first three persons, beneficiaries under the will of Mary Fox, late wife of Nevinson Fox deceased, release Dale of all obligations concerning the deceased's properties, particularly concerning a £20 life annuity formerly payable to Elizabeth Woolnough.

MXD579   Declaration and release (deed poll)   **5 Jan. 1722**

Thomas Barker of London, esq.

> the properties recently purchased by Robert Dale, as above. Occupiers names given are: Surrey Street houses: William White; *Talbot Inn*: Thomas Vernon and subtenant Thomas Carr; houses each side of the Talbot gate: Thomas Hathaway, cutler and [blank] a basket maker; north end of Surrey Street: Charles Danvers, woollen draper; Water Street: Mr Collier; Milford Lane, including houses, coach house and stables on former Green Dragon Alley: John Harding; further Surrey Street houses: Mrs Lane, Mary Pointer, Gabriel Lovis

Barker, as beneficiary under the will of Mary Fox, as above, releases Robert Dale from all obligations concerning the deceased's properties and the various former rent charges arising.

MXD580-581   Conveyance (lease and release)   **14-15 Mar. 1728**

William Dale, son and heir of Robert Dale late Richmond Herald, deceased, Thomas, Duke of Norfolk, Ann Lloyd of St James, Middx, widow, Jane Vernon of Twickenham Park, Middx, widow of Thomas Vernon deceased and John Anstis, esq., Garter Principal King at Arms

> Former premises of Nevinson Fox deceased, viz. nos. i) mansion house in Surrey Street, ii) The *Talbot Inn* and its surrounds, iii) House and vault on the west side of Surrey Street iv) two little tenements on the east side of Strand Lane v) messuage in Water Street

(ie as in the 1698 deed **MXD171** above. Occupiers as in **MXD579** above. Additional very detailed dimensions and abuttals are given.

Now it is acknowledged by all parties that by deed of 1-2 March 1726 i) and ii), the mansion house and the *Talbot Inn*, were sold outright to Thomas Vernon for £2,254 10s. For the rest, the trusteeship vested on the Duke's behalf in the late Robert Dale is transferred by his son (who is not of age) to John Anstis, with the consent of Ann Lloyd who still has a financial interest in the premises.   2 docs.

MXD582	Assignment	**15 Mar. 1728**

Parties as in **MXD580-581** above together with John Knight, esq. and William Knight, gentleman both of St Martin in the Fields, Walter Horneby of Chertsey, Surrey, esq. and Henry Weston of London, esq.

The Duke of Norfolk, Ann Lloyd and the Knights assign their interest in the premises as above (arising out of an earlier transaction) to Messrs Horneby and Weston as trustees for Ann Vernon.
Good signature of the Duke, and applied seal with his crest

MXD583-584	Draft deeds by the Duke of Norfolk's solicitors	**1721-1726**

– relating to the conveyance of Nevinson Fox's former premises to Robert Dale (**MXD575-576** above) and to the subsequent sale of the *Talbot Inn* and surrounding premises as in **MXD580-581** above by Thomas, [8th] Duke of Norfolk to Jane Vernon as above.   2 docs.

Charles Howard's properties
(for earlier deeds, see section 2.iv. above)

MXD585	Lease and agreement	**15 May 1702**

The Hon. Charles Howard, esq. and the Hon. Thomas Newport, esq.

Further to the lease of 27 April 1696 (**MXD145** above), it is agreed that Thomas Newport, who now lives in the house, shall have use of a certain cellar 10 x 6 feet in dimension;

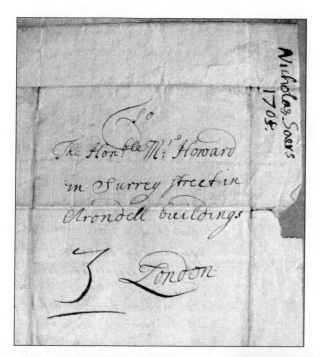

Fig. 5 The Howards in Surrey Street.
The Howards of Greystoke in Cumbria were
the only branch of the ducal family who had
a house on the new estate. Early plans for the
6th Duke to have a new mansion on the site of
the old garden, facing the river, had come to
nothing. These letters were written in the early
18th century to the Hon. Charles Howard and
to his son Henry Charles Howard, a time when
separate envelopes were not used and when a
standard address system had not been invented.
The second letter, from France, had presumed
that *Monsieur H. Ch. Howard, Londres* would
be sufficient, but someone had helpfully added
*In Surry Streatt furthest House butt one on the
rite hand.* The letters are part of an extensive
collection of family correspondence in the
archives at Arundel. (Ref. ACA/C88, C103.)

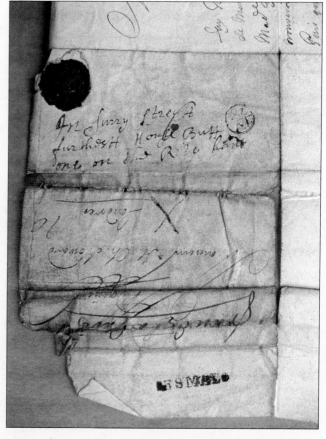

and that, for a rent of £100 a year he shall have the residue of the original 41-year lease on the premises, after his 9-year term (above) is finished

MXD586-587   Agreement, and counterpart   **3 Nov. 1705**

Thomas, (8th) Duke of Norfolk agrees with The Hon. Charles Howard, his great-uncle, and with Henry Charles Howard, the latter's son, re

> two parcels of ground on the west side of Surrey Street on which three houses now stand, built by Hon. Charles Howard, in the separate occs. of The Hon. Thomas Newport, esq., the said Charles Howard and Edward Porter, gentleman

Recites **MXD137** above, 11 August 1679, in which Joseph Hickes was acting as trustee for the Hon. Charles Howard. Now the present Duke, *out of his Great respect and Kindnesse* towards Charles Howard and his son, releases them from any future payment of rent during the remainder of the two 41-year terms on the premises.
The counterpart contains modern-style impressed seals with all three parties' crests.   2 docs., 1705

MXD588   Assignment of leases   **2 Feb. 1708**

The Hon. Charles Howard to the Rt Hon. Charles, Earl of Carlisle

> two houses with their gardens and all appurts., on the west side of Surrey Street, one in the occ. of the lessor, the other of Edward Porter, gentleman.

In return for a payment of £360 the premises are assigned to the Earl for the remainder of their respective 41- and 40-year leases taken out in 1677 and 1679.

Signature and seal, with crest, of the lessor

MXD589   Assignment of remainder of lease term   **2 Feb. 1708**

The Hon. Charles Howard to the Rt Hon. Charles, Earl of Carlisle

Messuage in Surrey Street in which the Hon. Thomas Newport dwelt, and still dwells, with the ground (60 feet) and garden at the lower end of Surrey Street [further details missing due to mutilation of the document]

Recites 41-year lease from Howard to Newport 15 May 1702.
Down payment £550; annual rent £100

MXD590   Quitclaim   **21 Jun. 1715**

Henry Charles Howard, of Greystoke, co. Cumberland, esq. for the benefit of his daughter, Mary Howard regarding:

Two messuages in Norfolk Buildings, Surrey Street, St Clement Danes, co. Middx

Howard releases his interest in an annuity of £100, as recited in an indenture of 20 November 1790, to his daughter.

MXD591   Declaration   **9 Jun. 1709**

Benjamin Muchall of St Andrew, Holborn, gentleman, concerning a deed of same day's date between himself and the Right Hon. Charles, Earl of Carlisle

two messuages on the west side of Surrey Street in Norfolk Buildings, one in the occ. of the Hon. Charles Howard, esq., the other in the occ. of Edward Porter, esq.

Muchall the premises were mortgaged, by assignment of the remainders of two 41-year leases to himself by the Earl of Carlisle to secure repayment of £360 plus interest; and that this money was put up by Thomas Howard, grandson of the Earl of Carlisle

MXD592   Lease for 13 years   **13 May 1710**

In return for a single payment of £50, Thomas (8th) Duke of Norfolk renews Thomas Newport's lease on premises as in **MXD585** above for 13 years starting from Lady Day 1718, at a rent of £100 a year

Charles Mawson's properties
*For earlier deeds see section 2.iii. above, and for a lease of
1710 see Appendix I.*

MXD593	Lease for 18 years	**26 Feb. 1708**

Mary Scott of Windsor, co. Berks., widow and relict of Matthew
Scott, gentleman deceased, and Charles Mawson to Abraham
Harrendine, perfumer

> messuage known by the sign of the *Naked Boy and
> the Jessamine Tree* in the Strand between Surrey Street
> and Norfolk Street, now in the occ. of the lessee

The premises are leased with Mawson acting as trustee, the
annual rent of £55 being payable to Mary Scott.
Room by room schedule of fixtures and fittings attached.

MXD594	Assignment of mortage and of a lease	**5 Aug. 1709**

Charles Mawson to James Pearce, gentleman

> i) moieties of a messuage on the west side of Surrey
> Street in occ. of Lady Longueville and of a little
> house behind it in occ. of Mr Powell; fifth parts
> of three messuages in Arundel Rents known as the
> *Whitehorse Tavern*, the *Cheshire Cheese* and the *Fox
> and Croune* in separate occs. of Captain George
> Jenkins, Mr Francis and Mr Willitt
> ii) old messuage and ground in The Strand in
> Arundel rents in a plot 13ft 4in (frontage) x 50ft 6in
> in depth

re. i): recites unredeemed mortgage of 26 March 1701 whereby
George Moore assigned his interest in the premises to Mawson
in trust for Matthew Scott of St James, Westminster, gentleman;
who has since died leaving a widow, Mary, and a daughter
Mary. James Pearce, party to this deed, is the executor of Mary
Scott's will and is half-uncle and guardian of the daughter
Mary. Mawson assigns to him the remainders of the several
terms on the premises, in trust for Mary Scott, together with
the ongoing liability under the mortgage.
re ii): recites lease of 10 Feb. 1691 for 40 years at £20 annual
rent (payable after the first year) by The Duke and Cuthbert
Browne to John Hodge, in trust for the same Matthew Scott;
which is now assigned to Pearce on the same trusts as for
property i).   2 docs.

Various persons' leases

MXD595   Assignment of lease   **5 Mar. 1708**

Nathaniel Piggott of Inner Temple, esq., Walter Raynes of Middle Temple, gentleman to William Smith of St Clement Danes, clerk

> parcel of ground in Arundel Street in Norfolk Buildings 17 x 53 feet; east to the street, west on a wall belonging to the Duke of Norfolk, south on ground demised to John Green and north on ground demised to Jonathan Wilcox

Recites lease 22 August 1679 by the 6th Duke's agents to Joseph Blowers [later cited as 'Bowers'] for 39 years at a peppercorn rent for the first year and thereafter at £9 7s. annual rent; that a house has since been erected on the plot, now in the occ. of Henry Playford; and that Piggott and Raynes are legally possessed of Blowers' former estate. Now, in return for a single payment of £150 they assign the remainder of the term to Smith at £9 7s. annual rent as before.

MXD596   Mortgage by assignment of lease   **20 Mar. 1712**

Timothy Macarty of St Giles in the Fields, perriwig-maker, and Elizabeth his wife to Elizabeth Dufton of St Paul, Covent Garden, spinster

> messuage on the east side of Arundel Street in a plot 24 x 44 feet in the occ. of Colonel Bond

Recites original 41½-year lease by the 6th Duke, 12 Feb. 1676, to Charles Stokes, assigned on 2 June 1677 to John Standbrook of Westminster citizen and surgeon of London and on 24 Feb. 1682 to Daniel Sheldon and Elizabeth Harrison alias Berenson. She has since married Macarty as her second husband and they both assign the remainder of the lease term to Dufton for a payment of £60.

Receipts of interest paid 1718-1734 are endorsed

MXD597- **MXD601**	Leases by Richard Chapman of St Clement Danes, apothecary	**1714-1721**

597   – to Francis Woodall, perriwig maker   **29 Sep. 1714**

> messuage being a corner house in Greyhound Court
> at the back of Milford Lane, abutting east on the
> *Golden Ball*, west on the court, north on a passage
> way from Milford Lane; formerly in the occ. of
> Bartholomew Brown, surgeon, now of said Woodall:
> for 7 years at £18 annual rent

598   – to Henry Gardiner, tailor   **9 Jan. 1718**

> brick house in Greyhound Court (no abuttals) now
> in the occ. of said Gardiner; for 7 years at £20 annual
> rent

599   – to John Style, of Milford Lane, baker   **20 Dec. 1715**

> messuage in Milford Lane fronting east on the Lane,
> north on a messuage in occ. of Edward Cole, victualler,
> west on a messuage in occ. of Richard Reeves, surgeon
> and south on coach houses of Sir John Darnell, knight:
> for 7 years at £30 annual rent.

Includes inventory of fixtures and fittings in various rooms.

600   – to Charles Lander, victualler   **8 Mar. 1721**

> messuage known by the sign of the *Golden Ball* in
> Milford Lane on the south side of a passage way from
> Milford Lane to Greyhound Court: for 11 years at
> £30 10s. annual rent

601   – to Oliver Peele of St Dunstans in the East, gentleman   **3 Oct. 1722**

> messuage as in **MXD599** abutting north on [blank]
> Lander, west on Henry Gardiner: – for 11 years at
> £30 annual rent

Inventory of fixtures and fittings.

MXD602	Lease for 21 years at £25 annual rent	**10 Mar. 1719**

Ann Loyd of St James without the Liberty of the City of
Westminster, widow to John Harding, victualler

stable on east side of Water Street, 17ft (frontage) x
61ft in depth x 29ft (width at back); with all rooms,
chambers and haylofts, etc.; east on a brewhouse in
Milford Lane, south Dr Robinson's stable, north a
stable of the Marquess du Cane

MXD603   Assignment of lease   **6 Nov. 1769**

Edward Wood of New Court, tailor & George Mills of Leather
Lane, St Andrew, Holborn, jeweller to Joseph Christian, linen
draper

messuage and appurts. in the Strand late in the occ.
of Christopher Cliffe, grocer; abutting east on John
Barrett, wax chandler and west on Ann Ware, milliner
[no dimensions given]

The premises are leased to Christian as from Midsummer last,
at £52 annual rent plus £5 for the first quarter already past.

MXD604-605 Assignments of lease interest   **13 Mar. 1782**

Edward Wood of Henrietta Street, St Paul, Covent Garden,
formerly of Woodford, co. Essex, tailor and Edward Parsons
of Aldgate High Street, London, 'mans mercer' [*sic*] to Joseph
Christian of the Strand, linen draper; and Joseph Christian to
Robert Delamotte of St Martin in the Fields, fan maker

messuage in the Strand in Arundel Rents known as the
Angel, 12ft 3in wide x 60ft in depth on the west side and
61ft on the [east] side and 13ft on the south side

Recites lease in 1724 by the 8th Duke to Ann Mills. Wood now
holds a moiety of the leasehold in right of his wife Elizabeth
(*née* Maurice).
In 1779, he and his trustee Parsons assign this to Christian for a
down payment of £120 subject to the rents payable to the present
Duke; and in 1782 Christian assigns again to Delamotte for a
down payment of £150.   2 docs.

MXD606   Assignment of lease for remainder of 60-year term   **28 Sep. 1775**

Montague Laurence of St Martin in the Fields, stationer and
Richard Williams of Bridewell Hospital, surveyor to Francis
Mearyweather of Gracechurch Street, ironmonger

messuage in a plot 15 x 31 feet; west Arundel Street, north John Harding, east Water Street and south John Culme, apothecary

Recites ducal lease to Hugh Mills 7 Nov. 1706, since assigned to Messrs Laurence and Williams; who now assign to Mearyweather for £170.

MXD607-608 Further assignment (lease and counterpart)   **12 Dec. 1778**

Francis Merryweather of Jerusalem Court, Gracechurch Street, blacksmith to William Taylor of Arundel Street, carpenter.

premises as in 606 above, formerly in the occ. of John Norcliff, barber and now of said William Taylor

Annual rent £30.   2 docs.

4. STRAND ESTATE, 1778-1815

i. Introduction

After the death of Edward, 9th Duke of Norfolk in 1777 the Dukedom passed to a second cousin, Charles Howard of Greystoke Castle in Cumbria and of the Deepdene near Dorking in Surrey. He was getting on in years, and so he generally engaged his son and heir apparent, Charles, Earl of Surrey, as his aide and unofficial agent. The latter succeeded as 11th Duke in 1786 and he died in 1815.

The task facing the 10th and 11th Dukes was the wholesale renewal of the 60-year leases made by the 8th Duke, which began to fall in around 1785-1791. A new Act of Parliament was applied for (23 Geo. III, 1783). The terms as to the actual leases are discussed in the introduction to 'Londoners' tenancies' (section 5.ii.) below.

The new Duke and his son had come to the ducal seat, Arundel Castle in Sussex, as strangers and found a town held firmly in the political sway of a rival family, the Shelleys of Michelgrove in Patching. They immediately set to the task of regaining a ducal foothold outside the Castle gates and, as a first project, started to build a new hostelry and meeting place, 'The Norfolk Arms'. The 1783 Act therefore ensured that the profits of the Strand Estate lease renewals could be put to their benefit in Arundel as well as London. After all expenses surrounding the new Strand Estate leases had been paid, the residue could be applied to *finishing and compleating a messuage or tenement, and buildings, now erecting in the town of Arundel, upon the scite of several old, ruinous and decayed buildings*. Additionally, the tenants' houses in Arundel and elsewhere in the Sussex estate might be repaired and improved. Thus began the long process whereby the Shelley family was routed, their seat at Michelgrove was acquired, and, by the 1830s, had been pulled down by the Duke of Norfolk.

As well as his designs for a meeting place in Arundel, the 11th Duke also had a social programme for the Strand Estate, centred, as in Arundel, on the provision of a modern meeting place. The *Crown*, an inn in Arundel Street was chosen, upgraded and transformed into 'the *Crown and Anchor Tavern*'. It emerged as one of the fashionable London meeting places – coffee house, debating club, and concert hall all in one, where discussion could be combined with good ale and wine. As a man known often to be 'in his cups', the 11th Duke must have thrown himself wholeheartedly into this particular memorial to his ducal reign. However, it became the scene of his disgrace, in the King's eyes, when his toast at a Whig Club dinner was taken as disloyal.[1]

---

1   J.M. Robinson, *The Dukes of Norfolk*, p.176 (Phillimore 1995)

The leases show that 'the *Crown*' lay on the east side of the street, just south of the Strand. By 1728 it enjoyed a 45ft frontage and was 81 feet in depth. The Duke, in collaboration with Thomas Simpkin, his tenant (described as a 'vintner' in the leases) acquired the adjoining premises to the east in Milford Lane, for which some title deeds survive (see Section iii below). A new access road for coaches, and stabling, could thus be provided, while the interiors were substantially revamped to provide a large assembly room and other public spaces. Much later, in 1852, the premises became 'The Whittington Club' under a lease made by the 13th Duke (**MXD917-920** below). However, the rooms described in that lease bear witness to his predecessor's, the 11th Duke's vision and achievement.

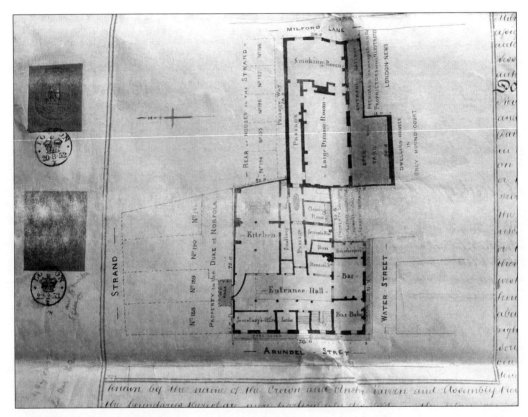

Fig. 6 The *Crown and Anchor* tavern.

The expansion of the old *Crown* inn in Arundel Street into a prestigious meeting place had been achieved by the purchase of additional premises to the east in Milford Lane. The extension, which is shown in this plan, was described in 1788 (ref. **MXD633-634**) as two large dining rooms on the ground floor and cellars underneath and a spacious Ball or Assembly Room above the same.

The ink and colourwash plan itself was drawn in 1852 by R.E. Philips and is typical of his work which decorates nearly all the mid-19th-century leases. (Ref. **MXD917**.)

ii. New building

MXD610   Copy Act of Parliament 23 Geo III   **1783**

– to enable Charles Duke of Norfolk to grant Building or repairing leases ... in the parish of Saint Clement Danes ... and in the Town of Arundel in the County of Sussex
14 printed pages loosely stitched

MXD611   Workmen's bills re the rebuilding of 24 Surrey Street   **1794-1796**

Includes detailed bills of bricklayer (Hugh Byrne) glazier (James Keir), iron smith (Thomas Hudson) and carpenter (John Davies), and schedule of works undertaken in 1794 and 1795 in building a new house and back offices at 24 Surrey Street. Paid in 1796. 1 file.

MXD612   Agent's notes as to bills on 24 Surrey Street, 1782-95   *c.*1795

iii. Appointments

MXD613   Watermen's appointments   **1790-1796**

Appointments, passes and lists of persons working as the 11th Duke's watermen between Surrey Stairs and Arundel Stairs. Some physical descriptions are given. One document is a petition for work signed by six referees.
Watermen's names are: John Barnett, George Place, John Woodcraft, Robert Edmonds, William Vallance, David Siday, James Dollett, John Law, Adam Spears, John Hollis. 1 file of 12 docs.

NB: *By deed poll of 20 Feb. 1802, Charles 11th Duke of Norfolk appointed Anthony Hunter of Norfolk House, St James's Square, gentleman, as his attorney for the collection of rents throughout the Strand Estate and in Charles Street and John Street near Norfolk House; as well as in 'two 'farmholds' in Little Stanmore, Middlesex and from all his houses in Southwark, co. Surrey. See Steer, vol. IV, p. 90 (ref. MD2382)*

iv. Acquisitions

MXD614-634   **Deeds of two houses in Milford Lane**   **1729-1788**

purchased in 1788 on behalf of Charles, 11th Duke of Norfolk

MXD614-615   Conveyance (lease and release) for £100   **7-8 Dec. 1742**

Richard Tidmarsh of St James, Middx, apothecary to Richard
Gem of Grays Inn, doctor of physick and Peter Shaw of
St James, doctor of physick (as mortgagor providing the
purchase money)

> Messuage called the *Forehouse* in Milford Lane in
> the occ. of Daniel Stokes; north, John Faithfull,
> south Richard Smith; and another messuage late
> in the occ. of Richard Pearce

Endorsed by a memo 6 Dec. 1746 by Peter Shaw as mortgagor
re transfer to the new purchaser Rayner Clark.   2 docs.

MXD616-619   Conveyance (lease and release) and (two) final concords   **2-3 May 1745**

Richard Tidmarsh, as above, sells the two houses to Rayner
Clarke of Strandgate Wall Lambeth for £140.   4 docs.

MXD620-622   Mortgage (lease and release) for £100, and bond   **19-20 Sep. 1748**

Rayner Clark of Walworth in St Mary, Newington, cowkeeper
and Mary his wife mortgage the two houses, as above, to
Bulkely Longbottom of St Giles, Middx, wine cooper.
The parties enter into a bond to levy a fine on the premises
to the use of the Longbottoms. A memorandum endorsed,
signed by Bulkely Longbottom 21 March 1749, concerns the
payment due upon transfer to John Lacy (below).   3 docs.

MXD623-626 Conveyance (lease and release) and assignment   **1729;**
22-23 March 1749

Bulkely Longbottom, Peter Shaw of Kensington, doctor of physick and Frances his wife, formerly Frances Tidmarsh, widow and executrix of the will of Richard Tidmarsh, Rayner Clark of St Mary Newington, and Mary his wife to John Lacy of St Ann, Westminster, cordwainer

Recites that Tidmarsh died in serious debt and that Shaw had paid these off on behalf of the executrix, now his wife. They, together with Longbottom and Clarke (who has paid off his debt on the premises) now convey the two houses as above to Lacy for £120 as absolute freehold. Longbottom receives £91 10 shillings of this sum and Clark receives the balance of £28 10s.

Associated documents are a copy of the will of Richard Tidmarsh 31 January 1729 and probate (PCC), April 1729 and a bond between Clarke and Lacy for performance of covenants.   4 docs.

MXD627-628 Conveyance (lease and release) for £180   **30-31 Dec. 1765**

John Lacy of Highgate, cordwainer to Thomas Fox of St Giles in the fields, victualler

> The *Forehouse*, as in 614-615 above; and the adjoining house, now described as in the occ. of widow Smallwood

The vendor also covenants to levy a fine, but copies of this are not present.   2 docs.

MXD629-632 Conveyance (lease and release) and fine (2 copies)   **13-14 Mar. 1787**

Thomas Fox of Great Queen Street, St Giles, victualler, to Thomas Simpkin of the Strand, vintner and Lancelot Burton of the Strand, plumber

> The *Forehouse*, now described as in the occ. of [blank] Chambers; and the adjoining house now also in the occ. of [blank] Chambers

The premises are conveyed to Simpkin and Burton for £315 in trust for Simpkin and his heirs. The fine was subsequently levied around Lady Day 1787.   4 docs.

MXD633-634   Conveyance (lease and release)   **11-12 Mar. 1788**

Thomas Simpkin of Arundel Street, vintner and Lancelot Burton of the Strand, plumber to Charles, Duke of Norfolk and Vincent Eyre of Sheffield, esq.

> Parcel of ground abutting west on the *Crown and Anchor Tavern* and on other property of the Duke of Norfolk; on which Simpkin, after taking down many ruinous old buildings hath lately in part covered with a very large erection annexed to the said *Crown and Anchor Tavern*, consisting of two large dining rooms on the ground floor and cellars underneath and a spacious Ball or Assembly Room above the same and the remainder thereof he hath appropriated to an open yard and other conveniences.
>
> The above ground was purchased by Simpkin partly from Thomas Fox (as in 614-632 above) and partly from Richard Andrews and Sarah his wife, as:
>
> i) parcel on which a messuage formerly stood, formerly in the occ. of Richard Newton Esq., deceased and late in the occ. of Joseph ?Raunant and then divided into several tenements
>
> ii) house plot formerly the *Three Horse Shoes*, and later used as a bakehouse in the occ. of Lasco Peele, baker
>
> iii) house plot in the occ. of Newton, then of Raunant as above, formerly known as the *White Horse* and later as the *Barley Mow*, since in the occ. of Walter White, collier and then of Jonathan Petit
>
> iv) house plot 12ft 6in x 16ft 3in taken out of the previous plot, on which a brick house had been built
>
> v) adjoining plot on which a little kitchen formerly stood adjoining the brick house, built by John Carryl, esq., former owner of the premises
>
> vi) toft on which a shed formerly stood 12 feet in length and a coal house 35 feet 9 inches in length
>
> vii) plot on which a little wash house formerly stood

The premises as developed by Simpkin are now conveyed to the Duke and Vincent Eyre for £760, in trust for the Duke. Burton confirms that the property is free from any demands on his part. The Duke additionally agrees to lease the premises back to Simpkin for an equable term as his lease on the *Crown and Anchor Tavern*, at £28 annual rent.   2 docs.

MXD635-656 Deeds of house purchased in 1785   **1719-1785**

635-638   Conveyance (lease and release) for £300   **22-3 May 1719**

> a) Katherine Fewtrell of St Botolphs without Aldersgate,
> widow and relict of George Fewtrell late citizen and
> ironmonger of London, deceased; b) George Fewtrell,
> gent. and Katherine Fewtrell, spinster, only son and
> only daughter of a) – to Richard Newton of the Middle
> Temple, London, esq.
> i) messuage called the *Three Horse Shoes*, in the
> occ. of Francis Buxton, victualler; messuage next
> door, late in the occ. of Michael Mazarine, tapestry
> maker
> ii) two messuages beyond the passage, in the yard
> behind i), in the occ. of Katherine Tunise, widow,
> John Caesar, Charles Davis, Mary Dawson, [blank]
> Nevill, [blank] James and Hester Morgan
> All in Milford lane and Crown Court; together with
> all yards, sheds, passages, etc.

Witnesses: Zeb: Clench (of St Botolphs without Aldgate),
Robert Woolley (late of Chancery Lane, glazier,
deceased), William Wills and J. Goddard
Two copies of final concord attached.   4 docs.

639-643   Conveyance (lease and release) for £260   **23-24 Nov. 1719**

John Caryll of Lady Holt [in Harting], Sussex, esq. and
Elizabeth his wife – to Richard Newton of the Middle Temple,
as above.

> Messuage in Milford Lane known by the name
> of the *White Horse*, late in the occ. of Matthew
> Fairless, wood monger and now of Walter White,
> collier; and the brick house newly-built in the garden,
> 12ft 6in x 16ft 3in, with a little kitchen adjoining,
> also newly built by John Caryll; and an old shed 12
> feet long, a coal house 12 feet 9 inches x 35 feet 6
> inches and a wash house; with all other buildings,
> ways and passages, etc.

Witnesses: Thornden Nevill and Austen Coom
With two copies of final concord and a further, enrolled, copy
of the lease.   5 docs.

644-652 Conveyance (lease and release) for £775   **2-3 Sep. 1765**

a) Samuel Alexander of Needham Market, co. Suff., merchant, John Cupitt, late of Spitalfields, silk dyer but now of Bishop Gate Street, city of London, innholder and Rosamond his wife, Thomas Potter of Goodmans Yard in the Minories, parish of St Botolphs, Aldgate, baker and Elizabeth his wife, James Whitely late of Bermondsey Street co. Surrey, innholder, but now of Little Queen Street, Grosvenor Square, co. Middx, weaver and Susan his wife

b) Richard Andrews, vintner

> i) Messuage in Milford Lane formerly in the occ. of Richard Newton, esq., deceased and lately in the occ. of Joseph Remnant and divided into several tenements
>
> ii) Messuage adjoining i), formerly called the *Three Horse Shoes*, now used as a bakehouse; late in the occ. of William Willis, victualler and now of Lasco Peele, baker
>
> iii) Messuage adjoining ii), formerly called the *White Horse* and now called *the Barley Mow*, formerly in the occ. of Richard Newton and lately of Joseph Remnant; with the brick built house in the garden, 12ft 6in x 16ft 3in and the little kitchen adjoining built by John Carryal, esq. [*sic*] former owner of the premises, a shed 12 feet long, a coal house 25ft 9in in length and a washhouse (size unspecified).

The vendors were heirs of James, brother of former owner Richard Newton who died in 1737. They also agree with the purchaser to levy a fine (or 'final concord') in order to strengthen his title to the premises.

Supporting documents are included with the conveyance, viz. copy marriage settlement of Richard Newton of Ipswich, esq. and Ursula, sister of Sir Richard Cust of Stamford, co. Lincs., 3 Aug. 1722; Newton's original will and codicil with note of probate 10 May 1737; copy conveyance for £1,050, 30-31 July 1764, by Mary Elliott of St Michael, Crooked Lane, widow, of her moiety of the above premises (and other premises in Darsham, Yoxford and Needham Market in Suffolk), as one of the nieces and devisees of the same Richard Newton, to Samuel Alexander as above; two copies of the fine levied in Trinity Term 1765; and a bond for performance of covenants, Sep. 1765.   9 docs.

MXD653-656 Conveyance (lease and release) for £400   **19-20 Oct. 1785**

Richard Andrews of Wood Street, London, only son of Richard Andrews as in 644-652 above, and Sarah his wife to Thomas Simpkin of the Strand, vintner and Lancelot Burton of the Strand, plumber

> Premises as in 644-652 above but the three plots have been conflated and all the buildings have been pulled down. **Marginal plan** shows a large plot 51ft 2in at the Milford Lane frontage (east) by 52ft 6in in depth, running into a further 30ft (approx) x 60ft plot which, itself adjoins west onto the *Crown and Anchor* inn (in Arundel Street)

The premises are conveyed to Simpkin and Burton in trust for Simpkin with a covenant to levy a fine, two copies of which are attached.   4 docs.

NB. *For further premises in Milford Lane and Water Street, purchased by the 13th Duke in 1852, see* 6. The Strand Estate 1816-1860 *below.*

v. Londoners' tenancies

60-year leases with building covenants 1785-1793
by Charles, 11th Duke of Norfolk

The preamble to these deeds no longer refers to the 17th-century Acts of Parliament which enabled the original housing development on the site of Arundel House, but to the Act of 1782-3) discussed above in the general introduction to this period of the Strand Estate's development. Its intention was *to enable Charles, Duke of Norfolk and others to grant building or repairing leases of certain tenements, houses and grounds in the County of Middlesex and in or near the Town of Arundel in the County of Sussex.*

The Duke's trustees empowered by the Act were Vincent Eyre of Sheffield, co. Yorks., esq. and Francis Wright of Henrietta Street, Covent Garden, banker. However, Wright had died by August 1786; after which, Eyre's name alone appears with the Duke's at the head of each deed. Lease terms of up to 60 years were to be made. The start of each term was to be no later than 29 September 1793 but in fact most of the actual leases were set up to run as from Michaelmas 1791 or Lady Day 1792.

Many of these leases were executed in the neat hand-writing of the Duke's surveyor, Joseph Hodskinson. He was probably the man responsible for the terms of reference (below) of this phase of development and rebuilding. He also appears in this part of the catalogue, as the lessee of two premises in Arundel Street and others in Water Street where he was building stables and coach houses. But his enduring legacy was not only to the Strand Estate but to all the ducal estates. In the archives at Arundel Castle there are several examples of his meticulous plans and books of reference, providing modern historians with an accurate perspective on the past.

The building covenants in these leases refer to a recent inquiry and report by the Duke's surveyors; in which the buildings that were *unfit to stand ... longer than 30 years* had already been identified. This ensured that the new leases were only granted on condition that they were rebuilt during that period. The new houses were to be *ranging and uniform with the best and most modern built houses in the said street.* The lessees were required to insure their houses against fire. Part of a draft agreement in 1796 with prospective tenant Peter Smith mentions that he was also obliged to erect iron railings outside his house and to pave the footway outside the entire frontage with good Yorkshire stones two and a half inches thick, with 'moorstones' (?granite) for the kerbs. He would be liable for the efficiency of his sewers and drains and to contribute to the costs of communal street lighting and night watching (Steer IV, p.89, MD2382). The lessees themselves were, as before, a mix of investors, widows and trades people, the latter perhaps sometimes using their premises at least as a retail outlet if not as a workshop.

Continuity from an earlier phase of development is provided by reference to the former tenants named in the 8th Duke's 60-year leases. These have all been noted in the catalogue. Houses still had no street numbers, but they were often located by reference to a fixed point in the landscape, eg., ... *being the 6th house from the house at the NE corner of Howard Street*. However, a (later) house number was sometimes added in pencil on the outside of the deeds. Where they occur, they are noted in the catalogue.

The list of proscribed trades for intended occupants is similar to those for the earlier periods. They include fishmonger, tripeman, dyer, pipe burner, melting or other tallow chandler, dealer in wood or timber or undertaker. Even carpentry could be forbidden (**MXD701**). There were also restrictions from stopping up a neighbour's light or obstructing any drains and watercourses. A clause for obligatory fire insurance is also included.

For some leases, no down payment was demanded, but this was usually offset by a higher annual rental. A few of these leases relate to the 10th Duke's period (September 1777-August 1786) and they tended to be for shorter terms than the 60-year norm. As for earlier decades, the bulk of the leases are the counterparts, signed by lessees rather than by the Duke and his agents, but where ducal signatures do occur, this is usually noted.

Witnesses to the leases were often the Duke's agents, clerks and servants as for example, William Seymour. Where several leases were executed on the same day a lessee of one might witness the lease of another. Other names, such as John Davis, Anthony Hunter, J.R. Pearson, Thomas Stewart, Uriah Madocks, J. Winder may have been legal clerks or employees of the Duke.

It is the norm in this part of the catalogue not to mention the length of the lease term if it was the standard 60-year term commencing in 1791 or 1792. Many of these leases have been water damaged, but most of the script is still legible.

Strand

MXD661   – to Elizabeth Chapman of Northumberland Street,   **18 May 1785**
Strand, spinster

> House plot 12ft 3in (frontage) x 62ft x 13ft 6in at
> the rear end, formerly leased to Mary Scott; being
> the 3rd house from the house at the NE corner of
> Arundel Street. (No. 192)

Down payment £245; annual rent £16

MXD662-663 – to Daniel Golden of the Strand, linen draper   **18 May 1785**

> i) House plot 16ft (frontage) x 43ft 6in formerly
> leased to Hugh Mills; being the 1st house from the
> NW corner of Norfolk Street. (No. 178)
> ii) House plot 13ft 6in (frontage) x 62ft, formerly
> leased to John Anstis; being the 4th house from
> the house at the NE corner of Arundel Street.
> (No.193)

Down payments £198 and £210 respectively; annual rents
£15 each.   2 docs.

MXD664   – to Martha Gumley of Grosvenor Square, widow   **25 Jun. 1785**

House plot having 17ft 9in frontage to the Strand x 44ft 6in, being the corner house on the east side of Norfolk Street, formerly leased to John Gumley. **Marginal plan.**

Down payment £490; annual rent £23

MXD665   – to George Vaughan of the Strand, esq.   **25 Sep. 1785**

House plot 16 feet (frontage) x 60 feet being the first house from the house at the NW corner of Arundel Street, formerly leased to Hugh Mills. Pencil addendum: 'No. 186'

Down payment £294; annual rent £15

MXD666-672 – to Tomkyns Dew of Cavendish Square, Marylebone,   **24 Feb. 1786**
Middx

i) House plot 15 feet (frontage) x 61 feet formerly leased to ?Mary Fleetwood; being the corner house on the west side of Arundel Street
ii) House plot 15ft 4in (frontage) x 45ft 3in formerly leased to Mary Fleetwood; being the corner house at the NE corner of Arundel Street. (No.188)
iii) House plot 12ft 3in x 60ft formerly leased to Mary Fleetwood; being the 1st house from the house at the NE corner of Arundel Street. (No. 190)

Down payments £259, £222 and £238; annual rents £16, £18 and £16 respectively. Includes a copies of schedules of works needing to be done to premises ii) and iii) in 1835, signed by Robert Abraham, the (12th) Duke's architect and agent. Names of tenants are given (no. 185 Edward Sherborn, draper; no. 188 Mr Szarka; no. 190 Joseph Partington, draper). 7 docs.

MXD673   – to George Edwards of Henlow Grange, co. Bedford, esq.   **20 Jun. 1786**

House plot 15ft 6in (frontage) x 58ft, formerly leased to Catherine Abram; being the house at the NE corner of Norfolk Street

Down payment £210; annual rent £18

MXD674   – to William Lingham of Bear Lane, city of London,   **12 Dec. 1786**
merchant

> Two new erected messuages in the Strand one on
> the east side and the other on the west side of a
> passage way leading from the Strand to the *Talbot
> Inn* including such part of the structures as is built
> over the passage way; with all appurtenances etc.
> belonging to the two messuages formerly on the
> same site but which were burnt down.

Leased for 65 years with immediate effect at £24 annual rent
but with no down payment (to recompense the lessee for his
building costs).

MXD675   – to Fenwick Bulmer of the Strand, chemist and druggist   **8 Sep. 1789**

> House plot 13ft 8in (frontage) x 57ft x 13ft at the
> rear, formerly leased to Hugh Mills; being the first
> house from the house at the NE corner of Surrey
> Street. (No. 173)

Down payment £273; annual rent £15

MXD676-678   – to Daniel Golden of the Strand, linen draper   **8 Sep. 1789-**
                                                                   16 Nov. 1790

> i) House plot 13ft 8in (frontage) x 75ft 6in x 13ft
> 6in at the rear, formerly leased to Mary Scott; being
> the second house from the house at the NE corner
> of Surrey Street. (No. 174)
> ii) House plot 21ft 9in x 48ft 3in fronting the Strand,
> with the two houses on it, being the 4th and 5th
> houses from the NE corner of Surrey Street, formerly
> leased to Hugh Mills.
> iii) House plot 12ft 3in x 61ft x 14ft at the rear,
> formerly leased to Ann Mills; being the 2nd house
> from the house at the NE corner of Arundel Street.
> (No. 191)

Down payments £255, £486 and £318; annual rents £18, £20
and £16 respectively

MXD679   – to John Cary of the Strand, map engraver   **8 Sep. 1789**

> House plot 16ft 6in x 43ft 8in, formerly leased to
> John Willett; being the first house from the house
> at the NE corner of Norfolk Street. (No. 181)

Down payment £243; annual rent £20

MXD680   – to William Cary of the Strand, mathematical instrument maker **1 Jun. 1790**

> House plot 12ft 9in x 60ft exclusive of a back house intended to be pulled down, formerly leased to John Bullock; being the second house from the house at the NE corner of Norfolk Street. (No. 182). **Plan in margin**.

Down payment £225; annual rent £16

MXD681   – to John and Robert Bury of the Strand, lacemen   **16 Nov. 1790–**
                                                                        20 May 1794

> House plot 16 x 60 feet exclusive of a back house intended to be pulled down, formerly leased to John Robinson; being the third house from the house at the NE corner of Norfolk Street. (No. 183). **Plan in margin**.

Down payment £260; annual rent £20
Endorsement, 20 May 1794: William Seymour, the Duke's *steward and surveyor*, states that the leased premises have been pulled down and replaced by a new brick house now erected by the lessees, which meets the standard for the rebuilding as specified in the lease.

NB. **Lease of No. 184 Strand** to George Burnett, bookseller for 60 years at £16 a year, (consideration £256) – see ACA/MD2576 in F.W. Steer (ed.), Catalogue Vol IV, p. 86.

Surrey Street and Strandbridge Lane

This run of deeds have standard-form headings and margins, sold by T. Combe at the *Mitre* in Bishops Court, facing Lincoln's Inn

60-year leases

Surrey Street, east side

MXD683-686   Leases   (as from Lady Day, 25 March, last) **24 Apr. 1785**

Four separate premises, being the first, second, third and fourth houses respectively from the SW corner of Howard Street, each formerly leased to William Ingram at £9 annual rent and each now with a newly-erected house, built by their respective present lessees. The small down-payments are presumably set against the lessees' building costs.   4 docs.

683   – to John Davis of Derby Street, Mayfair, carpenter

House plot 21ft 9in (frontage) x 54ft x 20ft 6in at the east end, (No. 13 Surrey Street)

Down payment £65; annual rent £10

684   – to Charles Evans of Farm Street [illegible] Square, co. Middx, carpenter

House plot 20ft 6in x 53in (No. 14 Surrey Street)

Down payment £55; annual rent £10

685   – to Lancelot Burton of the Strand, plumber

House plot 20ft 6in x 54ft. (No. 15 Surrey Street)

Down payment £54; annual rent £10

686   – to Philip Norris of Castle Yard, Holborn, builder

House plot 20ft 6in x 54ft. (No. 16 Surrey Street)

Down payment £53; annual rent £10.

MXD687   – to Philip Norris of Holborne, builder   **29 Sep. 1787**

House plot 18ft 6in x 54ft formerly leased to James Brown being the 5th house from the house at the SW corner of Howard Street (No. 17 Surrey Street)

Down payment £40; annual rent £16

MXD688   – to John Skinner of Surrey Street, gentleman   **3 Jul. 1790**

House plot 64 feet (frontage) x 54 feet (exclusive of a back house intended to be pulled down) formerly leased to Joseph Ashton; being the lowest house on the east side of the street, fronting the Thames (No. 19 Surrey Street)

Down payment £667; annual rent £31

MXD689 – to William Seymour of Norfolk House, St James, gentleman [the Duke's London agent] **1 Jun. 1792**

> House plot 23ft 6in x 54ft formerly leased to William Ingram; being the sixth house from the house at the SW corner of Howard Street. (No. 18 Surrey Street)

Down payment £40; annual rent £12

MXD690 – to Benjamin Dawson of Surrey Street, victualler **1 Jun. 1792**

> House plot 29ft 4in (frontage) x 15ft 10in formerly leased to John Bentley; being on the NE corner of Howard Street

Down payment £400; annual rent £12

Surrey Street, west side

MXD691 – to Hugh Byrne of Duke Street, Lincolns Inn Fields **1 Jun. 1792**

> House plot 19ft 6in x 67 feet, including a back house in the Strand Lane, formerly leased to Richard Millan; being the fifth house from the River Thames. (No. 25 Surrey Street)

Down payment £220; annual rent £16

MXD692 – to Thomas Nield of Surrey Street, silver smith **1 Jun. 1792**

> House plot 20ft 6in x 67ft 6in, formerly leased to Hugh Mills; being the 6th house from the River (No.26)

Down payment £288; annual rent £15

MXD693 – to James Howell of Surrey Street, tailor **1 Jun. 1792**

> House plot 28ft x 70ft 6in (north side) and 68ft 6in (south side), with two houses on it, formerly leased to William Draper; the 7th and 8th houses from the River (Nos. 27 and 28)

Down payment £598; annual rent £32

MXD694   – to Bloomer Ireland of Surrey Street, tailor   **1 Jun. 1792**

House plot 20ft 11in x 70ft 6in, formerly leased to Richard Guest; being the 9th house from the River. (No. 29)

Down payment £308; annual rent £15

MXD695   – to William Anderson of Surrey Street, vintner   **1 Jun. 1792**

House plot 34ft x 71ft 6in, formerly leased to William Congreve; being the 10th house from the River (No. 30)

Down payment £525; annual rent £25

MXD696-697   – to John Davis of Darby Street, May Fair, builder   **16 Jun. 1791-**
1 Jun. 1792

i) House plot 22 x 72 feet formerly leased to Lydia Warner, with the appurtenances newly erected on it by the present lessee; being the 11th house from the River, abutting north on a passage into Strand Lane. (No. 31)
ii) House plot 14ft 7in x 54ft, formerly leased to James Guidot; being the 12th house from the River. (No. 32)

Down payment for plot i) £45 and annual rent £16; for plot ii) £234 and annual rent £10

MXD698   – to William Seymour of Norfolk Street, gentleman   **1 May 1793**
                                        [the Duke's London Agent]

House plot 29ft 6in x 66ft with the house on it which 'being in a very ruinous state and condition is intended with all convenient speed to be rebuilt'; the fourth house from the River (No. 24)

Down payment £20; annual rent £20

MXD699-700   Unexecuted lease (2 copies)   **4 Jul. 1793**

– to William Seymour (as above)

plot of ground next to the river Thames 72 feet 8 inches (frontage) x 58 feet in depth (south side) and 64 feet (north side); and the three new houses erected on it by Hans W. Mortimer all formerly leased to Joseph Ashton at several rents amounting to £50 a year

Down payment £500; annual rent £80

Other leases: Surrey Street, east side

MXD701   Lease for 21 years at £28 annual rent   **8 May 1802**
– to John Wood, boot and shoe maker

> messuage in a plot 45ft 6in (frontage) by 9 feet (north end), 3 feet (south end) and 46ft 6in (back wall); in the occ. of the lessee. **Marginal plan.**

Other leases: Surrey Street, west side

MXD702   Lease for 12 years at £50 annual rent   **9 Jan. 1779**

Charles, 10th Duke to Robert Smith, esq.

> house in the occ. of the lessee, formerly of James Theobald, Esq; west Strand Lane, south a house lately erected by Hans Wintrop Mortimer, esq., north [blank] Moore

MXD703   Lease for 21 years at £54   **9 Aug. 1789**

– to Joseph Burnthwaite, linen draper

> house on the north west corner of Surrey Street having a 14ft frontage to the Strand by 57 feet in depth, the rear end being 7 feet 9 inches in breadth, in the occ. of the lessee.

No abuttals
(With later pencil additions as a template for a different lease)

Norfolk Street and Howard Street
60-year leases

Norfolk Street, east side

MXD704-705 – to Martha Gumley of Grosvenor Square, widow   **25 Jun. 1785**

i) House plot 25 x 65ft 4ins, including part of a back house intended to be pulled down; being the second house from the NE corner of Norfolk Street. (No. 41 Norfolk Street). **Marginal plan.**
ii) House plot 20 x 65 (approx) feet, including part of a back house intended to be pulled down; being the first house from the NE corner Norfolk Street (no. 42 Norfolk Street). **Marginal plan (staggered plot).**

Both properties were formerly leased to John Gumley.
Down payments £490 and £434; annual rent £22 and £16 respectively

MXD706   – to Thomas Simpkin of Arundel Street, vintner   **17 Aug. 1786**

House plot 27 x 65ft 4in on the south side x 69ft 6in on the north side, including part of a back house intended to be pulled down; being the third house from the NE corner of Norfolk Street and formerly let to John Gumley. (No. 40 Norfolk Street) **Marginal plan.**

Down payment £476; annual rent £20.

MXD707-708 – to James Cecil (the existing lessee)   **20 Jun. 1786**

i) messuage in a plot 40ft 6in (frontage) x 34ft (south towards the Thames), being the last house at the lower end of Norfolk Street; with a side passage leading to the house behind. **Marginal plan.**
ii) messuage in a plot 40ft 6in x 39ft (south towards the Thames), lying at the back of i). **Marginal plan.**

Down payments £380 and £400; annual rents respectively £15

MXD709-711 – to Thomas Simpkin of Arundel Street, vintner   **13 Sep. 1786–**
20 Feb. 1787

i) the 4th and 5th messuages from the north east end of Norfolk Street [endorsed: 'nos. 37 and 38'], formerly leased to William Mathews and Charles Longueville

ii) the 6th and the 7th messuages as above ['nos. 35 and 36'], formerly leased to Sarah Harrison and Charles Longueville
iii) the 8th and 9th messuages as above ['nos. 33 and 34'], formerly leased to Edward des Fountains and Hugh Mills

Down payments £539, £522 and £498 respectively for each pair of houses; with covenants for rebuilding ii) and iii); annual rents £38, £38, £36 respectively.   3 docs.

MXD712   – to Henry Creed of Hampstead, esq.   **28 Feb. 1788**

house at the back of premises on the SE side of Norfolk Street having 39 feet frontage to the River Thames by 46ft 6in in depth with liberty to use a passage way 34 feet x 5ft 6in in breadth out to Norfolk Street; formerly leased to Joseph Gascoigne. **Plan in margin**.

Down payment £400; annual rent £15

MXD713-716 – to Robert Hurst of the Middle Temple, barrister   **3 Sep. 1789**

i) the third house (20 x 71ft) from the house at the corner of Norfolk St and Howard St, formerly leased to Tancred Robinson. Endorsed 'No. 29'
ii) the fourth house (22 x 71ft) from (as above), formerly leased to Ann Carter. Endorsed 'No. 28'.
iii) the fifth house down (20 x 71ft) from (as above), formerly leased to Robert Weston.
Down payments £300, £455 and £300 respectively; annual rent £20; covenants to rebuild properties i) and iii).
3 docs., all water-damaged.

MXD717   – to Jane Mortimer of Norfolk Street, widow   **7 Sep. 1789**

house plot at NE junction of Norfolk and Howard Street having a 58ft frontage along Howard Street by 22 feet in depth; formerly leased to Thomas Hancock

Down payment £420; annual rent £20
This document is water damaged.

MXD718   – to John Wace of Pall Mall, St James, Esq.   **8 Sep. 1789**

the sixth house (20ft 7in x 71ft) from the house at the NE corner of Howard Street, formerly leased to Elizabeth Cockaine

Down payment £312; annual rent £20

MXD719   – to Robert Cawley of Norfolk Street, esq.   **8 Sep. 1789**

the second house (20 x 71ft) from (as above), formerly leased to Edmund Probyn. No. 30.

Down payment £300; annual rent £20

MXD720   – to Joseph Neild of St Paul, Covent Garden, esq.   **9 Sep. 1789**

the first house (25 x 71ft) from the house at the NE corner of Howard Street, formerly leased to Peter, lord King

Down payment £656; annual rent £20

MXD721   – to Henry Shaw of Norfolk Street, esq.   **20 Feb. 1790**

the seventh house (20 x 71ft) from (as above), formerly leased to William Shippen, esq.

Down payment £400; annual rent £20

Norfolk Street, west side

MXD722-723 – to Morgan Thomas, esq.   **24 Sep. 1785-**
16 Nov. 1785

Two house plots each 20 x 84 feet, each including part of a back house in Angel Court intended to be pulled down, formerly leased to Anthony Smith, being the 3rd and 4th houses from the house at the NW corner of Norfolk Street, fronting the Strand. **Marginal plans**.

Down payments £253 and £264; annual rents £22 and £20 respectively

MXD724 – to Ann Foley of Henrietta Street, Mary le Bone,
co. Middx, spinster   **5 Jun. 1785**

> House at the SW corner of Norfolk Street in a
> plot 37ft 7in x 52 feet in depth to Howard Street;
> formerly leased to Simon Lord Viscount Harcourt
> as from 29 September 1791. ?'No 20'

Down payment £490; annual rent £18

MXD725 – to William Johnson of Petworth, co. Sussex, esq.   **24 Sep. 1785**

> fourth house from the River Thames (21 x 71ft)

Down payment £258; annual rent £20

MXD726 – to Lancelot Burton, plumber   **24 Sep. 1785**

> House plot 25 x 90 feet on the north side and
> 86 feet on the south side including the greatest
> part of a back house in Angel Court, being the
> 2nd house from the house at the NW corner of
> Norfolk Street, all, except the back house, formerly
> leased to Susannah Whitechurch

Down payment £420; annual rent £30

MXD727 – to Isaac Heaton of Norfolk Street, esq.   **24 Feb. 1786**

> i) house plot 24ft 3in x 39ft 7in, with the yard at
> the rear, being the corner house at the SE end
> of Howard Street, formerly leased to Margaret
> Thompson. **Plan in margin shows staggered plot**.

Down payment £294; annual rent £16

MXD728 – to William Matthews of Green Lettice Lane,   **24 Feb. 1786**
                                  Cannon Street, Merchant

> ii) house plot 15ft x 59ft 8in (including part
> of a back house intended to be pulled down),
> the 8th house from the NW corner of Norfolk
> Street; formerly leased to Mary Warter. **Plan in
> margin**.

Down payment £270; annual rent £15

MXD729   – to Thomas Simpkin of Arundel Street, vintner   **20 Feb. 1787**

> Plot of land 44 feet (frontage) x 70 feet with the two houses on it and a back house, the 6th and 7th houses from the NW corner of the Strand, formerly leased to John Bullock, Thomas Smith and Grace Fuller

Down payment £618; annual rent £38

MXD730   – to the Rev. Arthur Robinson Chauvel of Stanmore, co. Middx and James Chauvel of Halton Bridge in Shepperton co. Middx   **1 Jun. 1787**

> house plot 22 x 70 feet (north side) and 79 feet (south side), (including part of a backhouse in Angel Court to be pulled down). **Marginal plan**. The 5th house from the house at the west corner of Norfolk Street, fronting the Strand.

Down payment £276; annual rent £20

MXD731   – to Albany Wallis of Norfolk Street, esq.   **18 Jun. 1788**

> house plot next to the River Thames 60 x 71 feet and the several houses on it together with a vault under the premises extending under the street, 40 feet in length. **Plan in margin**. Nos. 19-22 Norfolk Street.

Down payment £1,260; annual rent £66

MXD732   – to Philip Norris of Castle Yard, Holborn, builder   **8 Sep. 1789**

> house plot 22ft 6in x 71 feet in depth being the 4th house from the house at the NW corner of Howard Street; formerly leased to Sir John Williams. 'No. 16'.

Down payment £452; annual rent £22

MXD733   – to John Gotobed of the Inner Temple, London, esq.   **20 Feb. 1790**

> house plot 22 x 71 being the 3rd house from the house at the NW corner of Howard Street; formerly leased to Sir John Williams. 'No. 18'

Down payment £455; annual rent £20

MXD734   – to Samuel Dixon of Lincoln's Inn, esq., barrister at law **13 Mar. 1790**

house plot 20 x 72 feet, the 8th house from the River Thames; formerly leased to Edward Baker. No. 14'.

Down payment £470; annual rent, £20

MXD735   – to Fenwick Bulmer of the Strand, chemist and druggist **16 Nov. 1790**

house plot 18 x 49 feet formerly leased to John Walthoe, the first house from the house at the north west corner of Norfolk Street, fronting the Strand. **Marginal plan.**

Down payment £234; annual rent £10

MXD736   – to Alexander Brodie of Carey Street, Lincolns Inn, whitesmith **11 Sep. 1791**

house plot 20ft 9in x 71 feet, the 5th house from the River Thames; formerly leased to James Brown. 'No. 17'.

Down payment £300; annual rent £20

MXD737   – to Thomas Simpkin, vintner   **30 Mar. 1790**

the 9th house from the River Thames, formerly leased to Margaret Thompson. 'No. 13'.

Down payment £110; annual rent £18

MXD738   Abstract of Norfolk Street leases (many of the above)   **1785-1791**

Howard Street, north

MXD741   – to Robert Trotman of Ipswich, esq.   **18 May 1785**

House plot with 34ft 8in frontage by 38ft 6in in depth on the east side and 16 feet on the west side, being the 2nd house from the corner house in Arundel Street and formerly leased to John World. **See marginal plan.**

Down payment £280; annual rent £10

MXD742 – to Catherine Clark of Fleet street, widow   **24 Sep. 1785**

House plot with 16ft 4in frontage by 29ft 6in in depth on the west side and 44ft 9in on the east side, including part of a back house intended to be pulled down, being the first house from the house at the north-west corner of Howard Street, fronting Surrey Street; previously leased to Grace Fuller, except part of the back house. **Marginal plan**.

Down payment £175; annual rent £9

MXD743 – to Ann Howells of Howard Street, spinster   **24 Feb. 1786**

House plot 36ft 8in by 27ft 4in in depth being the corner house on the north east corner of Howard Street, formerly leased to Reginald Marriott. **Marginal plan**.

Down payment £216; annual rent £14

MXD744 – to Ann Bracegirdle Anderton of St George, Southwark,   **17 Aug. 1786**
widow

House plot 14ft 4in x 27ft being the first house from the corner house in Arundel Street; formerly leased to Ann Bracegirdle

Down payment £215; annual rent £6

MXD745 – to Thomas Glover of Howard Street, coal merchant   **8 Sep. 1789**

House plot 33ft 3in x 34ft being the second house from the north east corner of Norfolk Street; formerly leased to Elizabeth Abbutt

Down payment £210; annual rent £10

MXD746 – to Lancelot Burton, plumber   **1 Jun. 1790**

House plot 20ft 10in x 45 feet, the second house from the house at the NW corner of Howard Street fronting Norfolk Street, formerly leased to Hugh Mills. **Marginal plan**

Down payment £207; annual rent £10

MXD747   – to William Matthews of Green Lettice Lane,   **3 Jul. 1790**
City of London, merchant

> House plot 18 x 45 feet including part of a backhouse intended to be pulled down; formerly leased to Simon, Lord Viscount Harcourt. Marginal plan referred to but is not there.

Down payment £291; annual rent £10

Howard Street, south side

MXD748   – to John Pennington, glazier   **24 Apr. 1785**

> House plot 22ft 2in x 20ft 9in on the south west corner of Howard Street towards Surrey Street, formerly leased to William Ingram

Down payment £40; annual rent £8
The lease runs for 66 years from Lady Day last.

MXD749   – to William Norris of Ludgate Hill, London, glazier   **24 Apr. 1785**

> House plot 17 x 22 feet, being the first house from the south west corner of Howard Street, formerly leased to William Ingram

Down payment £45; annual rent £5; lease for 66 years as above.

MXD750   – to Henry Shaw of Norfolk Street, esq.   **7 Sep. 1789**

> House plot 15ft 9in x 22ft being the second house from the south west corner of Howard Street, formerly leased to Grace Fuller

Down payment £100; annual rent £5

MXD751   – to Isaac Heaton of Norfolk Street, esq.   **20 Feb. 1790**

> House plot 17ft 8in x 25ft being the fourth house from the house at the west corner of Surrey Street, formerly leased to Margaret Thompson

Down payment £135; annual rent £7

MXD752   – to Peter Flinn of Norfolk Street, gentleman   **30 Mar. 1790**

House plot 14 x 45ft 10in on the east side and 25ft on the west side; being the third house from the house at the west corner of Surrey Street, formerly leased to Margaret Thompson

Down payment £135; annual rent £8
Mark of lessee, not signature

MXD753-754 – to William Seymour of Norfolk House, St James, co. Middx [the Duke's London agent]   **1 May 1793**

House plot having a 13ft frontage by 11 feet on the west side and 22 feet on the east side, being the third house from the corner of Arundel Street; with the vault adjoining and extending under the street, 90 feet in length east to west; formerly leased to Thomas Hancock

Down payment £400; annual rent £5. Marginal plan cited, but not drawn.

Lease (signatures of the Duke and Vincent Eyre) and counterpart. 2 docs.

Arundel Street

60-year leases

Arundel Street, east side

MXD755   – to Mary Hodgson of Arundel Street, widow   **20 Feb. 1785**

No. 25: house plot 20ft x 56ft 8in, the 4th house up, formerly leased to Peter Walraven

Down payment £142; annual rent £15

MXD756   – to Thomas Ramsden of Upper Brook Street, co. Middlesex, esq. **[Blank] 1785**

No. 26: house plot 20 x 55 feet, the 5th house up, formerly leased to James Pearse

Down payment £198; annual rent £12

MXD757   – to Waring Willett of St Margarets, Westminster,   **16 Nov. 1785**
Master of Arts

>   No. 31: house plot 35 x 44 feet, the 10th house up,
>   formerly leased to Francis Willett

Down payment £276; annual rent £17

MXD758   – to John Rothery of Arundel Street   **16 Nov. 1785**

>   No. 32: house plot 18ft 10in x 45ft, the 11th house
>   up, formerly leased to Charles Johnson

Down payment £308; annual rent £11

MXD759-760   – to Tomkins Dew of Cavendish Square, St Mary le Bone, esq. **20 Feb. 1786**

>   No. 38: house plot 16 x 13 feet, the first house
>   from the house at the NE corner of Arundel
>   Street, fronting the Strand, formerly leased to Mary
>   Fleetwood

Down payment £72; annual rent £8
Later dilapidations report (1825) by Robert Abraham 'Architect
and Agent' to the Duke, no. 1 Torrington Street, Russell Square,
on work to be done in 1825 to the above premises.

MXD761   – to Lancelot Burton, plumber   **16 Mar. 1786**

>   House plot 15ft 10in (frontage) and 15ft 5in at the
>   back x 39ft, being the first house from the house
>   at the NE corner of Arundel Street fronting Water
>   Street, formerly leased to Hugh Mills

Down payment £100; annual rent £5

MXD762   – to Joseph Hodskinson, surveyor   **16 Mar. 1786**

>   No.35: house plot 17ft 5in (frontage) and 18ft 5in (at
>   the rear) x 40ft 6in, the 2nd house from the house
>   at the NE corner of Arundel Street, fronting Water
>   Street, formerly leased to Hugh Mills

Annual rent £10. Down payment waived because the premises
were burnt down some years ago and the land 'idle' but JH
has now built *a good and substantiall dwelling house* there.

MXD763   – to Joseph Hodskinson, surveyor   **17 Aug. 1786**

> Nos. 33 and 34: plots for two houses, 36ft 4in x 40ft 6in (north side) and 43ft 6in (south side), the 3rd and 4th houses from the house at the NE corner of Arundel Street, formerly leased to Richard Hawkins

Down payment £348; annual rent £22

MXD764   – to James Watson of Arundel Street, jeweller   **17 Aug. 1786**

> No. 24: house plot 23 x 56 feet (north side) or x 58 feet (south side), 3rd house up from the River, formerly leased to Henry Hankey; reserving to the Duke a passage way from Arundel Street to Water Street 56ft 8in x 4ft

Down payment £290; annual rent £15

MXD765   – to John Bellamy of Old Palace Yard, Westminster, gentleman   **20 Feb. 1787**

> messuage in a plot 16 feet 9ins x 36 feet in depth on the north side and 37ft 6ins on the south side, lying at the north east corner of Arundel Street fronting Water Street, formerly leased to Arthur Allibone

Down payment £210; annual rent £12

MXD766   – to Thomas Thomas of Arundel Street, victualler   **20 Mar. 1787**

> premises as in 765 above

Down payment £210; annual rent £12

MXD767   – to Thomas Simpkin of Arundel Street, vintner   **20 Mar. 1787**

> Plot of ground 78ft (frontage) x 85ft on the south side and 73ft on the north side, and the building on it known as the *Crown and Anchor Tavern*, together with the several other houses adjacent to it on the same plot, formerly leased to John Bullock, Joanna Baker, John Lifford and Thomas Hamerton.

Sketch plan endorsed showing its location in relation to the
Strand and Water Street
Down payment £1,450; annual rent £77

MXD768	– to Richard Trist of Arundel Street, tailor	**30 Mar. 1790**

Nos. 29 and 30: plot for two houses, 44ft 5in x 46ft
3in (north side) and x 51ft 10in (south side), the
8th and 9th houses up, formerly leased to Elizabeth
McCarty and Sarah Simonds

Down payment £481; annual rent £30 and covenant to repair
one house and rebuild the other.

MXD769	– to Jarvis Buck of Arundel Street, tailor	**3 Jul. 1790**

No. 28: house plot 14ft 4in x 51ft 10in (north side)
and x 52ft 8in (south side), the 7th house up, formerly
leased to Thomas Hamerton

Down payment £297; annual rent £14

MXD770	– to Peter Flinn of Norfolk Street, gentleman	**16 Nov. 1790**

No. 27: house plot 17ft 6in x 39ft 2in, the 6th house
up from the River Thames, formerly leased to Sarah
Bowtell

Down payment £193; annual rent £10

MXD771	Draft lease to John Ash of Arundel Street, St Clement Danes	**16 Nov. 1790**

– premises (details not entered, re **MXD786**
below)

Arundel Street, west side

MXD772	– to Angus McKinnon of Lincolns Inn fields, upholder	**18 May 1785**

No. 4: 3rd house plot down, 18ft 6in x 57ft 6in;
formerly leased to Hugh Mills

Down payment £166; annual rent £15

MXD773   – to Thomas Browne of Ealing, esq.   **18 May 1785**

> No. 5: 4th house plot down, 20 x 53 feet; formerly leased to George Tilsley

Down payment £224; annual rent £13

MXD774   Lease for 60 years   **25 Jun. 1785**

– to Martha Gumley of Grosvenor Square, widow of John Gumley

> plot of ground 16 x 60 feet, fronting to the Strand, with two messuages on it, formerly leased to John Gumley

Down payment £301; annual rent £27

MXD775   – to Charles Grave Hudson of Arundel Street   **25 Jun. 1785**

> house plot at the south end of Arundel Street 61 x 53 feet; formerly leased to James Pearse

Down payment £490; annual rent £25. Signatures cut out

MXD776   – to Jonathan White of the Strand, hatter and Thomas White   **24 Feb. 1786**
of Aldersgate, oil and colourman

> No. 2: 2nd house plot from the north west corner of Arundel Street, 22 x 60 feet; used and enjoyed with another plot fronting the Strand; formerly leased to Hugh Mills, now in occ. of George Vaughan

Down payment £245; annual rent £15

MXD777   – to Samuel Brewerton of Arundel Street, merchant   **20 Jul. 1786**

> No. 17: house plot 17ft 2in x 53ft 8in, 3rd house up from the River Thames, formerly leased to George Gindott

Down payment £210; annual rent £11

MXD778   – to Thomas Simpkins, vintner   **17 Aug. 1786**

> No. 6: 5th house plot down, 22ft 2in x 51 feet, formerly leased to John Bullock

Down payment £224; annual rent £13

MXD779   – to Richard Trist of Arundel Street, tailor   **16 Nov. 1789**

> Parcel of ground 17 feet 6 inches x 13 feet with the messuage on it which it is now intended to convert into a stable; formerly leased to Thomas Hammerton

Down payment *a competent sum of money*; annual rent £5

MXD780   – to Anne Leech, spinster   **25 Jun. 1785**

> No. 7: house plot 20 x 51 feet, formerly leased to John Shaw

Down payment £200; annual rent £13

MXD781-782   – to Stephen Skillern (or Skellern) of Arundel Street, tailor   **20 Feb. 1790**

> i) No. 11 Arundel Street and no. 8 Howard Street: house plot 34 x 30 feet, at the NW corner of Howard Street, formerly leased to John Robinson and George Calvert
> ii) Nos. 12 and 13: plot 40 x 53½ feet, being the first and second house from the NW corner of Howard Street; formerly leased to Jane Loggan

Down payments £270 for i) and £450 for ii); annual rents £15 and £30 respectively; with covenants to rebuild.
Duke's signature as well as tenant's.

MXD783   – to John Meakings, attorney at law   **1 Jun. 1790**

> No. 8: house plot 20ft 4in x 51 feet, the 3rd house from the house at the SW corner of Howard Street, formerly leased to Charles Austin

Down payment £162; annual rent £15

MXD784-785 – to Fenwick Bulmer of the Strand, chemist and druggist **1 Jun. 1790**

>i) No. 9: house plot 20 x 51 feet, the second house from the house at the SW corner of Howard Street formerly leased to John White
>ii) No. 10: house plot 19ft 10in x 51 feet, the first house from the house at the SW corner of Howard Street, formerly leased to Hugh Miles

Down payments £240, £250; annual rents £13 and £12 respectively,

MXD786   – to John Ashe of Arundel Street, esq.   **16 Nov. 1790**

>No. 15: house plot 17 x 53 feet, including the passage at the side, the fourth house up from the River Thames, formerly leased to Tabitha Marshall

Down payment £204; annual rent £15

MXD787   – to William Cook of Dean Street, Soho, gentleman   **16 Nov. 1790**

>No. 18: house plot 19ft x 53ft 10in, 2nd house up from the River Thames, formerly leased to Edward Mountney

Down payment £217; annual rent £15

MXD788   – to John Prince, of Water Street, mason   **16 Jun. 1791**

>No. 14: house plot 20 feet x 53 feet 7 inches, formerly leased to William Barnsley and George Jenkins

Down payment £154; annual rent £15

For a further lease re Arundel Street, 1786, see Appendix I

Water Street
60-year leases

Water Street, east side

MXD791   – to Elizabeth Raikes of Water Street, widow   **18 May 1785**

>Plot of ground 132 feet (frontage) by 38ft 3in on the north side by 136 feet at the rear against Milford

189

Lane and 40 feet against the river Thames on the south side; formerly leased to Thomas Syms. **Marginal plan**.

Down payment £791; annual rent £22

MXD792 – to Thomas Simpkin of Arundel street, vintner   **17 Aug. 1786**

Piece of ground 34 feet (frontage) by 30 feet 8 inches including a piece to be opened up as a passage into ground leading into Milford lane; and the three messuages built on it, being the first houses next to a stable and coach house at the north east corner of Greyhound passage fronting Water street

Down payment £298; annual rent £25

MXD793 – to George Prince of Water Street, carpenter   **20 Feb. 1787**

Piece of ground 85 feet 3inches (frontage) by 33 feet on the south side and 38 feet 3 inches on the north side, formerly leased to Thomas Syms; with the second, third and fourth houses from the River Thames built on it.

Down payment £275; annual rent £36

MXD794 – to John Robinson Pearson of Water Street, coal merchant   **5 Sep. 1789**

Parcel of ground at the south end of Water next to the river Thames 20 feet 9 inches by 60 feet 2 inches, with the platform of stone and stone steps leading up to it, formerly leased to Honoria Dutton; with the house on it, the lowest house at the bottom of Water Street

Down payment £192; annual rent [illegible, ?£20]
Text states there is a marginal plan, but there is not.

MXD795-796 – to Joseph Hodskinson of Arundel Street, surveyor   **1 Sep. 1786-**
                                                                 12 May 1835

> i) parcel of ground having a frontage of 49ft 6in x 31 feet east to west by 65ft 6in north to south, with the house and coach houses on it being the 3rd and 4th houses from the NE corner of Water Street; formerly leased to William Curryer; reserving to the Duke a passage way from the premises into Greyhound Court. **Plan**.

Down payment £210; annual rent £21

Duke's copy as well as tenant's counterpart survives containing signatures of the Duke, Vincent Eyre (the Duke's agent), Edward Christian and Edward Darley (Hodskinson's executors); with later endorsement, 12 May 1835 assigning the remainder of the lease term to John Boykett Jarman of Roseneau House, Datchett, Bucks., esq.
See also **MXD841** *and Appendix I,* **MXD1353**, *below*

MXD797-798 – to Joseph Hodskinson as above   **7 Sep. 1789**

> House plot 32ft 10in (frontage) x 20 feet east to west at the north end and 32ft 9in at the south end and 14ft 11in at the back part, formerly leased to William Curryer; with the stable and coach house newly erected by the lessee, being the 5th and 6th ones from the NE corner of Water Street. **Plan**.

Down payment £50; annual rent £8
Some water damage to the text. Duke's copy, with his signature, survives, witnessed by Henry Thomas Howard and (agent) Joseph Hinde, but is extremely water-damaged.

MXD799-800 – to Joseph Hodkinson as above   **1 Jun. 1790**

> Parcel of ground 29ft 10in frontage x 59ft 6in east to west at the north end and 61ft at the south end with the stables, coach houses and lodgings newly erected on it by the present lessee

Down payment £65; annual rent £31
NB: Joseph Hodskinson's sublets are in section v below.

Milford Lane

For further premises in Milford Lane, see
MXD614-656 *above and* **MXD801-806** *below*

Leases of various terms: Milford Lane, west side

MXD801-802   – to Alexander Brodie of Carey Street near Lincoln's Inn,   **18 May 1779**
whitesmith

> two timber-built messuages having a combined
> frontage of 40 feet, late in the occ. of Wharton
> Collier, esq., deceased and now of the lessee, west
> on a yard and brewhouse in the occ. of the lessee,
> north on stables in occ. of Samuel Breeden, livery
> stable-keeper

In return for the costs incurred by the lessee in repairs, the
premises are leased for 21 years as from Lady Day last at
£25 annual rent.
One copy found with the Syms family deeds of 1706-1725, the
counterpart with Surrey Street leases. Ducal signature.
2 docs.

MXD803   – to Thomas Simpkin of Arundel Street   **10 Mar. 1788**

> Parcel of ground extending from the west side of
> Milford lane to the back of the *Crown and Anchor
> Tavern*, late in the possession of Richard and Sarah
> Andrews and Thomas and Christine Fox. The plot
> is partly covered with a building erected by the
> present lessee consisting of two large dining rooms
> and cellars underneath and *a very large handsome
> ball or assembly room over the same* ...

Down payment nil, in consideration of Simpkin's expenses
in building the said rooms; annual rent £28 and 40s. a year
payable to the poor of the parish living in Milford lane and
20s. to the minister of the Parish.
Term 63½ years.

MXD804-805   Rough jottings, draft lease and a sketch plan relating to the above   *c.*1788

> – showing a dog-leg plot with frontage of 51ft 2in, depth
> 79ft 7in and 85ft 3in at the rear towards the *Crown and
> Anchor.*   2 docs.

MXD806   – to Alexander Brodie as above   **30 May 1788**

Two new-erected messuages on the above site;
abutting as above except north is in the occ. of
Thomas Plant, livery stable keeper

Leased from Lady Day last at £30 annual rent but without a
down payment, in return for Brodie's costs in pulling down
the former houses and erecting anew.
Term 63 years.

vi. Sublets

MXD807-809 Leases by Joseph Hodskinson of Arundel Street, surveyor: **1791-1804**

807 – to Isaac Heaton, esq. for 61 years at £10 annual rent **20 Dec. 1791**

> Coach house, stables, with the lofts and rooms thereon erected, on the east side of Water Lane 20ft 4in (frontage) by 32ft in depth on the north side and 17ft on the south side; west on stables in Milford Lane, south William Adey, north on stables of Joseph Robinson and premises of ?William Robinson. **Plan.**

This deed is severely water damaged, barely legible.

808 – to Thomas Bolton of Norfolk Street, gentleman for 50 years at £58 annual rent **1 Dec. 1802**

> Coach house with the lofts and rooms over in Water Street in the occ. of the present lessee [no further details but **plan is endorsed** with dimensions

Two witnesses' signatures, both Ann Hodskinson.

809 – to John Kelly of Water Street [occupation illegible] or 49 years at £42 annual rent **6 Sep. 1804**

> Messuage with the yard, workshop and premises on the east side of Water Street.

Much water damage to this deed

MXD810 Lease for 21 years at £80 annual rent **20 Jun. 1796**

William Seymour of [Norfolk House], St James's Square, gentleman to Andrew Lovering Sarel, gentleman

> Messuage or dwelling house on the east side of Surrey Street, late in the occ. of Elizabeth Rakes

The Duke leased the premises to Seymour on 1 June 1792. *See also Appendix I below.*

vii. *Private Deeds*

MXD811-812 Copies of lease for 40 years at 5 shillings annual rent   **29 June 1795**

The Duchy of Lancaster to Hans Winthrop Mortimer of [blank], Daniel Parker Coke of Inner Temple, esq. and Alexander Luders of Lincolns Inn, esq.

> Small slip or screed of land in Strand Lane 72 feet in length by 20 inches in breadth at the south end and diminishing to a point at the north end; east on premises in the occ. of H.W.Mortimer and south on the river Thames

The fair copy was enrolled in the Duchy office 29 Sep. 1795. 2 docs.

For H.W. Mortimer's premises in Surrey Street, see **MXD368-372** *above.*

For correspondence and papers concerning rents due to the Duchy of Lancaster for premises near the Strand, see Steer IV, p. 89, MD2382.

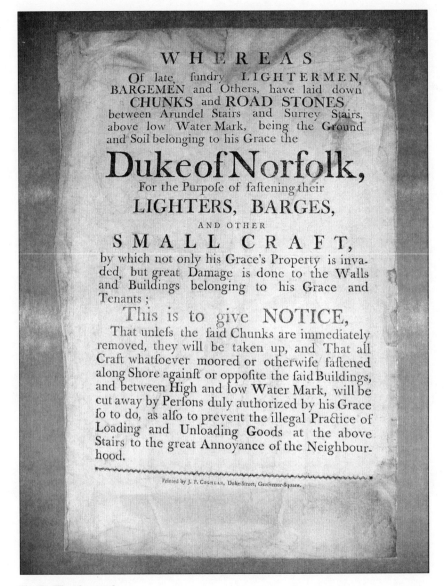

WHEREAS

Of late, sundry **LIGHTERMEN**, BARGEMEN and Others, have laid down **CHUNKS** and **ROAD STONES** between Arundel Stairs and Surrey Stairs, above low Water Mark, being the Ground and Soil belonging to his Grace the

Duke of Norfolk,

For the Purpose of faftening their

LIGHTERS, BARGES,

AND OTHER

SMALL CRAFT,

by which not only his Grace's Property is invaded, but great Damage is done to the Walls and Buildings belonging to his Grace and Tenants ;

This is to give NOTICE,

That unlefs the faid Chunks are immediately removed, they will be taken up, and That all Craft whatfoever moored or otherwife faftened along Shore againft or oppofite the faid Buildings, and between High and low Water Mark, will be cut away by Perfons duly authorized by his Grace fo to do, as alfo to prevent the illegal Practice of Loading and Unloading Goods at the above Stairs to the great Annoyance of the Neighbourhood.

Printed by J. P. COGHLAN, Duke-Street, Grofvenor-Square.

Fig. 7 The river trade.
The Strand Estate, like Arundel House before it, enjoyed a private river frontage as fig. 2 shows. There is evidence throughout this catalogue that its wharves and stairs had long been policed by the Earls' and Dukes' own liveried watermen. This printed notice issued by the 12th Duke makes it clear that he is prepared to deal forcefully with offenders who have 'invaded' his private property. (Ref. **MXD814**.)

5. THE STRAND ESTATE, 1815-1842

The 12th Duke

Bernard Edward, the 12th Duke had very little to attend to on the Strand Estate due to the comprehensive rebuilding leases executed by his predecessor. Because the 60-year leases did not generally fall in until after his death, the next round of renewals will be found in Section 6 below. However, he did appoint Robert Abraham as Surveyor to the estate (see **MXD957-960** below).

i Appointments etc.

MXD813   Appointment of water bailiff   **21 Dec. 1827**

The Duke appoints Henry Richardson, waterman as his:

> surveyor, water bailiff and agent in charge of Arundel Stairs and Surrey Stairs and all the shore belonging to the Duke between high and low water mark from the end of Water Street westwards to Surrey Stairs.

Duties include the proper maintenance of the shore and prevention of unwanted vessels from landing.

MXD814   Printed notice (J.P. Coghlan, Grosvenor Square, printer)   **Undated (?c. 1820)**

– forbidding unauthorised bargemen and lightermen from landing stone and other goods between Arundel Stairs and Surrey Stairs.

ii. Londoners' tenancies

For two further leases, 1835, see Appendix I.

Surrey Street, east side

MXD815 Lease for 21 years at £52 10s. annual rent   **30 Nov. 1825**

– to Charles Pain, gentleman

> House numbered 5 formerly in the occ. of James
> Hunt and now of the lessee

MXD816 Lease for 21 years at £28 annual rent   **13 Oct. 1831**

– to James William Barrier of Burlington Arcade, St James,
Westminster, bootmaker

> House plot 45ft 6in x 45ft 6in, no. 4 Surrey Street
> in the occ. of the lessee. **No plan.**

Surrey Street, west side

MXD817 Lease for 21 years   **23 Mar. 1833**
– to The Company of proprietors of the Grand Junction
Canal

> Premises having a 31ft frontage on Surrey Street
> by 58 feet south to the river Thames; west Strand
> Lane and north the Rev. Mr Fearnley. **Large plan
> in margin** showing ground-floor meeting room and
> strong room, and staircase.

The premises were leased on 22 June 1773 to Hans Winthrop
Mortimer (see above) of Caldwell co. Derbs., who had erected
them at his own expense. A **schedule of fixtures and fittings**
is included.

Down payment £500; annual rent £105
This deed is badly water-damaged.

MXD818 Lease for 21 years   **6 Jul. 1833**

– to John Copland of Harrow, Middx, esq.

No. 22 Surrey Street (21 x 59 feet); west on Strand
Lane, south on premises of the Grand Junction
Canal Company, north on [blank]. **Marginal plan**.

Down payment £200; annual rent £100
Water-damaged but mostly legible.

Howard Street, south side

MXD819 Lease for 21 years at £45 annual rent   **5 Jun. 1829**

– to Cornelius Donovan of Howard Street, wine and spirit
merchant

No. 6 Howard Street late in the occ. of [blank] Stabb
deceased; south on premises fronting the Thames in
occ. of Anthony Spedding., esq., east Henry Blake,
west George ?Beale, Lodging House Keeper

Duke's signature and crest on seal
Surrender endorsed, 25 Mar. 1841.

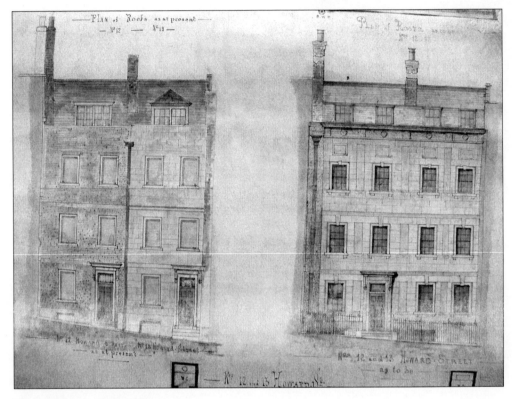

Fig. 8 Houses in Howard Street.

These architectural drawings are attributed to Robert Abraham, and his son H.R. Abraham, agents for the estate in the 1840s and 1850s. They were based at the 'Arundel Estate Office' which was itself in Howard Street. The plans show two houses to be thrown into one, the rooflines, windows and front aspect to be redesigned in classical symmetry and finished off with iron railings. Brickwork, formerly seen as a statement of worth and durability in the estate, was now to be covered up.

    The conflation of narrow individual houses into larger premises was just beginning in the estate at this time. As fig. 10 shows, by the end of the 19th century there were virtually none of the old houses left. (Ref. ACA P5/51.)

6. THE STRAND ESTATE, 1842-1868

The 13th and 14th Dukes and Estate trustees

i. Introduction

Henry Charles Howard succeeded as 13th Duke in March 1842 and died in 1856. One of his first acts as Duke was to get the old family name Fitzalan added, by Royal warrant, as a prefix to his children's surnames. When his son and heir, Henry Granville, finally became 14th Duke in 1856 he had long been known, familiarly, as Fitz. His ducal span lasted only four years until 1860, leaving an eldest son and heir, Henry, who was still under age. Henry's mother Augusta Mary Minna Catherine, generally known as Duchess Minna, took up the reins along with other trustees until 1868 when her son came of age and became the 15th Duke. This section of the catalogue deals with the Strand Estate administration until 1868 when the 15th Duke became responsible for his own affairs.

As the 60-year leases of the 11th Duke's era were mainly due to expire between 1845 and 1851, it was important that the power to lease the settled ducal estates was again renewed. The 'Arundel Estate Act' which gained assent on 26 August 1846, relating to the settled estates in Sussex and in the parish of St Clement Danes, thus underpinned the Strand Estate leases of this period. It enabled the 13th Duke of Norfolk and his successors to make 31-year leases of sound existing premises and 99-year leases for the building of new premises. Provision was made in the Act for new premises to have yards or gardens and some sort of water supply and connection to the local sewers. The usual rights of landlords to enter premises and terminate leases where tenants had not fulfilled their part of the agreement were secured. A catalogue of furnishings and effects in one of the houses in 1865 (ACA MD 838/14), towards the end of this period, describes a comfortable residence of five storeys with nine bedrooms for the family and their guests over and above the accommodation for several servants.

It was in the 15th Duke's era, 1868-1917, that the Strand Estate was transformed from one of residential properties to one of large commercial and institutional premises. This was done by throwing together several narrow residential houses to create grander premises, in response to London's changing needs. Yet the trend had been identified and embraced by his father and grandfather. Architectural plans of Robert Abraham and his son H.R. Abraham as ducal agents for the Strand Estate demonstrate that this trend was already in place in the 1850s (ACA P5/51, 53).

The 13th Duke was also granted the power to raise a sum up to £10,000 out of the Strand Estate, or out of other parts of his settled estates, against the planned Thames Embankment development – a project which had been *for some time in contemplation, and in case the same should take place* ... The money thus raised would be spent in works to ensure that the approaches of his streets running down to the River and the infrastructure of the estate were not harmed by the new embankment, but rather enhanced. The trustees appointed by the Act to oversee these measures were Edward Howard Howard-Gibbon of Arundel, esq., John Abel Smith of Dale Park [Madehurst], esq. and Sir Charles George Young, knight, Garter King of Arms.

The leases during Duke Henry's minority were executed by his guardians, his mother Minna and James Hope Scott of Abbotsford, co. Roxburgh, (described as) 'North Britain'. Judging by witnesses' names, various different firms of solicitors had been engaged to produce the leases. They included Henry Smith, solicitor of no. 33 Norfolk Street, Strand and John Isaacson of no. 40. Other witnesses during this period include Jacob Ratcliffe, clerk to James Hope Scott and W. Gordon, a clerk at the Brompton Oratory in Knightsbridge.

An 'ancient lights' case arose during this period on behalf of a property in Surrey Street, concerning the 'Theatre' building on the Kings College complex just west of the Duke's estate. It resulted in an agreement about the maximum height of the College building, adjudicated in 1847 by architect Edward I'Anson (ACA FC632-634).

ii. Appointments

MXD820   Appointment   **25 Jun. 1856**

Henry Granville, Duke of Norfolk appoints Henry Joseph King of the Thames Police Station, Norfolk Street, inspector, as his

> Attorney, surveyor, water bailiff and agent to look after the several stairs called Arundel Stairs and Surrey Stairs and all the foreshore between high and low watermarks from the end of Water Street in the east to Surrey Stairs in the west, viz. by preventing any fixing or mooring of boats there, and by looking after the landing places, etc.

MXD821   Re-appointment of the same H.J. King as waterman   **8 Apr. 1861**

Henry, 15th Duke of Norfolk makes the appointment with the consent of his trustees (the Duke was only 13 years of age).

Confident signature

iii. Ducal purchases (deeds, 1738-1852)

MXD822   Registered copy of a conveyance for £160   **9 Mar. 1852**

The Guardians of the Poor of the Strand Union to Henry Charles [13th] Duke of Norfolk

> Parcel of ground in Tweezers Alley, 229 feet in length with the cottage standing on it in the occ. of Messrs. Butterfield; bounded south by part of Tweezers Alley and the site of supposed stairs leading down to the Thames, north on another part of Tweezers Alley, east Joseph Holl, west on premises leased to Thomas Godfrey Sambroke, esq.

The cottage was formerly used as a house for one of the four beadles appointed for the parish and as a watch house and a 'plying' house.

MXD823-852 **Premises in Milford Lane and Water Street**   **1738-1852**

purchased by Henry Charles, 13th Duke of Norfolk, in 1852. 39 docs.

823 **<u>The purchase deed</u>**   **2 Jun. 1852**

William Henry Norton of the Strand, button maker and trimming seller, George Smith Norton of Bell Yard near Lincoln's Inn, law book seller and William Wilkinson of the Strand, chemist to Henry Charles, Duke of Norfolk

> i) yard or parcel of ground between Milford Lane and Water Street 66 feet east to west by 33 feet north to south and the four stables on it, formerly dwelling houses, formerly in the separate occs. of Messrs Champion, Thorogood, Howell and Robert Norton (now deceased) and the covered shed or building for carriages also on it

ii) entrance passage 3 feet in width from Milford Lane on the east, into the said yard

ii) free use and right of way through a roadway leading out to Water Lane on the west through land belonging to the Duke.

Detailed marginal plan: giving dimensions and details of the plot and names of neighbours and showing the adjoining leasehold premise in Water Street (property ii below).

Recites that the vendors are heirs of the said Robert Norton, deceased, formerly of Pickett Street, Temple Bar, trimming seller; who now sell the premises to the Duke for £500.

Contains vendors' signatures and witnesses by clerks to the solicitors of either party.

Sequence of earlier title deeds to the premises

i) **Freehold** messuage in Milford Lane 39 feet (frontage) x 50 feet in depth east to west in occ. of Joseph Remnant; east on the house called the Parsonage in Milford Lane, west the Duke of Norfolk's stables, south Edward Middleton, brewer, north on the house formerly of Nicholas Barley in occ. of Canon John Hind and [blank] Kingrove with a passage 3 feet wide leading into Milford Lane between Edward Middleton and the Parsonage

ii) **Leasehold (already in the Duke's possession as part of the Strand Estate)** parcel of ground on the east side of Water Street in breadth north to south 19½ feet exclusive of all walls at the front and 7ft 6in; in depth 32 feet on the north side and 17ft 6in on the south side; west on stables in Milford Lane, north on a coach house and premises lately built by Joseph Hodskinson and south on ground of the same Joseph Hodskinson, with the coach house, stables and rooms over now built on the said ground

---

824-825   Conveyance for £100 (lease and release)   **5-6 May 1738**

The Hon. Alexander Denton, esq., one of the Justices of the Court of Common Pleas to Joseph Remnant, carpenter (property i)

826   Conveyance in trust   **15 July 1757**

Joseph Remnant of Lambeth, citizen of London and carpenter and Ann his wife with Richard Remnant of St Giles in the

Fields, citizen of London and carpenter to William Hayhurst of St Ann in the Liberty of Westminster, colourman

> Parcel of ground, stable, yard, lodging rooms and premises on the west side of Milford Lane; south George Tisdale, peruke maker, west on a freehold stable, yard and workshop of Joseph Remnant (property i)

The premises are conveyed to Hayhurst as trustee for Joseph and Ann Remnant for lives with remainder to Richard Remnant

827-828   Conveyance for £500   **20-21 Dec. 1774**

Richard Remnant to John Thurgar of Surrey Street, victualler

> Premises as above now described as six stables with a workshop over in the occ. of [blank] Spence (property i)

829   Assignment and quitclaim   **21 Dec. 1774**

William Hayhurst and Richard Remnant to John Thurgar

> Messuage called the Parsonage in Milford lane. formerly in the occ. of Abraham Shuttleworth and now converted into two stables, with all rooms and chambers etc., in the occ. of Martha Collier (property i)

Recitals include a lease of the Parsonage from the Bishop of London, 13 Mar. 1737

830-831   Copies of final concord on the above transactions.   2 docs.

832   Copy of will and codicil of Joseph Remnant proved (London) **23 May 1767**

833-835   Mortgage (lease and release) for £200, and bond   **24-25 Mar. 1775**

John Thurgar and his trustee, Tobias Williams to John Rockett of St Mary, Islington, victualler (property i).   3 docs.

836-837   Copy and extract of will of John Rockett, proved (London) **22 Mar. 1776**
2 docs.

838-839   Conveyance (lease and release) for £200   **25-26 Feb. 1795**

John Rawlin Thurgar and the other devisees of John Thurgar
deceased to Alexander Brodie of Carey Street in the Liberty
of the Rolls, co. Middx   2 docs.

840   Bond in £900   **26 Feb. 1795**

– between Alexander Brodie and William Young Knight of
Great Marlborough Street, Westminster for repayment of
mortgage loan. All above are property i)

841   Sub-lease   **20 Dec. 1791**

– from Joseph Hodskinson (the Duke's lessee) to Isaac Heaton,
of Norfolk Street, esq.

            Property ii) is leased for 61 years at £10. **Detailed
            plan**.

842-844   Extracts from PCC wills   **1761-1792**

– of William Gee, 1761, John Coxe, 1783 and John Stracy,
1792 in connection with evidence cited in **MXD845** below.
3 docs.

845   Reply by Isaac Bargrave of Eastry Court, Sandwich, Kent   **20 Oct. 1799**

– to the letter from ?J. Brown and Co. re ruinous houses in
Milford Lane formerly the property of Joseph Ashton

846   Assignment of remainder of lease term   **8 Jun. 1802**

Heaton assigns property ii) to Alexander Brodie (as in
MXD838-839 above) for £430 with no future liability to pay
rent

847-848 Conveyance (lease and release) for £470   **10-11 Jun. 1816**

Richard Barry of Fleet Street in the City of London, esq., the Rev. Henry J. Symonds late of Upper Tooting, Surrey but now of Gibraltar, clerk, Francis L. Clason of Lincoln's Inn, and William Wingfield of the same, esqs., trustees of the estates of the late Alexander Brodie, to Robert Norton of Pickett Street, Temple Bar, trimming seller

Premises between Milford Lane and Water Street (property i. above)

The property is sold under a decree of the High Court of Chancery (details in the recitals) and at the same time the lease on property ii) is assigned to Norton.   2 docs.

849 Assignment of the bond **MXD840** above to Robert Norton   **11 Jun. 1816**

850-851 Draft deed and plans (Messrs Few and Co)   **Dec. 1835-**
Feb 1836

– for a settlement of a disputed right of way, the plan showing the freehold and leasehold parts of the premises purchased and the passage way leading in from Milford Lane, described as 'in dispute'.   2 docs.

852 Agreement and counterpart   **14 May 1836**

The Duke, Robert Norton and John Bellingham of the *Rising Sun Tavern*, Hackney Road (the Duke's tenant of premises in Milford Lane adjoining the passage) agree that while Norton does have a right of way from Milford Lane to his freehold premises, he will, during the remainder of his lease of the premises in Water Street (which will expire in 1852) use that entrance instead.

Detailed plan.   2 docs.

iv.   *Londoners' tenancies*

Introduction

As discussed in the Introduction to this section, the Arundel Estate Act 1846 underpinned the lease renewals of this period. Despite the thoroughness of the 1783-1791 rebuilding leases, it was claimed that many properties were again in a bad state of repair. In some cases one suspects this was a convenient plea, masking the real concern – a simple desire to modernise. However, the claim did have some foundation in truth. A dispute in 1851-53 refers to the ruinous state of nos. 7, 8 and 9 Norfolk Street and an order against the Duke that they be pulled down for the sake of public safety (ref. ACA FC641).

The documents in this section are leases except where otherwise indicated. The preambles state they were drawn up in accordance with the terms of the Act. The usual clauses against the making of nuisance now included such things as the setting up of steam engines on the premises, converting the frontage to shop windows or the blocking of ancient lights. Subletting without licence was forbidden and lessees were required to have fire insurance. By 1857 maintenance of the gutters, drains and drain covers was specified and the lessee was also required to whitewash, repaper or paint the interior walls as appropriate every seven years of the lease term ... *in good oil and proper colours.* The schedules of fixtures and fittings routinely made by the Duke's agents now covered window sashes, water pipes and cisterns.

The parchments on which the deeds were entered were generally supplied with ready-printed decorative headings by various London law stationers such as J.R. Hale and H.B. Moseley. As before, most of the documents are the counterparts, signed by the lessees, though the lessors' copies are sometimes also present, containing the Dukes' or trustees' signatures. The leases are witnessed in general by solicitors' clerks. The houses were mostly already occupied by the lessee when these new leases were issued, unless where indicated otherwise in the catalogue. House numbers were standard by now, so that the abuttals and so on are no longer noted in the catalogue.

Terms

The usual term is 31 years in this series and this is not generally noted in the catalogue. Deviations from this norm are noted.

The annual rents

Annual rents differ from property to property and the sums are therefore given in the catalogue, but expressed as 'a year' for brevity. No down payments were asked for in this series, but the rents were often higher than before. However, it is noticeable that in the 1860s many new leases were issued at low rents of around £40 or less. In these cases it is stated in the 'consideration' clause that the lessee has already laid out considerable sums in repairs and improvements. This is simply noted in the catalogue by the words 'low rent' after the annual sum.

Plans and property details

All leases have fine ink and colourwash plans inset, drawn by R.E. Philips of the Arundel Estate Office in Howard Street. They show the ground floor, including staircase, and give room names; with outside ground plan. Measurements of the plot and names of leasehold neighbours either side and at the rear of the premises are also given. These abuttals are written into the text of the leases, as before, but have not generally been transposed into the catalogue as there are now proper house numbers and good plans. However, if there is anything unusual about the premises, this has been noted in the catalogue.

Mr Philips' draft plans and other draft papers were sent to be approved by E.S. Dendy (Edward Stephen Dendy, 1812-1864, Chester Herald). He became the 13th Duke's Private Secretary and the Official Secretary to the 13th and 14th Dukes in 1849 [W. Godfrey, *The Survey of London: College of Arms*, 1963].

Further plans and papers re alterations occur in section v, *Agents papers*, below.

Strand

MXD853   No. 175, to George William Bartley of King William Street, tea dealer at £151 a year   **30 May 1851**

MXD854-856 A building lease of no. 179, to Jeremiah Down, tailor   **31 May 1851**

Term 99 years at £63 a year, reciting that the house previously leased to Fenwick Bulmer on the site has been pulled down; with mortgage for £1200 to Thomas Mutlow Williams of 155 Oxford Street, tailor. Endorsements in 1881 between Olivia Williams of 37 Foxley Road, North Buxton, Surrey and James Down of 55 Lady Somerset Road, Highgate Road, Middlesex, gentleman, paying off the mortgage; and assignment of the remaining term 1899 to George Herbert White of Hastings House, Norfolk Street, contractor
3 docs.

MXD857   No. 180, to Henry Burfield, chemist and druggist,   **31 Dec. 1855**
at £200 a year

MXD858   No. 176, to William Dickens late of 34 Arundel Street but now **9 Sep. 1857**
of 2 Norfolk Street, lodging house keeper, at £105 a year

MXD859-860 No. 178, to James Clarke Lawrence of Pitfield Wharf,
Commercial Road, Lambeth, builder at £100 a year.
Lease and counterpart   **8 Oct. 1860**

Endorsement, 5 Apr. 1899, records assignment of the remaining term to George Herbert White of Hastings House as in 854-6 above.

MXD861   No. 177, to Samuel Sainsbury, chemist at £125 a year   **20 Mar. 1861**

MXD862-863 No. 181: two unexecuted leases at £130 a year   **[blank] 1860**

– to Charlotte Gould, widow and administratrix of the goods of Henry Gould, optician and maker of mathematical instruments, deceased

MXD864   No. 181, to Charlotte Gould, widow at £130 a year   **20 Mar. 1861**

MXD865   No. 173, to Mary Morgan, widow at £145 a year   **31 Dec. 1864**
The lease is for 18 years only (see introduction above)

MXD866-867 No. 183, to Henry Palser at £145 a year   **1857, 1867**

-with previous agreement to lease, 9 Oct. 1857 to Thomas Palser, printseller, as from 1852, containing clauses for the replacement of the shop front and for insuring the premises to £1,200; and lease 4 Aug. 1865 for 18 years; with a memorandum of a mortgage endorsed in 1867 by John Abel Smith, esq. (presumably the then leaseholder).

Surrey Street, east side

MXD868   No. 10, the *Cheshire Cheese* public house   **28 Jul. 1855**

– to the existing publican, Thomas Newsom, licensed victualler, at £75 a year, low rent

MXD869   No. 5, to George Booth, gentleman at £50, low rent   **20 Mar. 1861**

MXD870   No. 5: counterpart of above, with later endorsements   **1861-1880**

By the first endorsement, 23 Apr. 1864 George Booth assigns the lease to himself and Samuel Alfred Lane late of Whitehall Place but now of No. 5 Surrey Street, gentleman; by the

second endorsement, 25 Mar. 1865, Booth surrenders his
interest in the lease to Lane for £25; by a third endorsement,
24 Jul. 1865, Lane assigns the lease to William Lay of No. 8
Surrey Street, private hotel keeper for £110; and by a fourth
indenture, 12 May 1880, Lay surrenders the lease to the Duke
that he may be re-granted a lease of nos. 4 and 5 together.

MXD871-872 Nos. 14 and 15, to Edward Lowe, private hotel and boarding **20 Mar. 1861**
housekeeper at £55 a year low rent.   2 docs.

MXD873 No. 16, to Charles Lewis Gruneison, gentleman   **16 Jul. 1861**
at £50, low rent

Surrey Street, west side

MXD874 No. 23, formerly in the occ. of the Guardians of the Poor **[blank] 1845**
of the Strand Union

– to the Rev. William Webb Ellis of Grafton Street, Bond
Street, Master of Arts, Rector of St Clement Danes and one
of the managers of the St Clement Danes, Holborn Estate
Charity [blank] 1845

The premises are now in the occ. of Mr Willoughby; and are
leased at £105 a year. Space for a plan, blank.

MXD875 No. 30, the *Norfolk Hotel*   **26 Feb. 1857**

– to Joseph Moore Palmer, (the present) hotel keeper at £90
a year low rent. The premises abut on the north on a passage
way from Surrey Street to Strand Lane (shown on the plan
as 'Surrey Place').

MXD876 No. 31: agreement to lease to Sarah Bousfield, widow at   **16 Mar. 1852**
£70 a year

MXD877 No. 31: lease for 14½ years at £70 a year to Mary Bunyard of
19 Norfolk Street, lodging house keeper   **7 Apr. 1860**

Norfolk Street, east side

MXD878 No. 30, to Hannah Cram, widow at £70 a year   **20 Nov. 1851**

MXD879 No. 31, to Robert Dunn, surgeon at £90 a year   **29 Nov. 1851**

MXD880-881   No. 32: to Benjamin Kent, gentleman at £40 a year   **28 Sep. 1851**

Kent is granted a 60-year lease in consideration of the £1,900 spent by him on improvements to the property.

In an endorsement, 14 Mar. 1867, the surviving mortgagee surrenders the premises to the trustees of the 15th Duke due to unpaid mortgage.   2 docs. (lease and counterpart)

MXD882-883   Agreement   **29 Sep. 1852**

a) Benjamin Kent, as mortgagor, Charles George Bannister and Edward Bannister of 13 John Street, Bedford, gents. (mortgagees)   b) The Duke

Recites the previous day's lease and that the Bannisters have loaned Kent £1700 for the improvements. Now Kent and his mortgagees undertake that these financial arrangements do not compromise the Duke's legal rights as freeholder. Two copies, the second containing endorsement recording a further loan, 1855; by residuary mortgagor, 1880 assigning the mortgage to himself and Charles James Walker of Furnival's Inn, Holborn, esq.; and in 1884 assigning it additionally to Charles Oakleigh Walker junior of Furnival's Inn.

MXD884   No. 29, to Mary Ann Levett, widow at £70 a year   **24 Dec. 1852**

MXD885   No. 35, to James Dixon, tailor, at £70 a year   **7 Aug. 1857**

MXD886   No. 40, to John Frederick Isaacson, gentleman at £95 a year   **12 Dec. 1857**

MXD887   No.18, to Joseph Scarlett, plumber at £80 a year   **20 Jun. 1860**

MXD888   No. 33, to Brownlow William Knox, esq., of 28 Wilton   **11 Jul. 1860**
Crescent, MP, late Lieut. Colonel; and Henry Pournall
of 63 Russell Square, at £70 a year

MXD889   Counterpart of **MXD888** above with 14th Duke's signature   **11 Jul. 1860**
Surrender endorsed, 24 Mar. 1866

MXD890   No 27, to John T.N. Barnand, solicitor at £64 a year
Signature of Duchess Minna   **5 Aug. 1865**

213

MXD891   No. 41 to William Henry Smith of No. 186 Strand, esq.   **1 May 1866**
The premises are leased for 16¼ years at £110 a year

MXD892   No. 28, to Nathan Jacob Calisher, jeweller at £90 a year   **27 Feb. 1867**

Endorsement of surrender of the remainder of the term   **25 Mar. 1868**

– by Phoebe Calisher of 30 Sackville Street, Piccadilly, widow
and executrix of her late husband's estate, to Henry, 15th Duke
of Norfolk

MXD893   No. 33 Norfolk Street and no. 11 Howard Street,   **21 Nov. 1867**
now converted into one building

– lease for 16 years to the Rt Hon. Thomas Heron Jones,
Viscount Ranelagh of No. 7 Burlington Street, City of
Westminster and John Chevalier Cobbold of Ipswich, co.
Suff., esq.

MXD894   Reassignment of the above lease on no. 28 to Henry Benthall   **25 Mar. 1869**
of Chatham Place, Blackfriars, contractor

Norfolk Street, west side

MXD895   No. 3: – at £131 a year   **23 Jun. 1854**

– to Samuel Boydell of Queen's Square, Bloomsbury, esq., the
Rev. Henry Edward Knatchbull, clerk of Elmham vicarage,
Thetford, clerk and Bettesworth Pitt Shearer of Swanmore
House, Bishops Waltham, co. Hants, esq., the present trustees
of the Farmers and General Fire and Life Insurance and Loan
and Annuity Company

MXD896   No. 9, to Louisa Bruce, widow at £60 a year   **31 May 1851**

MXD897   No. 17, to George Rose Innes of No. 20 Billiter Street,
city of London, gentleman at £80 a year   **9 May 1853**

MXD898   No. 16, to Miss Rosina Johnstone, spinster at £85 a year   **8 Jun. 1854**

MXD899   No. 3, to the trustees (names given) of the Farmers and General
Life Insurance and Loan and Annuity Company, at £130   **23 Jun. 1854**

MXD900   No. 10, to Jean Pierre Cornu, used as a private boarding   **30 Apr. 1857**
               house, at £110 a year; abutting south on Howard Street

MXD901   No. 5, to George Slyfield, boarding house keeper, at £105 a year   **29 Apr. 1859**

MXD902   No. 4, to Elias Morgan, lodging house keeper, at £85 a year   **5 Jul. 1859**

MXD903   – to Richard Allerton of 36 Norfolk Street, Land Surveyor   **12 Mar. 1860**

               No.13, at £50 a year; abutting south to no. 14 occupied by
               the Commissioners of Inland Revenue

MXD904-905   No.2, to James Clarke Lawrence of Pittfield Wharf,   **8 Oct. 1860**
               Commercial Road, Lambeth, builder, at £40 a year, low rent

               The lease is granted for a 60-year term as from 1851 and
               an assignment of remainder of the term to George Herbert
               White, 5 Apr. 1899, endorsed. The counterpart has the Duke's
               signature.   2 docs.

MXD906-909   Nos. 7 and 8, at £60 a year each   **24 Nov. 1863**

               A 99-year lease is granted on each of the two properties to the
               Rev. Christopher Wordsworth of the Cloisters, Westminster,
               DD., Thomas Godfrey Sambrooke of 32 Eaton Place, Middx,
               esq. and William Bowman of 5 Clifford Street, Bond Street,
               Middx, esq.; the low rent against lessees' repair costs; with
               covenants for the stopping up of communicating access
               between the two houses (details are shown on the plan).
               Counterparts have Duchess Minna's signature.   4 docs.

               Howard Street, south side

MXD910   Lease for 21 years at £35 annual rent   **9 Aug. 1845**

               – to Morrice Levy of No. 25 Norfolk Street, wine merchant

               No. 6 Howard Street, having a frontage of 13ft 11in, in occ.
               of the lessor, formerly of Mr Cross; east on No. 7 (Henry
               Appleby), west on No. 32 Norfolk Street (Mr Kent); with
               the vaults or cellars in front and under the premises 83 feet
               in length under Howard Street from east to west by 12 feet
               north to south

MXD911   No. 7, to Joseph Rowley Porter, linen draper at £55 a year   **13 May 1852**

MXD912   Nos. 12 and 13, at £40 a year, low rent   **8 Aug. 1865**

A 19-year lease is granted to Joseph Westbroom of no. 4
Howard Street, lodging house keeper.

Howard Street, north side

MXD913   Nos. 9 and 10 (as one house) at £80 a year   **1 Mar. 1853**

– to Thomas Chapman, boarding and lodging house
keeper

MXD914   No. 8 at £45 a year   **6 Aug. 1855**

– to Arthur Edward Obbard of no. 1 Howard Street, glass
merchant

MXD915   No. 2 at £35 a year   **11 Jun. 1856**

– to Arthur Edward Obbard as above, now described as
gentleman

MXD916   No. 4, to Joseph Westbroom, lodging house keeper at £45   **8 Aug. 1865**
a year

No. 11 – see **MXD893** *in Norfolk Street, East side, above*

Arundel Street, east side

MXD917-920 The *Crown and Anchor Tavern*   **31 May 1852**

– to Charles Lushington of Palace Gardens, Kensington, esq.,
Richard Monckton Milnes of Pall Mall, esq., James Wyld
of Park Village west, esq., Joseph Alfred Novello of Dean
Street, Soho, esq., John Humffreys Parry of Southampton
Buildings, barrister at Law, and Douglas Jerrold of Douglas
Lodge, Putney, esq.

Plan shows an elaborate complex with a 78ft frontage and
depth of 154 feet, running east as far as Milford Lane; all

lying due south of nos. 188-191 and nos. 194-198 Strand. Includes a room by room schedule of fixtures and fittings, including chimney pieces.

Lease with ducal signature and counterpart signed by the lessees and witnessed by the librarian and the Secretary of the Whittington Club; 37 Arundel Street; with two later receipts, 1857, relating to an award of arbitration re the premises which are now known as The Whittington Club.   4 docs.

MXD921-922 No. 24, to Thomas Godfrey Sambrooke, coal merchant   **29 Jul. 1853**

The house, in the occ. of Charles Henry Gabriel, is leased for 60 years at £45 a year (low rent) in consideration of the £470-worth of improvements and repairs to be expended by the tenant. The premises include (along the north side) a private passage way to Water Street and a cottage on Water Street in the occ. of John Batho, lighterman as tenant to T.G. Sambrooke.

Two copies, lease and counterpart, one endorsed, 6 Apr. 1872, with assignment of the remainder of the term by Robert Cheere, executor of the will of T.G.Sambrooke, deceased. See also **MXD931** below.

MXD923   No. 31, at £63 a year with £150 down payment   **30 Dec. 1853**

– to John Child and James Turnbull of no. 1 Water Street, lodging house keepers. Premises include a cottage at the rear (east side) in Water Street.

A 10ft wide access way running on the north side against the *Howard Arms* public house (no. 32, agreed to be leased to George Webster, victualler) is also shown in the plan, with rooms over as part of the present lease. The lessees shall respect its use by horses, carts, carriages and foot passengers.

MXD924   No.27, to Richard Massey of no. 19 Norfolk Street, plumber **6 Jun. 1855** at £38 a year, low rent.

MXD925   No. 32, to Francis Kirby Evans at £75 a year, low rent.   **21 Oct. 1857**

The premises are the *Howard Arms* public house, already in occ. of the lessee. Includes cellars under Water Street at the rear (see plan).

MXD926   No. 22, to John Gilliam Stillwell and Thomas Stillwell,   **29 Jul. 1859**
navy agents
Down payment £200; annual rent £125.

Plan shows a substantial building with a large courtyard
lying behind nos. 21 and 23, approached by a passage way
between them.

MXD927   No. 23, to John Gilliam Stillwell (as above) at £30 a year   **29 Jul. 1859**

Down payment £100. Plan shows a square building 20 x
22 feet (approx).

MXD928   No. 36, to Katherine Green Warren and Sarah Warren,   **18 Oct. 1860**
spinsters, at £35 a year, low rent.

MXD929   No. 35, to George Cocking, builder at £38 a year, low rent   **16 Dec. 1860**

MXD930   No. 29, to Hannah Mather, spinster at £80 a year, low rent   **31 Dec. 1864**

MXD931   No. 24, as in **MXD921-922** above   **20 Jun. 1865**

Sublease of the main house by T.G. Sambrooke to the
existing lessee, Alexander Gordon Dunbar for 7 years at
£80 a year.
Plan and **schedule** of fixtures and fittings.

MXD932   No. 30, at £45 a year, low rent.   **?May 1866**

– to Henry Ratcliffe of no. 30 Arundel Street, lodging house
keeper

Arundel Street, west side

MXD933   No. 18, at £52 a year, low rent.   **30 Dec. 1854**

– to Major Richard Culverwell, of no. 21 Arundel Street,
gentleman

MXD934   No.17, to Major Richard Culverwell as above at £40 a year
low rent   **26 Jan. 1855**

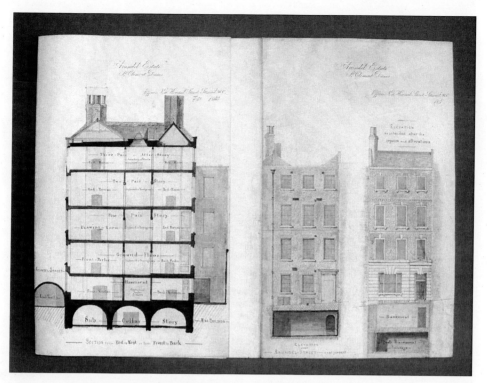

Fig. 9 A house in Arundel Street.

The task of upgrading and improving houses in the Strand Estate had engaged the Dukes' agents since the mid-18th century. It is doubtful whether any of the medieval timber-framed houses in the Strand survived into the 19th century. We have to rely on the deeds and leases themselves to tell their story, for there are no drawings extant. However, R.E. Philips' ground plans decorate the 1860s leases, and a few of his drawings survive. This one is interesting for the details of the cross-section and the below-street details. It forms part of a specification for improvements to a house in Arundel Street. (Ref. **MXD972**.)

MXD935	No. 5, to Walter Hamilton Davis, gentleman at £50 a year, low rent	**10 July 1858**

MXD936	No. 13, at £45 a year, low rent	**31 Dec. 1858**

– to James Russell Williams of nos. 13 and 14 Arundel Street, private hotel and boarding house keeper

MXD937	No. 6 at £47 10s. a year, low rent	**28 Apr. 1859**

– to George William Vickers of No. 1, Angel Court, bookseller

MXD938	No. 6: pre-lease agreement, terms and conditions	**1856-1886**

– with letters from the Duke's agent, E. Mesnard, re rent collection and letters and a bill from Messrs. Few and Co.

MXD939	No.14, to Henry Levy, gentleman at £45 a year, low rent	**15 May 1860**

MXD940	No. 9, at £50 a year, low rent	**31 Jul. 1860**

– to James Turnbull of 31 Arundel Street, and John Child of no. 1 Water Street [occupations not given]

MXD941-943	No. 19, at £90 a year, low rent	**20 Aug. 1860**

– to James Russell Williams of no. 13 Arundel Street, gentleman

Plan shows a substantial house with a 53ft frontage and bow window overlooking the River Thames; with a copy lease, 20 Mar. 1861.   3 docs.

MXD944	Mortgage of no. 19 for £710	**4 Mar. 1868**

– by James Russell Williams of Sutton Street, York Road, Lambeth, gentleman to Thomas Berkeley of 12 Grays Inn Square, gentleman

MXD945   Surrender of the above mortgage   **23 Jun. 1884**

– back to James Russell Williams of Margate, Kent, Hotel Keeper by Mary Angellick Berkeley of 8 The Cedars, Clapham Common, widow, all principal and interest having now been repaid.

MXD946   No. 8, at £35 a year, low rent   **27 Jul. 1863**

– to Eleanor Turnbull of no. 31 Arundel Street, widow and John Child of no. 1 Water Street

MXD947   No. 7, at £50 a year, low rent, to Christina W. Sheppard,   **22 Aug. 1865**
               spinster

MXD948   Letter from D. Cubitt Nichols to R. Bingham   **7 Jan. 1874**

– that repairs at no. 7 had not been done

Water Street

NB. *There was a dispute in 1859-1860 between the lessees of one of the premises in Water Street and other locals due to the noise of a steam engine or printing press installed by lessee 'Mr Smith' (William Henry, founder of W.H. Smith Ltd), operated by his subtenant Mr Tallis (ACA FC 641).*

MXD949   – to Herbert Ingram of no. 198, Strand, gentleman,   **22 Dec. 1852**
               at £68 a year

Ground on the east side of the street which nos. 1-4 Water Street lately stood, now occupied by a warehouse currently being built.

Plan shows the premises as 'The Printing Warehouse'; north and east the Whittington Club; south and east Greyhound Court.

MXD950-951 Norfolk Wharf: lease and counterpart   **1853-1872**

Lease   **29 Jul. 1853**

– to Thomas Godfrey Sambrooke of Eaton Place, co. Middx, coal merchant for 60 years at £105 a year, in consideration of £950 to be spent by the lessee in repairs and improvements

Premises comprise a dwelling house, coach house, other buildings now built but unoccupied and wharfage. Dimensions given, and plan.

Endorsement   **6 Apr. 1872**

The lease is assigned for £1,146 the residue of the term by Robert Cheere of no. 31 York Terrace, Regents Park, esq., executor of the will of T.G. Sambrooke, deceased, to William Henry Smith of no. 2 Hyde Park Street, co. Middx, MP.

MXD952   – to Robert Child, licensed victualler, at £84 a year   **10 Dec. 1855**

The *Kings Arms* public house; north and east on Water Street and west on Arundel Street

MXD953-954 Lease for 60 years, and counterpart   **16 Mar. 1857**

– to Thomas Godfrey Sambrooke as above, now described as of Arundel Wharf, Water Street, coal merchant

Dwelling house, coach house, stabling and buildings on the east side of Water Street in the occ. of the lessee; on J. Bellingham east and part south, and on W.H. Smith on the rest of the south and north

Down payment £250; annual rent £35

MXD955-956 Law Fire Insurance certificates on: **1853, 1869**

24 Arundel Street and 15 Water Street, owned by Thomas Godfrey Sambrook of 32 Eaton Place, esq.   2 docs.

See also 'Water Street' in *7: Strand Estate 1868-1917* below.

iv. Agents' papers

The Agent's office was no. 11 Howard Street. Some correspondence survives, the notepaper embossed with the Duke's crest (two different motifs). Until around 1850-2 the agent was Robert Abraham, but retirement was imminent, as his shaky handwriting in **MXD957** below testifies. For a short while his son Henry Robert Abraham took up the reins but he was soon was succeeded by E.S. Dendy (see introduction to ii above, *Londoners' Tenancies*). However, most papers in this section are drafted in the hand of R.E. Philips. The ducal agents were professional persons in their own right, engaged on the strength of their reputations as architects or surveyors.

Whereas the following papers give the names of a handful of subtenants, this is by no means the full picture. Further subtenants of the 1840s during Robert Abraham's stewardship, are named in other Strand Estate papers for which there is a Box List at Arundel (prefix MXE).

MXD957	Letters concerning estate business. 1 gathering	**1848-1852**

Mainly addressed to E.R. Dendy, the Duke's agent, including two from ?retiring agent Robert Abraham, from a disgruntled tenant James Dixon and printed form of lease terms under the 1846 Arundel Estate Act.

MXD958	Terms of renewals	**1849-1852**

Signed agreements in printed format, giving the outline of terms to be agreed upon in a forthcoming lease; and including the cost of specific repairs and alterations to be undertaken. All streets except Arundel Street

These docs. were found in original files (**MXD960** below). 1 file.

MXD959	Signed agreements to accept a lease.	**1850-1858**

Details as in **MXD958** above, but only relating to 13 premises throughout the estate.

MXD960   Examples of the original filing system of **MXD958-9** above

MXD961-971 Draft papers for licences to sublet or make alterations,   **1860-1865**
prepared by R.E. Philips of the Estate Office in Howard
Street; **with colour plans of several floors and charming
elevations by R.E. Philips**.

961   Nos. 168-9 Strand, 1865

962   No. 180 Strand: including correspondence and elaborate
plans 1864

963   No. 182 Strand: **plan only** (elevation of proposed new shop
front)

964   No. 190: Henry Smith to sublet to Thomas Tucker, a tallow
chandler (with prohibitions re trading); in 1864 to John
Sercombe of Lloyds Coffee House, ship owner and Charles
Aitken of Clifton Place, Hyde Park, surgeon to David and
Robert Laidlaw of Edinburgh and Glasgow, gas engineers.
No plans

965   No. 10 Surrey Street: various licences to sublet the public
house called the *Cheshire Cheese* on the NE corner of Howard
Street. Main tenants are Thomas Newsom, William Hales,
and Mrs Sharp, and various sub-tenants are named. No
plans.

966   No. 18 Surrey Street, referring to building works to be done
(no details, no plan), 1860

967   No. 14 Norfolk Street: draft licence for Murray Jack Davis
of Piccadilly, dentist, to assign to Eliza S. Richards, 1864.
No plan

968   No.16 Norfolk Street: draft licence for Rosina Johnstone to
assign to William Dickens, Lodging House keeper, 1862

969   Unnamed property in Norfolk Street: booklet of coloured
plans, viz. several floors and roof, and different elevations

970   Nos. 12-13 Howard Street: agreement to let to Joseph
Westbroom, 1861 and licence to sublet to George Hollingham,
1865; with some receipts. Includes plan

971   No. 21 Arundel Street: floor plans and covering letter to
E.S. Dendy from R.E. Philips, 1861

MXD972   Plans of a house in Arundel Street   **1860**

R.E. Philips' floor plans and elevations, in colour, of all storeys
from the sub-cellar to the roof of a house on the west side of
Arundel Street (next door to no. 13). Elevations show front
face 'as at present' and intended repairs and alterations in an
up-to-date style.

1 foolscap gathering

7. THE STRAND ESTATE, 1868-1917

i. Introduction

This section of the catalogue spans the era of Henry, 15th Duke of Norfolk from the year he gained his majority until the year of his death. Some of the deeds and leases were found in the collections brought to Arundel from Norfolk House. Others have been retrieved from the tin trunks at Arundel which had come in direct from the premises of Messrs Few and Co. in Covent Garden, London. This catalogue thus covers all known Strand Estate deeds and leases at Arundel down to 1917. The ongoing post-1917 administration of the Estate remains in the hands of ducal solicitors and agents and is not the subject of this catalogue. The pre-1917 leases are supplemented by the London material in the papers of Messrs. Few and Co., catalogued (vol. IV) by Dr Francis Steer as 'FC', and by a small amount of further material now classified as Strand Estate (prefix MXE), not yet catalogued.

The incoming Duke was able to start straight away on changes and improvements in his settled estates by virtue of a new Act of Parliament, *The Arundel Estates Act 1863*, obtained a few years earlier during his minority, by his mother and the other trustees. In Sussex it enabled him to sell off outlying parts of the hereditaments and to bring in other newly acquired premises as desired. Long schedules of affected premises are appended, including the Strand Estate – in which lessees names and annual rents are given. The Strand Estate was included among those the Duke might sell, but he also had power to renew leases for 31-year terms or to pull down, enlarge or build premises anew and to make new leases. It seems, from the subsequent development of the estate, that, rather than sell, he chose to enhance its commercial potential by the development of new hotels and business premises at the expense of private housing. Thus, for example, the firm of W.H. Smith were able to establish their publishing empire in the Strand itself and in warehousing behind, while for the proprietor himself there was a brand new house in Norfolk Street (**MXD1072** below).

The funds for these developments were also provided for in the Act. As well as the £10,000 made available in 1846 for development of the Thames Embankment, a further £10,000 might be raised out of the Settled Estates, on top of the profit from any land sales that the Act allowed. The original sum had not yet been spent, since the Embankment project was still in early stages, the *Thames Embankment Act* having only been passed the previous year. Significant clauses in the latter prevented the new Metropolitan Board of Works from erecting any premises along the Duke's river frontage or interfering in any way with his footways and accesses onto the proposed embankment. The £10,000 might now be spent not only on protecting his interests in the matter of the embankment, but throughout the estate more generally. A specification (no costs given) by D. Cubitt Nichols in April 1875 shows that the interface between the new Embankment and the Duke's estate was, by then, on the drawing board. It related to new iron railings at the bottom of Surrey Street and the building of new premises for Messrs. Few and Co. and mentions the embellishment of the ducal coronet on the proposed railings. The costs for this were to be shared equally between the Board and the Duke (ref. ACA MD839/3).

The existing trustees under the 1846 Act were invited to continue under the new 1863 Act. They were James Robert Hope Scott of the Inner Temple, London, esquire, Richard Garnett Bellasis of Lincolns Inn, co. Middx, esq. and Edward Henry Mostyn of Arundel, Sussex, esq. Hope Scott and Bellasis were replaced after their deaths by the Right Hon. Marmaduke Francis Baron Herries of Carlaverock Castle co. Dumfries and of Everingham co. York and The Hon. Ralph Drury Kerr of Castlegate House, York.

The Duke's agent responsible for leases and estate management at the start of the 15th Duke's era was Reuben Bingham, gentleman, acting from the office described as No. 1 John Street, by Norfolk House, St James's Square. He was followed by Edward Mesnard, who was in turn succeeded by John Dunn in the early 1900s. The postal address of their office had, by then, been re-styled as No. 33a Norfolk Square.

John Dunn was a son of John Quinn Dunn, born in Ireland, who had become secretary to the 14th Duke of Norfolk and later to his widow, Duchess Minna. In 1884 one James Dunn was a 'surveyor at the Arundel Estate Office' (**MXD1004** below). Before becoming the Duke's main agent, John Dunn was engaged for the design of some of the tudor-style new buildings on the Strand Estate, which the 1863 Act made possible. Dunn became an associate of the R.I.B.A. in 1876 and correspondence in the archives (ref. ACA MD456) shows that he had become a Fellow by 1884. As well as the deeds and leases catalogued here, the archives at Arundel Castle also contain various series of architectural plans and drawings. Among them are some very fine coloured drawings of Dunn's work on the Strand Estate, including *Schrams Private Hotel* in Arundel Street and Surrey House, on the 'Approach Road' facing the River. We have now had these items professionally conserved.[2] There is also a book of photographs by Lemere of Bedford Lemere and Co., showing interiors on the estate in Dunn's era [ACA MD2228].

Street and house plans made in the late 1800s and early 1900s survive in the archives at Arundel, as for example ACA MD1941, to demonstrate how the Strand Estate had changed under the 15th Duke's hand. He had carried forward his late father's project to develop the commercial potential of the estate. Demographic trends were changing and the Strand was no longer the desirable residential area it had been at its conception in the late 17th century. Leafy suburbs were burgeoning, connected to the Metropolis by reliable train services. Fleet Street's newsprint empire was on the estate's eastern doorstep, Covent Garden on its north, each a hub of commercial activity. The Metropolitan Board of Works had brought the convenience of a new underground railway station, Temple, to his southern doorstep, and beyond it the River Thames fetched and carried the materials of an industrial age in and out of London. The Duke had responded to these challenges. He had created an area of hotels, company and institutional headquarters, society meeting places and commercial premises. He had thus enabled the estate to find its proper position in late-Victorian society and to look forward to the new challenges the 20th century would bring.

---

2 Ref. MD 2208; Acc 48/31; PhD student Kornelia Robertson (Oxford Brookes) was working on these papers in July 2008 and brought our attention to them.

ii. Title deeds

MXD981-988   Deeds and papers of Messrs Few and Co.   **1867-1872**
re Strand Estate matters

Includes a valuation for sale (under the Thames Embankment
Act 1862), by the Metropolitan Board of Works of a strip of land
between the Strand Estate and the River Thames.   8 docs.

MXD989-991   Deeds of release by Duke of Norfolk to the Strand Estate   **1875-1886**
trustees

Relates to sums of money reclaimed out of the estate during
the Duke's minority, which he now settles in favour of the
estate trustees.   3 docs.

MXD992   Release from land tax charges re a house in Norfolk Street **31 May 1886**

– to the Strand Estate trustees by Mary Ratcliffe Bolton of
Windsor, co. Berks. and Thomas Dolling Bolton of 3, Temple
Gardens, London, gentleman

MXD993   Deed of covenants and grant   **14 Nov. 1883**

The Duke, Joseph Walker of the *Cheshire Cheese*, Surrey
Street, licensed victualler and Fenwick La Terriere of Alston
Lawn, Cheltenham, co. Glos., esq. and William Lay of Surrey
Street, licensed victualler

Relates to proposed new building on No. 9 Surrey Street and the
protection of ancient lights on the Duke's premises (the *Cheshire
Cheese* in Surrey Street and no. 10 Howard Street). **Plans**, including
elevation of the yard adjoining the *Cheshire Cheese*.

MXD994   Deed of covenants   **13 Feb. 1893**

The Duke, the Law Land Company Ltd. of Talbot House,
Arundel Street, Strand and Henry Charles Benyon Barton, esq.,

William James Bulmer La Terriere of the Wyndham Club co. Middx and Harriet Ann Lay of Surrey Street, widow

Concerns proposed alterations to nos. 8 and 9 Surrey Street and no. 8 Howard Street. **Large fold-out plans** showing, inter alia, the flank wall of the *Cheshire Cheese* (inn) in Surrey Street.

MXD995 Conveyance of No. 5 Strand Lane **5 Jul. 1893**

Mary Price Hughes of 59 Cheriton Road, Folkestone, co. Kent, wid. conveys to the Estate trustees for £1,375. **Plan.**

MXD996 Articles of agreement **6 Dec. 1893**

The Duke, the Law Land Company Ltd, George Herbert White of No. 12 Sherlock Road, South Hampstead and the Board of Works for the South Strand District. The agreement relates to the pulling down and rebuilding of the *Norfolk Hotel* in Surrey Place and alterations in the adjoining Surrey Place (lying between Strand Lane and Surrey Street). **Plan.**

MXD997 Deed of covenants **30 Dec. 1905**

Henry, Duke of Norfolk and the Rev. James Fleming of St Michaels vicarage, Ebury Square, London, a canon of the Cathedral Church of York, Edward Stafford Howard of Thornbury Castle, co. Gloucs., esq. and C.B. and William Hind Smith of the Chestnuts, Copers Cope Road, Beckenham, co. Kent, esq., Trustees of the United Kingdom Temperance and General Provident Institution of 1, Adelaide Place, London Bridge

Nos. 194, 195, 196, 197 and 198 Strand

The Trustees own the freehold of the premises on which they intend to erect a new building. They agree with the Duke as to the heights of the party wall on the western side of the plot, and other matters, so as not to prejudice the existing covenants in the Duke's leases of premises on the western side. Details given. **Four plans attached** (two in colour).

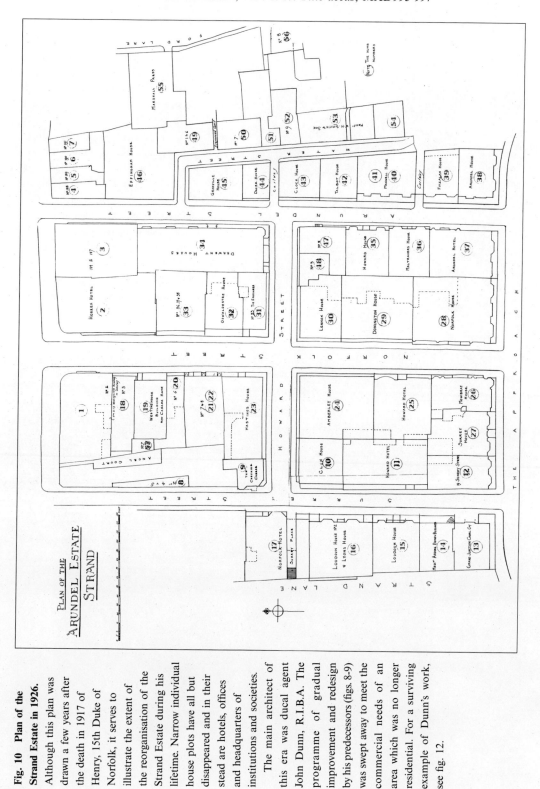

Fig. 10 Plan of the Strand Estate in 1926.

Although this plan was drawn a few years after the death in 1917 of Henry, 15th Duke of Norfolk, it serves to illustrate the extent of the reorganisation of the Strand Estate during his lifetime. Narrow individual house plots have all but disappeared and in their stead are hotels, offices and headquarters of institutions and societies.

The main architect of this era was ducal agent John Dunn, R.I.B.A. The programme of gradual improvement and redesign by his predecessors (figs. 8-9) was swept away to meet the commercial needs of an area which was no longer residential. For a surviving example of Dunn's work, see fig. 12.

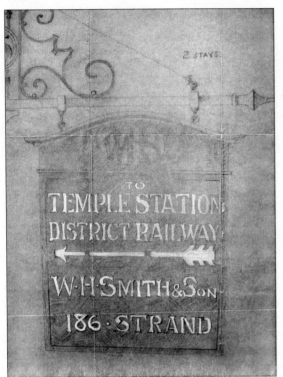

Fig. 11 Premises in the Strand.

Shops and commercial premises were not permitted in the residential streets of the Estate but they had existed in the Strand since the earliest times. However, the leaseholders did not have a free rein in the design of shop fronts and signs and plans had to be approved by the Estate Office. It is surprising, therefore, that the two illustrations shown here are virtually the only examples in the ducal archives. The firm of W.H. Smith, stationers, spread to almost every high street in the land from origins at No. 186 Strand. Regrettably, none of the old-fashioned shop fronts like that of No. 182 Strand still exists today. Temple tube station lies immediately south of the Estate and its construction impinged so closely on the Duke's land that there is a set of plans for its development among the ducal archives. (Refs. ACA/MD1894 [W.H.Smith sign] and **MXD963** [shop front].)

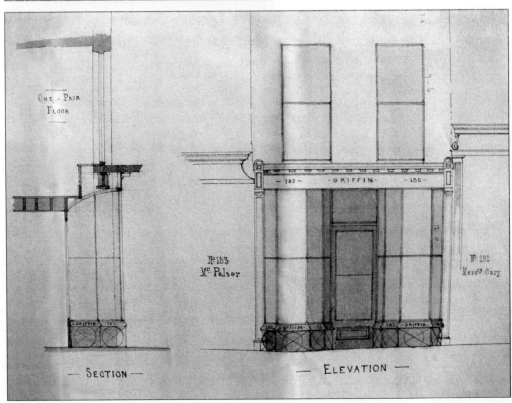

iii. Londoners' tenancies

As in earlier periods, most of the documents in the series are the counterparts signed by the lessees but the copy containing the Duke's signature is sometimes also present. **The leases are for 21 years except as otherwise noted** in the catalogue and, as in the previous series, they cite the Arundel Estate Act 1846. Excellent ink and colourwash ground plans are inset as previously, naming the rooms and showing some details as staircases and outside features. Dimensions of the premises and names of neighbouring leaseholders are also given.

The leases at the start of this series have the usual clauses re maintenance, drains, etc. Prohibited trades on the premises were: scavenger or nightman, bagnio [brothel] keeper, fell monger, soap boiler, varnish maker, flayer of horses, dealer in old iron, marine stores or second-hand clothes; blacking maker, baker, brewer, distiller, vintner, victualler, butcher, slaughterer, poulterer, fishmonger, tripeman, fruiterer, herb seller, dyer, brazier smith, farrier, pipe burner, melting or other tallow chandler, wax chandler, undertaker, carpenter, joiner, sawyer, or dealer in timber or wood of any sort. No advertising placards were allowed higher than the ground floor. Fire insurance was compulsory, as before, and a timetable for repairs and redecoration was set out.

From the 1880s onwards a less-formal lease had been introduced, as for example **MXD1054-1056** below for no. 28 Norfolk Street, Strand. In this the Duke and the prospective tenant agreed terms as to rents, other outgoings, sub-letting and repairs. Nuisances were to be avoided by the tenant as before, but were not specified. The term was set for an initial six months and the rent was payable quarterly. After this initial period the Duke had the power to terminate the agreement as from the end of the current quarter.

Strand

MXD998	No. 174, to James Reynolds, publisher for 12 years at £140 a year	**28 Jul. 1870**
MXD999	No. 182, to the *Sunday Times* Company Ltd, whose offices are at 52 Farringdon Street, city of London; at £300 a year	**9 Jul. 1883**
	Signatures include the company chairman and secretary.	
MXD1000-1001	No. 183, to the Right Hon. William Henry Smith, of 3, Grosvenor Place co. Middx, MP for 21 years at £235 a year	**17 Mar. 1885**
	Surrender of lease in 1891 endorsed. 2 docs. (lease and counterpart)	

MXD1002-   Deeds and papers relating to no. 179 Strand (on the   **1880-1898**
1014   north-east corner of Norfolk Street)

1002-   – sublease of the shop, parlour and cellar, 24 Dec. 1880, by
1003

> the Duke's tenant James Down, gentleman to William Ellis Lawrence of 70 Halton Road, Canonbury, co. Middx, hosier for 21 years at £200 a year; assignments endorsed: May 1882 to George Rees of 74 Cheswell Street, Dec. 1883 to Sydney Herbert Palfreyman, hosier and Aug. 1891 to George Herbert White of Hastings House, Norfolk Street, contractor.

1004   – elevation and section of staircase features by James Dunn,   **15 Apr. 1884**
          surveyor, Arundel Estate Office,

1005-   – licenses first by agent E. Mesnard to James Down of   **May 1885**
1006   55 Lady Somerset Road, Highgate Road then by Down to his under tenant S.H. Palfreyman to alter the shop front; **each with a plan**. The shop's trading sign was 'Palfrey and Bowen – hosiers, glovers and shirt tailors'.

1007-   – licences to sublet the first-floor office at the side of the   **1891, 1897**
1008   premises (No. 1 Norfolk Street) first to S.H. Palfreyman, then to Edward Vickers of 42 Foxbourne Road, Balham, Surrey.

1009-   – Licence to assign, duplicate and assignment.   **Mar. 1898**
1014

> James Down assigns to George H. White, as above, for the residue of a 99-year lease term first granted on 31 May 1851, for a purchase price of £7,000. Associated docs. include a copy of the death certificate in 1860 of Eliza Down of No. 1 Norfolk Street, wife of Jeremiah Down, master tailor.   6 docs.

MXD1015   No. 178 Strand and No. 2 Norfolk Street   **28 Jul. 1898**

> Assignment by Edwin Durning Lawrence and others to George Herbert White of Hastings House, Norfolk Street, contractor, of the remainder of a 60-year lease by the 14th Duke to James Clarke Lawrence (now deceased) in October 1860. Purchase price £2,000.

MXD1016-   No. 7 Angel Court   **1890-1913**
1022

> Lease for 7 years to William Edward Vickers and George Frederick Vickers of No. 1 Angel Court on a renewable option

up to 21 years at £35 a year. **Plan endorsed**; with associated deeds and documents concerning the under-tenancy to Diana Maria Bridgwood of Abbotts Bromley co. Staffs., widow (1895-1899); and licence to lessee John Arnold Einem Hickson to sublet to Lilian Vickers in 1913.   7 docs.

Surrey Street, east side

MXD1023   No. 32 to Lucy Jane Belsey, spinster   **20 Jul. 1871**

Leased for 11 years at £44 a year

MXD1024   Nos. 4 and 5 to William Lay (status not given)

Leased for 13 years at £70 a year   **13 May 1881**

The premises occupy a narrow strip having a frontage of 86ft 9in and a depth of 5ft at the north end by 13ft at the south.

MXD1025   Counterpart, having the Duke's signature; and endorsement **1881, 1885**

Endorsement, 8 Nov. 1885 surrendering the lease

MXD1026   Nos. 4 and 5, to William Lay, hotel keeper   **9 Nov. 1885**

Leased for 21 years at £70 a year. Covenants specify that the connecting door between nos. 5 and 6 shall be stopped up before surrender of tenancy.

Surrey Street, west side

MXD1027-   No. 21, for 61 years   **31 Dec. 1874**
1028

– to the company of Proprietors of the Grand Junction Canal. The crest and logo of the company, impressed under a paper cover, are appended in place of a signature on the counterpart. The lease has the Duke's signature.

MXD1029   No. 3, for 21 years at £300 a year   **9 Jul. 1883**

– to the Royal Farmers and General Insurance Company. Ducal signature. Surrender of lease, 5 October 1901, endorsed.

| MXD1030-1037 | Assignments of lease | 1888-1901 |

– to Nathan Mayer, Baron Rothschild and others, 1888, then to the Law Land Company Ltd., 1901; and associated papers. 8 docs.

MXD1038-1041 No. 3: licence, lease and counterpart **15 Feb. 1886**

– for James Clarke Lawrence, existing lessee, to sublet; and lease and counterpart from Clarke to Mrs Louisa Dunn of No. 5 Norfolk Street, widow. 4 docs.

MXD1042 No. 3: release of rent claims **29 Jul. 1898**

– by the Duke to George Herbert White, present lessee of the premises and of 187 Strand (see above)

MXD1043-1044 Assignments of under-tenancy **1892, 1899**

– from Mrs L. Dunn to Miss Annie Farley, spinster and from her to George Herbert White. 2 docs.

Norfolk Street, east side
For No. 1 Norfolk Street: see 179 Strand, above

No. 27

MXD1045 Assignment of remainder of 31-year lease (made in 1864) **25 Mar. 1878**

Miss Ellen Newman of 193 Camden Road, spinster assigns to Mary Jane Sampson of 24 Norfolk Street, lodging house keeper and Francis Bishop of 37 Colverstone Crescent, West Hackney, co. Middx, clerk for £1,050.

MXD1046-1047 Mortgage for £500 **20 Dec. 1881**

Mrs M.J. Sampson to Moritz and Emil Winter of the city of London trading as Winter Brothers Merchants; and affidavit as to the mortgagor's income. 2 docs.

MXD1048 Assignment of remainder of lease term for £1,468 **3 Apr. 1884**

Mrs Sampson to Elizabeth Goult of 32 Surrey Street, hotel keeper

MXD1049-1050   Licence to assign and assignment of same for £1,400   **3-4 Jul. 1888**

Mrs Goult of 32 and 33 Surrey Street, hotel keeper to Miss Annie Meggy of *Bacon's Hotel*, Fitzroy Square, co. Middx

MXD1051   Mortgage of the same premises for £1,400   **5 Jul. 1888**

Miss Annie Meggy to Arthur Wolton of Fern Lodge, Atkins Road, Clapham Park, co. Surrey, esq.

MXD1052   Schedule of relevant deeds received (?by Messrs. Few and Co.)   **22 Jun. 1894**

MXD1053   Lease Agreement   **23 Jun. 1894**

The Duke and Miss Annie Meggy of 27 Norfolk Street, private hotel keeper, agree terms re an indeterminate lease of the premises at a rent of £64 a quarter. *See also re 31-32 Norfolk Street below.*

Nos. 28-30

MXD1054-1056   Agreements for indeterminate leases   **22 Mar. 1894**

– between the Duke and Mrs Mary E. Slaughter of 6 Norfolk Street, Miss Matilda Mc Curdy of 29 Norfolk Street, private hotel keeper and Mr Samuel Bond of 30 Norfolk Street, private hotel keeper, at quarterly rents of £50, £42 and £45 for nos. 28, 29 and 30 respectively. *See also re 31-32 Norfolk Street below.*

Nos. 31-2

MXD1057   Reconveyance of no. 32   **23 Sep. 1889**

C.J. Walker and C.O. Walker (the mortgagees of the premises) reconvey to Henrietta Kent of Kents Hotel, Norfolk Street on repayment of £500 and interest

MXD1058   Mortgage for £700   **23 Jun. 1890**

Henrietta Kent and Henry, her son, to John Jackson Sudbury of Wonersh Park, Surrey, esq.; endorsed with a reconveyance in 1898 by Mary Sudbury, widow, on repayment to her of all capital and interest due on the loan, by Frederick George Beech of Myddelton Lodge, Weston Park, Eltham, Kent, beneficiary of Henrietta Kent, deceased.

MXD1059   Deed of covenant as to erection of buildings   **1 Dec. 1897**

– between (a) the Duke, (b) George Herbert White of Sherlock Road, South Hampstead, gentleman and   (c) Henry Frederick Nicholl of no. 1 Howard Street, solicitor, Frances Sarah Newman of no. 40 Russell Square, London, widow and the Rev. Francis Brown Newman of The Wilderness, Baldock, Herts., clerk.

Nos. 31-2 are in the occ. of Benjamin Kent and another as lessees. The sites of nos. 27-30 Norfolk Street are about to be redeveloped as a new building to be called Donington House. Party (c) are leaseholders of the adjacent nos. 1 and 3 Howard Street. All parties agree as to covenants re ancient lights, etc.

MXD1060   Plans, elevations and sections re premises as in **MXD1059**   *c.*1897

Ground plan of 27-32 Norfolk Street and 1 and 3 Howard Street; and elevations and sections of intended new building; all by D. Cubitt Nichols, Sons and Chater, architects.
4 docs.

MXD1061   Sale of the remainder of a 60-year lease on no. 32   **1 Feb. 1899**

Frederick G. Beech of Eltham, Kent, warehouseman sells to George Herbert White of Hastings House, Norfolk Street for £2,000 (the original lease granted to Benjamin Kent in 1852)

MXD1062-   Further minor evidence in support of **MXD1061** above.   **1899-1901**
1066   5 docs.

No. 33

MXD1067   Lease for 21 years at £125 a year   **9 Jul. 1883**

– to Thomas Heron, Viscount Ranelagh of No. 18 Albert Mansions Victoria Street and Nathaniel W.N. Strode of Cranmore Lodge, Chislehurst, Kent, esq. [trustees of the

Conservative Benefit Building Society also known as the
Conservative Land Society]

MXD1068-
1069
Licence to assign and assignment for £800
May, Jun. 1891

The liquidator for the Conservative Benefit Building Society
assigns the remainder of the above lease to The Engineer Ltd.
of no. 163 Strand (their registered office).   2 docs.

MXD1070
Further copy of the 1883 lease
24 Jun. 1903
– with surrender by The Engineer Ltd endorsed

Nos. 34-35

MXD1071
Agreement for tenancy of no. 34 by J.A. Bertram at
£200 a year
23 Mar. 1882

– concerns alterations affecting nos. 34 and 35 Norfolk Street
in 1905, then known as Oswaldestre House. *See also* No. 2
Arundel Street below.

Nos. 36-38

MXD1072
Lease for 61 years at £225 a year
24 Dec. 1869

New house known as **no. 37** Norfolk Street, to William Henry
Smith of 186 Strand, esq., MP. The house replaces nos. 36,
37 and 38 Norfolk Street which were recently pulled down
by the lessee at whose cost the present house was built.

MXD1073
Licence to make alterations
23 Mar. 1896

Recites as above and that the new combined plot is 59ft
4in frontage by 70ft depth. The present leaseholder of these
premises, William Frederick Danvers Smith of no. 3 Grosvenor
Place, Middx, MP, is instructed to allow G.H. White of
the adjoining nos. 40-41 Norfolk Street permission to make
cornices in the manner shown on a plan (**plan endorsed**).

MXD1074
Licence to W.F.D. Smith to erect additional floor.
9 Nov. 1897

Plan: large fold-out floor plan and exterior elevation by
D. Cubitt Nichols, Sons and Chater, architects, 3 Howard
Street, Strand, June 1897.

No. 41

MXD1075-
1076

Lease for 21 years at £225 a year   **17 Mar. 1885**

– to the Rt Hon. William Henry Smith of 3 Grosvenor Place, Middx, MP; with counterpart (signatures of both parties) **Plan**.

Surrender of lease, 24 Jun. 1891, endorsed.   2 docs.

Norfolk Street, west side

No. 3

MXD1077

Lease for 21 years   **9 Jul. 1883**

– to the Royal Farmers and General Insurance Company at £300 a year. Signature of the Director and modern-style crest and logo of the Company

No. 4

MXD1078

Agreement to lease to W. Horrex (no personal details)   **24 Mar. 1882**

MXD1079

Letter from W. Horrex (headed notepaper showing engraving   **5 Jul. 1897**
of *Horrex's Hotel*) asking to give up the tenancy

Nos. 7 and 8

MXD1080-
1086

Assignments of residues of two 99-year leases on   **1 Sep. 1898**
nos. 7 and 8

Sir William Paget Bowman, Bt. of Corporation House, Bloomsbury, London, and John Frederick Bowman, of 21 Bedford Row, London, esq. to The Rt Hon. John Gilbert Talbot of Falconhurst, Edenbridge, Kent, MP, the Rev. Prebendary Arthur John Ingram of St Margaret's Rectory, Ironmonger Lane, clerk and Laurie Frere of Allerford House, Taunton, Somerset, esq. [Trustees of the House and Sisterhood of St John the Evangelist for the training of nurses.] The original lease was granted in 1863.

Additional documents include licences to assign and a copy of the rules of the St John House Sisterhood, 1878.   7 docs.   **1878-1898**

MXD1087- **1088**	Licences to the Trustees assign the leases of nos. 7 and 8. 2 docs.	**7 Jul. 1905**

MXD1089-
1090   Declaration   **6 Jun. 1907**

– by E.R. Frere, Secretary of the House and Sisterhood of
St John the Evangelist, as to their reasons for sale, etc.; and
copy of resolution re same.   2 docs.

MXD1091   Assignment of residues of lease eases of nos. 7-8   **10 May 1907**

The Trustees of the Sisterhood assign to George Herbert
White, Esq. for £11,500.

MXD1092   Surrender of lease by G.H. White to the Duke of Norfolk   **31 Jul. 1907**

Howard Street

Nos. 1 and 3: *see* 27-32 Norfolk Street

No. 2: *see* 5-10 Arundel Street

Arundel Street

No. 2

MXD1093-
1094   Licence and consent for alterations   **29 Jun. 1905**

– to The Hon. William Frederick Danvers, tenant of the
premises.
2 copies each with large fold-out plans showing, *inter alia*, a
proposed new opening from Derwent House (no. 2 Arundel
Street) into Oswaldestre House (nos. 34-5 Norfolk Street).

Nos. 5-10

MXD1095-
1096   Agreement re nos. 5-10 Arundel Street and no. 2
Howard Street   **2 May 1889**

The Duke agrees with the Law Land Company Ltd. of the
Royal Courts of Justice Chambers, Strand that he will lease
the premises to them for the purpose of pulling them down and
rebuilding them as residential chambers and offices to be called
Derwent Houses. Details, restrictions etc., and **plan**.   3 docs.

MXD1097-1098   Sale of the above premises for £4,314   **31 Dec. 1889**

The Law Land Co. sells the premises, now designed to be rebuilt as a private hotel on a new 79-year lease, to George Herbert White, MP; with separate draft re electricity supply.
2 docs.

No. 24

MXD1099   Licence to assign   **30 Dec. 1870**

Robert Cheere of York Terrace, Regents Park, esq., executor of the will of T.G. Sambrooke, deceased, is granted licence to assign the premises to William Henry Smith of 186 Strand, esquire.

MXD1100-1103   Agreement to sublet to Maria Dunbar, widow   **24 Jun. 1882**

With notice to quit on 24 Jun. 1882, and schedule of documents re the property, 1853-1882.   4 docs.

Re cottage at the rear of the premises, see 15 Water Street, below.

No. 28

MXD1104   – to William Henry Smith of No. 186 Strand, esq., MP   **23 Jun. 1873**

Lease for 15 years at £20, low rent

No. 37

MXD1105   Surrender of lease   **18 Oct. 1877**

– by Joseph Alfred Novello and the other lessees (names given) of **The Whittington Club**, as in **MXD917-920** above). No plan but detailed description of the premises and its bounds.

MXD1106-1107   Lease for 50 years   **19 Oct. 1877**

The Temple Club (formerly the Whittington Club and before that the *Crown and Anchor Tavern*)

The premises are leased for 50 years to Charles Henry Russell of the same address, the proprietor of the Club, at £900 a year for the first seven years of the lease, £1,000 a year for the next seven years and £1,100 a year for the residue of the term. Plan shows a building of the same extent as in 1852 (**MXD49-52** above). Room by room schedule of fixtures and fittings.

Two copies, lease and counterpart

MXD1108   Consent and covenants re **The Temple Club**   **19 Oct. 1877**

The Duke agrees with lessee C.H. Russell, as above, and Ann Ingram of no. 198 Strand, widow as to shared access through an open yard and gateway opening onto Milford Lane between Russell and Ingram (she as proprietor of adjacent premises in the occupation of the *Illustrated London News*). Russell agrees to block up stairways giving onto the yard and to remove sheds, etc. **Plans and elevations** are endorsed.

Nos.19-20

MXD1109-   Surrender of lease by C.H. Russell   **4 Aug. 1884**
1111

With supporting papers of same date.   3 docs.

Water Street

MXD1112-   Licence to sublet and lease   **11-12 Jun. 1869**
1115

– to Thomas Godfrey Sambrooke of Water Street, esq., (licence to sublet); with subsequent lease, and counterpart, for 21 years to Charles Farlow of 191 Strand, fishing rod and tackle manufacturer at £63 a year

> Dwelling house called '**Norfolk House**' on the east side of Water Street. **Plan** shows a plot with a frontage of 67ft 9in and depth of 38 feet to Tweezers Alley, previously leased on 29 July 1853.

With fire insurance policy on the premises issued by the Law Fire Insurance Society, 12 Sep. 1876

MXD1116   Licence to assign   **30 Dec. 1871**

Robert Cheere of 31 York Terrace, Regents Park, esq., executor of the will of Thomas Godfrey Sambrooke, esq. is permitted to assign to William Henry Smith, esq.

Parcel of ground known as **Norfolk Wharf** with the house, stables and buildings on it

See also **MXD1124** *below.*

MXD1117   Agreement to sublet at £7 rent a year (term not stated)   **25 Dec. 1872**

W.H. Smith to James Jones of the Arundel Hotel, Arundel Street, hotel keeper

> Cottage and premises No. 15 (at the rear of 24 Arundel Street) in the occ. of Mrs Standgroom

Endorsement 25 Mar. 1882 extending the lease of the premises (described as 'Stand Groom's Cottage') from week to week at 12s. 6d. a week

MXD1118-   Notices to quit the above premises.   2 docs.   **1881, 1882**
1119

MXD1120-   Agreement to sublet at £42 a year   **1872-1882**
1123

– William Henry Smith to James Jones (as above)

> Coach house and a three stall stable with two rooms over on the east side of Water Street, abutting north on Norfolk House. **Plan**.

An initial open-ended one-year lease is renewed to 25 March 1882, followed by notice to quit in August.   4 docs.

MXD1124   Surrender of lease by W.H. Smith to the Duke   **30 Jun. 1882**

– on **Norfolk Wharf**, as in **MXD1116** above

MXD1125   Lease to W.H. Smith as above for 72 years   **9 Jul. 1883**

The Duke leases a plot on the east side of Water Street with a 34ft frontage x 40 feet 4 inches; east on Tweezers Alley, south on the London School Board at £20 a year until 1912 and £80 a year thereafter. **Plan**.

MXD1126   Assignment of the residue of a 30-year term for £3,000   **17 Jul. 1882**

W.H. Smith assigns i) part of '**Arundel wharf**' together with a house known as no. 14 Water Street and ii) part of '**Norfolk**

Fig. 12 Arundel House.

This view, taken from across the river, shows Arundel House on the corner of Arundel Street and the Embankment as a solitary representative of architect John Dunn's work in the late 19th century. Brick had triumphantly re-emerged in Tudor-Gothic style, its warmth contrasted by decorative stone mullions and courses.

Another example of Dunn's work, the *Norfolk Hotel*, survives in Surrey Street. For other buildings in the estate, such as Surrey House on the river front, which sadly have not survived, there are his plans and drawings in Arundel Castle archives. (Photo: H. Warne, Autumn 2009)

wharf', held at £85 and £90 rent respectively, to the London School Board. **Plan** shows land in question and adjoining land not to be built upon.

MXD1127   Mutual covenants as to building   **31 Dec. 1891**

The Duke agrees with Ann Ingram, widow, William James Ingram, esq. and Charles L.A.N. Ingram, all of 198 Strand, newspaper proprietors, as to their respective rights to erect and alter buildings in and between Water Street and Arundel Street under the supervision of John Dunn, the Duke's surveyor.

Large **plan** shows elevation of a house the Duke intends to erect on the site of the old *King's Head* public house (between Arundel Street and Water Street) and shows the position, and an elevation of the premises of the *Illustrated London News* in Water Street and a proposed additional storey.

Signatures of all parties.

Milford Lane

MXD1128   Agreement   **11 Dec. 1890**

a) The Duke,   b) George C. Madge of no. 4 Ashburn Place, Kensington, esq. and William T. Madge of 74 West Cromwell Road, esq. and   c) Ann Ingram, widow, W.J. Ingram, esq. and L.N. Ingram, esq., proprietors of the *Illustrated London News*
The parties agree as to building permissions and rights of way on the boundary between their two properties. Details given. **Plan**.

MXD1129   Nos. 11 and 12: Licence to make a communicating door   **20 Mar. 1894**

The two houses are leased to the Hon. W.F. Danvers Smith and undertenanted by the city of London Saddlers Company. The Duke, by his agent E. Mesnard, permits the Company to make a communicating door between the two properties. **Plan**.

8. NORFOLK HOUSE, ST JAMES'S SQUARE, PICCADILLY

i. Introduction

Once Arundel House in the Strand had been demolished in the 1670s the Dukes of Norfolk lacked a London residence. The original intention had been to build one within the new Estate, but this did not materialise. As discussed in the introduction to Section 2 (Strand Estate 1672-1701), more money than expected had been spent on the first phase of housing development. Maximising the rental by infilling the designated land with further houses for Londoners may well have seemed a good long-term solution. Both the 6th and the 7th Dukes had the benefit of a 'palace' at Norwich and perhaps did not feel a particular need for a permanent base in London. Moreover, the new 'West End', which was beginning to be developed on open land west of St Martin in the Fields, might well have seemed more attractive than the hustle and bustle of the Strand. A 'wait and see' policy seems to have been deployed.

The house eventually chosen as the ducal residence in London had started life around 1670, contemporary with the first phase of the Strand Estate development. It lay at the south-east corner of St James's Square, a new residential development. The land it stood on was described in various deeds as *part of the Pell Mell or Pallmall Field alias St James Field, parcel of the bailiwick or manor of St James in the Fields, co. Middlesex*. It was also mentioned as *formerly parcel of the possessions of the late Hospital of St James and since of the Provost and College of Eaton*, which had since been surrendered by them to the Crown.

At the Restoration of the Monarchy, the Earl of St Alban, the lessee of the land, had petitioned the King for a grant of the freehold. His plan was for a prestigious housing development. He cited the need for the King's courtiers to live near his Court, there being a deficit of suitable housing for *noble men and other Persons of good quality*. The King duly granted the freehold to St Alban and his trustees in April 1665, although not without protest from various quarters, including the City of London. Fuller details of this phase as well as histories of the individual properties in the square can be read in the Survey of London, vol. XXIX, part one, 'South of Piccadilly', pp.56-210. In 1699 the 7th Duke himself had rented one of the new houses in the Square, on part of the site from which Norfolk House later sprang (**MXD1197** below).

The deeds in this collection date from 1670 and relate to the site of Norfolk House and to adjacent premises on the south-east side of St James's Square, which is referred to in early deeds as *the Piazza*. Another property on its north side is also mentioned in passing. The evolution of 'Norfolk House' is complex, beginning with the Earl of St Alban's own dwelling house, known as St Alban House, and adjacent buildings and

247

ground, purchased piecemeal. In 1676 the main house, which had a 65ft frontage onto the Square, was described as that in which the Earl *formerly dwelt*. The name *St Alban House* had evolved by the early 18th century into *St Albans House*.

Mortgages were raised on the premises by successive owners from 1676. These sums were still outstanding in 1722 when Thomas, 8th Duke of Norfolk offered £10,000 for absolute title, all debts repaid – and a further £1,600 for the fixtures and fittings. He and his trustees simultaneously acquired two sets of coach houses and stables held with the premises, in St Alban Street and Charles Street.

It was Edward, 9th Duke of Norfolk who created 'Norfolk House' as it is remembered. First, in 1738, he obtained from the Crown further ground at the rear of the premises and in 1741 he took a long lease on a small adjacent house in John Street. His main opportunity came in 1748 with the purchase of the adjacent house northwards from his own. Its frontage was 44 feet, which, added to his, gave him a combined frontage of 109 feet. Both houses, including their rear offices etc., were around 40 to 50 feet deep and they sat in plots 200 feet in depth. With the new house there came further stabling with access north onto Charles Street. Though it is only mentioned retrospectively in 1771, it is clear from the property description (i) in that deed (**MXD1244-1245** below) that he had combined the two premises to create one grand house. In 1751 he added some rental houses in Charles Street to complete the estate and in 1771 he obtained possession of the ground rents of Norfolk House and two houses northwards, to the corner of Charles Street.

On the eve of his succession as 10th Duke, Charles Howard of Greystoke Castle in Cumberland paid £1,000 for possession of the lease of one of the Charles Street houses – perhaps to be on hand to attend to the succession – but it was returned to the pool after he became Duke. His son Charles, as 11th Duke, made the final acts of consolidation of the Norfolk House estate by the purchase of some extra land in 1802 and by getting the freehold of the John Street house for £840 in 1810. This house became the office of the main ducal agent who directed and oversaw the work of the local agents on the Sussex estate and elsewhere. Its address was changed during the 19th century. The name 'John Street' disappeared and the house became 33A St James's Square. It survives today as the only unaltered part of the Norfolk House complex.

The acquisition of additional coach houses and stables in the mid-18th century, with access out to Charles Street, allowed the Norfolk family a freer hand with the existing stabling at the rear of Norfolk House. It was converted to provide a first-floor garden room or assembly room, around 85 feet in length north to south by 25 feet in width. This later became a laundry downstairs, while the ducal archives, now at Arundel Castle, were stored on the first floor. The archivist was encouraged to light a good fire each day to keep off the damp! This building was wrongly labelled as 'Old Norfolk House' in sales particulars prepared by Hampton and Sons in 1930 and a catalogue of illustrious occupants, from the Earl of St Alban onwards, was cited as part of the sales pitch (ref. ACA EO Box 179).

Norfolk House remained in the family for nearly two hundred years but death duties and other financial pressures in the early 20th century caused the family to consider its sale. The main ducal estates had largely descended from the medieval period and were strictly tied to the inheritance of the Dukedom by parliamentary acts and settlements. Norfolk House was one of the later acquisitions and was not thus tied. On the eve of its sale in the 1930s, photographs published with the sales particulars show that the interiors looked very much as they would have done in the 9th Duke's day. The house remained on the market for several years, failing to meet its reserve price at auction, until it was finally sold in 1938. The interior of the music room has been re-assembled at the Victoria and Albert Museum as a memorial to one of London's most distinguished houses.

Fig. 13 Norfolk House.

Norfolk House lay at the south-east corner of St James's Square and was created, as this section of the catalogue demonstrates, from the footprint of two earlier houses. Architect John Dunn, R.I.B.A., created this drawing of the front (west-facing) elevation while working as the 15th Duke's surveyor at the Norfolk Estate Office, no. 31A St James's Square, which still exists just south of the main house. The drawing was recently found among the Arundel Archives in uncatalogued plans of Norfolk House dating from around 1895 to 1910.

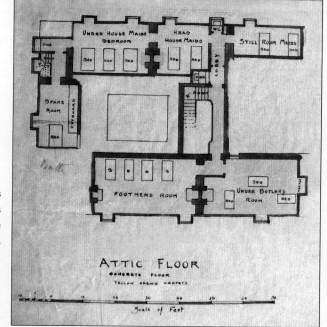

Fig. 14 The attics at Norfolk House.

This undated plan was found in the same source as fig. 13 above. While there are many photographs at Arundel Castle and elsewhere to illustrate the glorious principal interiors of the house, this unsigned scrap allows us a small glimpse behind the scenes. The 14 members of staff for whom beds were provided in the attics would not have been the whole workforce. The butler, cook and housekeeper would have had rooms elsewhere.

ii. St Alban House, 1670-1731

MXD1131   Assignment in trust   **24 Mar. 1670**

a) Henry, Earl of St Alban and the Hon. Baptist May, master
of the Privy Purse   b) the Rt Hon. John Lord Belasyse,
Baron of Warlaby   c) the Rt Hon. Thomas, Lord Viscount
Fauconberge and George, Viscount Castleton

> Parcel of ground in St James Field in St Martin-
> in-the-Fields, co. Middx, in front 133ft, in depth
> 200ft, abutting N. on intended street called Charles
> Street, S. on house and stable of the said Earl of
> St Albans, W. on the intended piazza, and E. on
> a messuage of Edmund Wansell, gentleman

The premises are assigned by a) to c) in trust for b) at an
annual rent of £30 on an indefinite term.

MXD1132   Conveyance   **9 Mar. 1676**

a) Henry, Earl of St Alban, knight, The Hon. John Hervey
of Ickworth, Treasurer Generall to the Queen Sir John Coell
of Lincolns Inn, kt., The Hon. Baptist May, Master of the
Privy Purse,   b) Sir Thomas Bond of Peckham, knight and
baronet., Caesar Wood, lately Cranmer of Astwood Bury,
co. Bucks., esq.   c) Richard Frith, citizen and bricklayer of
London, John Grosvenor, citizen and goldsmith of London,
Richard Hayburne, citizen and carpenter of London

> Capital messuage in Pall Mall Field alias St James
> Field called St Alban House, wherein the Earl of
> St Alban formerly dwelt with all buildings, yards,
> stables, coach houses (etc.), having a 65ft frontage
> west by 200 feet in depth, formerly in the occ. of the
> Rt Hon. Sir John Duncombe; abutting the intended
> piazza west and lying between the premises of John,
> Lord Bellassis north and Mr Wandsell's ground
> and five (back)yards of the tenements of Isaac

Harper, Mr Hawkinson, Mr Hobbs, Mr Harris
and Anthony Ellis east

Recites that the land was part of the manor or bailiwick of
St James in the Fields in the King's possession, and before
that, part of the possessions of the Abbot of Westminster.
The premises are to be held for the remainder of terms of
21, 10 and 29 years at an annual rent of £36, provided the
said Richard Frith builds for the Earl a mansion house on N.
side of St James Piazza, in front 120ft; and on other trusts.
Recitals include details of the building plots set out around
the new square.

MXD1133   Release and quitclaim   **7 Sep. 1676**

a) Henry, Earl of St Alban, K.G., Privy Counsellor   b) Richard
Frith, citizen and bricklayer of London   c) John Cholmeley,
of London, gent., Thomas Fowle, citizen and goldsmith, James
Bridgeman, of St Martin-in-the-Fields, co. Middx, esq. and
William Masemore, of Middle Temple, London, gentleman

> i) Capital messuage in Pellmellfield alias St James
> Field called St Alban House, with buildings, yards,
> gardens, stables, coach houses (etc.)
> ii) messuage being built (120ft frontage) on the
> north side *of a greate square place in St James Field
> otherwise Pell Mell field called St James Piazza.*

Recites deed of 9 March 1676 in which the Earl conveyed ii) to
his trustees (named) as security on a £2,000 bond for Richard
Frith to complete the building of the house; and he conveyed
i) to Frith and his trustees (named) for the remainders of
lease terms of 21 and 29 years originally granted to St Alban
by 'the late Queen mother [Henrietta Maria, d. 1669] at £36
annual rent'. This was done in trust for St Alban until Frith
had finished tiling the roof, had *plaunchered and plastered*
the house and had finished the vaults. The Earl now releases
from all these previous trusts so as to allow Frith to convey
the premises to his own trustees (party c) of this deed.

MXD1134-   Lease and release   **8-9 Sep. 1676**
1135

a) Richard Frith (as above)   b) John Grosvenor, citizen and
goldsmith of London, Richard Hayburne, citizen and carpenter
of London   c) the Right Hon. Lewis, Lord Duras, Baron of
Holnby alias Holneby co. Northants., John Cholmley of London,

gentleman, Thomas Fowle, citizen and goldsmith of London
d) James Bridgeman and William Masemore (as above)

St Alban House as described in **MXD1132** above

Recites the earlier history of Pell Mell field and what was
excluded from the development. Now, for £3,000 in hand paid
by c), and the promise of a further £3,000 to be raised by
mortgage to Martin Folkes and David Lloyd, the premises are
conveyed by a) and b) to c) and d) in trust for c)

MXD1136	Assignment of furnishings in St Alban House	**9 Sep. 1676**

Pursuant to the above sales, the Earl of St Alban and Richard
Frith assign the contents of St Alban House to Lord Duras.

Schedule attached: room contents range from the mundane (e.g.
'three binns') to the lavish (eg., 'a suite of tapestry hangings').

MXD1137-1138	Mortgage by lease and release, for £3,000	**12-13 Sep. 1676**

Pursuant to **MXD1134-1135** above, Lord Duras conveys to
Edward Bourne, citizen and woollen draper of London and
John Molins of St Martins in the Fields, gentleman in trust for
Martin Folkes of Grays Inn and David Lloyd of St Martins
in the Fields, gentleman to secure repayment of the capital
sum plus interest (specified).

MXD1139	Release and quitclaim	**24 Mar. 1677**

Richard Frith has now finished building the new house for the
Earl of St Alban who now releases him from the trusts specified
in a document annexed [but not present] to **MXD1137-1138**
above.

MXD1140-1142	Assignment of mortgage	**25 Mar. 1677**

Repayments have been made by Lord Duras to the various
existing mortgagees, by raising a further £2,500 from the Rt
Hon. Sir Edward Villiars, esq., Henry Savyle of St Margaret's,
Westminster, esq., Henry Guy of Dunsley in Tring, co.
Herts., esq. and Sir Christopher Musgrave of St Margaret's
Westminster, knight. Lord Duras now assigns St Alban House
to Sir Thomas Bond of Peckham, co. Surrey, knight and

baronet and William Crofts of St Martins in the Fields, esq.
as trustees for the new mortgagees.
With Lord Duras' bond and a receipt for £2,500 signed by
Richard Frith.   3 docs.

MXD1143   Release and quitclaim   **20 Apr. 1677**

Sir Christopher Musgrave releases his interest in St Alban's
House to the other mortgagees.

MXD1144   Further mortgage by lease and release   **8-9 Mar. 1679**

The existing mortgagees are paid £800 by Lord Duras, now
styled Earl of Feversham and £700 by Martin Folkes (as in
1137-8 above) in full satisfaction of the outstanding debt
on St Alban House. Now, at the direction of the Earl of
Feversham, the house is conveyed to Symon Folkes, esq. and
Andrew Card, gentleman, both of Grays Inn in trust for Martin
Folkes subject to future redemption by the Earl.

MXD1145-   Assignment of mortgage by lease and release   **23-24 Dec. 1681**
1147

Martin and Simon Folkes and Andrew Card assign St Alban
House to the Rt Hon. Sydney Godolphin, esq., one of the
lords commissioners of His Majesty's Treasury, and to William
Legg of St Martins in the Fields, his trustee, reserving Lord
Feversham's power of redemption. With receipt for £835 12s.
signed by Martin Folkes.   3 docs.

MXD1148   Release   **4 Nov. 1682**

A Chancery case is pending between the Rt Hon. Mary,
Countess dowager of Feversham, relict and administrator of
the goods of the Rt Hon. George, late Earl of Feversham and
the Rt Hon. Louis, Earl of Feversham, Viscount Sondes of
Lees Court, Lord Duras, Baron of Holdenby and Throwley.
Now, following a decree of 10 Feb. last, *inter alia*, for £1,103 4s.
paid to the Countess by the present Earl, she and her trustees
release to him, his trustee and his mortgagees, any claim she
has in St Alban House.

MXD1149-   Assignment of mortgage   **5-6 Sep. 1683**
1151

For £1,500 paid by Matthew Locke of St Martins in the Fields,
esq. to the Earl of Feversham, he, with the Rt Hon. Sydney

Godolphin and his trustee William Legg, assign St Alban House to Locke and to his trustees William Dobbins of Lincolns Inn, esq. and James Smith, citizen and haberdasher of London. The earl is then bound in £3,000 to Locke for the performance of covenants.   3 docs.

| MXD1152-1154 | Assignment of mortgage | 1685 and 7-8 Dec. 1688 |

The various previous mortgages on St Alban House are held on three separate lease terms of 21, 10 and 29 years all of which are now assigned to the Rt Hon. Sir Stephen Foxe, one of the Commissioners of His Majesty's Treasury, Thomas Foxe of St Martins in the Fields, esq. and Nicholas Fenn of St Margaret's, Westminster, esq.

A receipt by Matthew Locke dated 24 Sep. 1685 for £1,549 10s. in full payment of all principal and interest is attached. 3 docs.

| MXD1155-1157 | Assignment of mortgage | 29-30 Jul. 1692 |

The mortgage terms, above, are assigned for £1,000 to Sir Thomas Fowle, alderman of the city of London and his trustee, Reginald Bretland, Serjeant at Arms; with a bond in £2,000 for performance of covenants.

| | Endorsements of further charges | Dec 1693, Nov. 1695 |

For further loans of £400 and £1,000 from Robert Fowle, citizen and goldsmith, exor. of the will of Sir Thomas Fowle, decd., the premises are assigned to Fowle and Reginald Bretland as trustee.   3 docs.

| MXD1158-1159 | Agreement as to further loan and bond | 30-31 Jul. 1692 |

A further loan of £600 to the Earl of Feversham on the security of St Alban House by one George Seigniour of the Middle Temple, gentleman, is acknowledged by Sir Thomas Fowle. Seigniour is bound to Sir Thomas Fowle for the performance of covenants.

| MXD1160 | Further loan of £500 | 21 Nov. 1695 |

– to Robert Fowle (as in 1155-7, endorsement, above)

MXD1161-1163	Further assignment of mortgage	**12-13 Mar. 1696**

Existing mortgagees as in **MXD1155-1160** above and Anne Windsor of London, widow, assign their interest in St Alban House to Sir Stephen Fox (as above) and his trustees Martin Folkes and Andrew Card (as above) for £500 paid to Robert Fowle, £500 to Anne Windsor and £4,000 to the Earl of Feversham, now also styled Viscount Sandys.

Recites that, following Sir John Duncombe's tenancy, the house was occupied by the Countess of Penalva, then Edward, late Earl of Conway and now the Right Hon. Robert, late Earl of Sunderland.   3 docs.

MXD1164-1165	Assignment of Mortgage	**1-2 Apr. 1696**

Recitals state, *inter alia*, that Sir Stephen Fox and Martin Folkes of the above deed were acting as trustees for the Rt Hon. Ann, Countess Dowager of Bristol. She and they now assign the remainders of the various lease terms for £2,000 to James Vernon of St Martin in the Fields, esq. and his trustees Robert Yard of St Martin in the Fields, esq. and William Welby of Gedney, co. Lincoln, esq.   2 docs.

MXD1166	Assignment of mortgage	**1 Jun. 1702**

Ann, Countess of Sunderland, wife of Robert, Earl of Sunderland, Charles, Lord Spencer, their son and heir apparent, the Rev. Henry Godolphin, provost of Eaton, Edward Sayer of Berkhamsted, co. Herts., esq. and Fennes Whitwrong of Lincolns Inn, esq.

A further £700 has been raised by the Countess of Sunderland, as acknowledged by Lord Spencer and the Rev. Godolphin, from Sayer and Whitwrong, to whom the remainder of the lease term in the property is assigned; while the previous mortgagee James Vernon, on the promise of receipt from the Countess of his £2,000 plus interest, also assigns his interest in the property to them.

MXD1167	Assignment of interest	**2 Dec. 1703**

Sir Henry Bond, son and heir of Sir Thomas Bond late of Peckham, assigns to Robert Yard and William Welby (as above) any interest he might hold in the property.

MXD1168 Assignment of interest   **23 Dec. 1703**

The Right Hon. Charles, Earl of Sunderland and his trustee the Rev. Henry Godolphin, DD assign to Ann, dowager countess of Sunderland such interest as they may hold in the property.

MXD1169 Conveyance and assignment of mortgage   **28 Jan. 1704**

Ann, dowager countess of Sunderland and her current mortgagees (as above) assign St Alban House for £3,500 as an absolute purchase price (in trust for Edward Stracey of London, gentleman who had provided £1,500 of the purchase money) to Sir Richard Hoare of the City of London, knight and alderman and his trustees William Cook and John Arnold of the City of London, goldsmiths.

MXD1170- Conveyance (lease and release)   **10-11 Jun. 1709**
1172

Edward Stracey of London, gentleman, Sir Richard Hoare with his trustees William Cook and John Arnold (as above) to the Rt Hon. Henry Bentinck, esq., commonly called Lord Woodstock, son and heir apparent of William, Earl of Portland and trustee John Smith of Beaufort Buildings, St Clement Danes, esq.

St Alban House is conveyed to John Smith in trust for Lord Woodstock for £3,300 of which £1,000 went to Sir Richard Hoare and £2,300 to Edward Stracey.

By a separate deed (1172) Edward Stracey indemnifies Lord Woodstock in the sum of £800 at six per cent interest against any claim for arrears or loss of rent by the representatives of Henry, late Earl of St Alban's [sic] until 29 Sep. 1711.
3 docs.

MXD1173- Mortgage for £5,000 (lease and release) and bond **12-13 Sep. 1717**
1175

The Earl of Portland, as above, to Edward Harrison of St James parish, esq.

> St Alban House (as described on 9 Mar. 1676 above, cited as most recently in the occupation of the Earl of Portland)

3 docs.

MXD1176 Memorandum of agreement **21 Feb. 1722**

Henry, Duke of Portland agrees to sell to Thomas, Duke of Norfolk

> i) Messuage with the back houses, offices, stables, coach houses and other buildings in St James's Square in the possession of Henry, Duke of Westminster
> ii) House in St Alban Street *comprehended in the purchase deed of the said stable* [*sic*]

The sale would be executed by March 1723 with a good freehold title free of all incumbrances. Purchase price, £10,000.

MXD1177 Conveyance and declaration of trusts **31 May 1722**

Henry, Duke of Portland conveys to the Rt Hon. Thomas, Lord Howard of Effingham and the Rt Hon. Lord Frederick Howard, one of the sons of Henry, late Duke of Norfolk, deceased

> St Alban House (as described in **MXD1132** above)

The house is conveyed to the lords Howard in order to give them freehold possession at a peppercorn rent.

MXD1178 Declaration of trust **31 May 1722**

John Lucas of St Brides, gentleman and John Fielding of St James, Westminster, esq., administrators of the goods of Francis Edwards, a bankrupt, and the lords Howard as above

Reciting the bankruptcy judgement of £8,000 made in 1719 in favour of Messrs Lucas and Fielding, they now declare that this sum shall stand to the lords Howard in order to protect their purchase of St Alban House.

MXD1179-1180 Bargain and sale and release **1 Jun. 1722**

Henry, Duke of Portland and Edward Harrison, mortgagee (as in **MXD1173-1175** above), assign their rights in St Alban House to the lords Howard for £5,000.   2 docs.

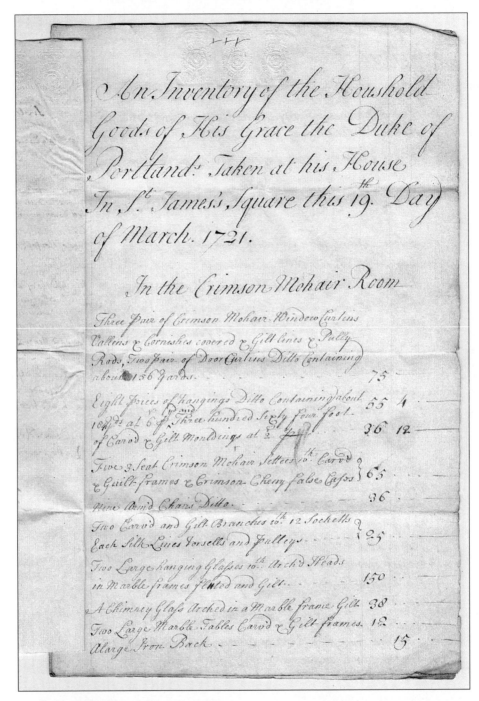

Fig 15 The Duke of Portland's furnishings.
By 1676 the Earl of St Albans had invested in the land on which Norfolk House later stood and
had built himself a house there called St Alban House. In 1722 Thomas, 8th Duke of Norfolk,
not only bought the house but, for an additional sum of £1,600, he obtained its furnishings and
fittings as well. The first page of the accompanying inventory is shown. (Ref. **MXD1182**.)

MXD1181   Declaration of trust   **20 Nov. 1723**

The lords Howard declare that they hold St Alban House to
the sole use of Thomas, Duke of Norfolk.

MXD1182   Bond with inventory attached   **Mar.-Jun. 1722**

*An inventory of the Household goods of His Grace the Duke
of Portland; taken at his House in St James's Square this 19th
day of March 1721.*   4 folios
Room by room details of significant fittings and furnishings such
as gilt mirrors, curtains, cushions, etc. and some furniture. By
the bond, 6 June 1722, the Duke of Portland releases everything
specified in the inventory to the Duke of Norfolk for £1,600.

MXD1183   Grant and release   **15 May 1730**

Thomas Fowkes, surviving trustee under the will of Sir Henry
Jermyn, late Lord Dover, deceased and the devisees under
the will [21 names] grant to John Anstis, Garter Principal
King at Arms the ground rent of £36 a year issuing out of
St Alban House.

MXD1184   Papers supporting Fowkes' claim and the above rent. 6 docs.   **1722-1730**

MXD1185   Declaration of trust   **10 May 1731**

– by John Anstis that he holds the rent, as above, in trust for
Thomas, Duke of Norfolk, by whom the purchase money of
£972 was paid.

iii. *Premises on north side of St James's Square*
This property is unrelated to the Duke of Norfolk's title
(see **MXD1133** *above)*

MXD1187   Assignment of residue lease term   **7 Apr. 1713**

Sir John Newton of Barrescourt, co. Glos., Bt., sole executor
of the will of Carey Coke, deceased who was executrix of the
will of Edward Coke late of Holkham, co. Norfolk, deceased
to Daniel Woodroffe of London, upholder

> Capital mansion house with the chapel, offices,
> buildings, gardens, yard, ground and appurts. in
> St James's Square; abutting south on the Square,
> north on Auger Street, east on the capital messuage
> of the Earl of Radnor, and west on York Street;
> and the stables used with the house which lie on the
> north side of Auger Street and are in the occ. of Lord
> Cornwallis; abutting south on Auger Street, north on
> the houses of Mrs Dorothea Chamberlain and Mrs
> Emera Cross, east on a house called the *Apple Tree*
> and west on York Street

Schedule of fixtures and fittings indoors and out (best rooms
excluded). The premises were leased in 1699 to Edward Coke for
21 years by Thomas, Lord Jermyn, Baron of Bury St Edmunds
and the Rt Hon. Henry, Lord Dover, Baron of Dover. The
remainder of the term is now assigned to Woodroffe for £550
at £300 annual rent. Note of insurance for £2,000 endorsed.

MXD1188   Lease for 5 years at £260 annual rent   **7 Apr. 1718**

Robert Clarges of St James's, esq. to the Right Noble Peregrine
Hyde, Lord Marquis of Carmarthen

> Brick messuage on the north side of St James's
> Square with the garden, coach houses, stables and
> appurts., late in the occ. of the Rt Hon. George,
> Lord Lansdowne; abutting east on the messuage of
> the Rt Hon. Thomas, Earl of Pembroke

Schedule (room by room) of fixtures and fittings is included.

iv. Premises in St Alban Street

MXD1189   Assignment of lease   **10 Apr. 1701**

a) the Rt Hon. Henry, Lord Dover, Baron of Dover
b) The Rt Hon. Thomas, Lord Jermyn, Baron of St Bury
Edmunds,   c) Sir Robert Danvers of Rougham, co. Kent
and   d) Baynbrig Buckeridge of St Giles in the Fields, co.
Middx, gentleman

> Messuage, yard, stable, three stables, four coach
> houses on the west side of St Alban Street in Pell
> Mell Field; west on a house in the occ. of Sir Henry
> Colt, south on houses and grounds in the several
> tenures of Mr Knight, Mr Mosse, Mr Brewer and
> Mr Mockett, north on the stable yard in the occ.
> of Nicholas Baxter and on the passage way leading
> to it. Dimensions: the house – 16ft frontage at the
> ground floor and 20 feet 6ins. at the dining room
> floor, the same being built over the said passage way
> of 4 feet; the yard is 16 feet in breadth, the stables
> and coach houses 20 feet in breadth and the entire
> ground is 134 feet 6 ins east to west. **Ground plan**
> of stables and coach houses only.

The house was leased in 1663 by the Earl of St Alban to John
Grove, plasterer for 43 years at £7 16s. 4d. a year with the
use of the stables and coach houses; and also of the stable
in the occ. of Nicholas Baxter on the north side of the dung
place and pond.

Recites the will, 6 Dec. 1681, of the Earl of St Alban, deceased,
in which he bequeathed the premises to b), who in 1684 settled
it upon c) as trustee for himself and a). Now, for £200, a),
b), and c) assign to d) for the remainder of a lease term of
29 years

Endorsement states Buckeridge's name was used in the deed
as trustee for William Minors of the Inner Temple and Joan
his wife.

MXD1190   Mortgage by assignment of lease   **17 Jun. 1708**

William Minors and Jane his wife (see endorsement above) assign the remainder of the lease term to Rachell Frye of St Giles in the Fields, co. Middx, spinster, for £300 plus interest.

Endorsement (partly illegible with illegible date) records the re– assignment of the lease by John Cranmer of Eccleshall, co. Staffs., gentleman and Rachell his wife to William and Jane Minors as above on receipt of the principal sum plus interest.

MXD1191   Assignment of remainder of 29-year lease term   **25 May 1709**

Baynbrig Buckeridge and William Minors, as above, and Andrew Card of Grays Inn, esq. to Daniel Malthus of St James, Westminster, apothecary

> Stable and coach house (32 feet 4 ins in length east to west and in breadth north to south 17 feet 10 ins.) in St Albans [*sic*] Street in a stable yard called Hubbard's Yard (on the north side of it); south on the said yard, north on the house of Elizabeth Hastings, widow, east on ground and buildings of Mr Rack and west on a stable of Sir Henry Dutton Colt

Recites mortgage for £800 19 Nov. 1707 to Andrew Card. Minors now sells the remaining lease term to Malthus for £125 and the other two parties indemnify the property against any claims from themselves.

MXD1192   Assignment of remainder of lease term for £630   **17 Apr. 1712**

William and Jane Minors (as above) to the Rt Hon. Henry, Earl of Portland

> Messuage (as in 1189 above), now with five separate stables and four separate coach houses built on its adjacent land, making in all a plot of 134 feet 6 ins. in depth east to west; with the stable in the occ. of Nicholas Baxter on the north; and all ways and easements and the use of the pond and dung place in the yard and the passage way out into St Alban Street, in common with Lord Dover, Lord Jermyn and Sir Robert Danvers and sharing with them the

costs of keeping the paving of the yard and passage
way in good repair and of carrying away the dung
and of paying the water rent

MXD1193 Assignment of part of the above premises   **3 May 1712**

Daniel Malthus (as above) to the Rt Hon. Henry, Earl of
Portland

Stable and coach house as in 1191 above

Recites that the premises were leased by the late Lord Dover
and Sir Robert Danvers for 29 years on 20 Aug. 1705 for £1,710
to William Minors and his trustee Bainbryg Buckeridge. It
was mortgaged on 19 Nov. 1707 to Andrew Card (as recited
in **MXD1191**). Now Daniel Malthus assigns it to the Earl of
Portland for £125.

MXD1194- Conveyances for a nominal sum   **1 Jun. 1722**
1195

Henry, Duke of Portland to Frederick, Lord Howard, one of
the sons of Henry, late Duke of Norfolk

Premises as above

Recites that the said house, coach houses and stables are used
in conjunction with St Alban House (above); and recites the
previous mortgages to William Minors and Daniel Malthus

MXD1196 Declaration of trusts   **1 Jun. 1722**

Lord Frederick Howard declares that he holds the house, coach
houses and stables as above and of the stables in **MXD1217**
below on various leases (details) in trust for Thomas, Duke
of Norfolk

Fig. 16 Sales particulars, 1930s.

This shows the Music Room at Norfolk House. Edward, 9th Duke, inherited St Alban House in 1733 but it was not until 1748, when he was able to buy the house next door, that he was able to create 'Norfolk House' on both plots. Rooms such as the Music Room, illustrated, were used for lavish entertaining. Although the house was sold in 1938 and demolished, the Music Room interior can still be appreciated at the V&A Museum, where it has been reconstructed. (Ref. EO/Box179.) Below: Sales Particulars.

The Music Room

A room of rare and refreshing charm enjoying outlook over the Square and having French windows opening to the balcony. Contained in the panels of the ceiling are emblems of the arts and crafts and the paraphernalia of war. Plaques of musical instruments and masks are set in the panels of the walls which are further decorated by scrolls, ribbons, feathers and the Ducal crest. The mouldings are picked out in gilt and the fireplace is surmounted by carved statuary marble mantel having central plaque of musical instruments. Set at each end and between the windows, and contributing to the air of exceptional beauty, are three handsome mirrors decorated in gilt *en suite*. Approximate measurements 33ft. by 20ft. 9in.

v. House on east side of St James's Square; and stabling with access to Charles Street

MXD1197   Lease for three years at £200 annual rent   **20 Feb. 1699**

The Rt Hon. Honora, Lady dowager Bergevenny, John Webb of Odstock, co. Wilts., and Barbara his wife, John Talbot of Longford and Katherine his wife and Thomas Stoner of Stoner [*sic*, Stonor] co. Oxon. and Isabella his wife to Henry [7th] Duke of Norfolk

> Messuage or mansion house with a coach house, stable and other outhouses now in the occ. of the lessee

Schedule has room by room list of fixtures and fittings, viz. in the kitchen, cellar, laundry, servants' hall and pantry next the great back stairs, passage from the street door, parlour, drawing room, bed chamber and closet; on the second storey (via the great stairs), the great dining room, withdrawing room, bed chamber, great closet, inner closet, dressing room; on the third storey the first room, the front room, the next room and a closet; garret; stable with chambers over.

MXD1198-   Lease, release and bargain and sale   **5-6 Mar. 1728**
1200

John Talbot of Longford, co. Salop, esq. and Catherine, his wife, one of the daughters of John, Lord Bellasis, Baron of Worlaby, deceased to Joseph Banks of Revesby Abbey, co. Lincs., esq.

> i) Messuage with the outhouses, stable, coach house in St James Field, par. of St James (formerly St Martins in the Fields), having a frontage of 44 feet 2 inches west onto St James's Square, by 40 feet 2 inches north to the Earl of Lincoln's house, and 47 feet 4 inches south on the Duke of Norfolk's house
> ii) a coach house 22 feet 1 inch (south) by 12 feet 3 inches (west), by 12 feet 8 inches (east)

265

iii) a stable 15 feet 3 inches (west next the stable yard) 9 feet 7 inches (next the party wall of the Earl of Lincoln's stable), 14 feet 11 inches (on the south side next the lay stall or dung place), 7 feet 7 inches (next another party wall of the Earl of Lincoln) and 22 feet 6 inches (on the north side next the coach house)

iv) a single coach house on the north side of the stable: 8 feet 9 inches (west to the said stable yard), 22 feet 6 inches in depth and 10 feet 8 inches in height; with one lodging room over the coach house and over part of a coach house of Mr William Abdy, 17 feet 10 inches (fronting the stable yard to the west), 10 feet 9 inches east to west

All lately in the occ. of the Countess dowager Strafford Talbot sells to Banks for £2,550 and an ongoing annual ground rent of £5 and declares that the fine he has levied during the current Hilary Term shall stand to the use of Joseph Banks and his heirs. Endorsement states that the deeds were registered pursuant to an Act of Parliament on 9 March 1728.   3 docs.

| **MXD1201-1203** | Memoranda concerning **MXD1198-1200** above | **1727-1729** |

– containing signatures of John and Catherine Talbot and Joseph Banks and others.   3 docs.

| **MXD1204-1205** | Copy marriage settlement (lease and release) | **15, 16 Oct. 1731** |

– of Joseph Banks of Reavesby, co. Lincs., esq. and Catherine Wallis of the Close, Lincoln, widow

i) House and premises (as above) in St James's Square and Charles Street, now in the occ. of the Count of Dagenfield, His Prussian Majesty's Ambassador
ii) several properties (details) in Haltham and Wood Enderby, co. Lincs.
iii) premises in Leics. (places mentioned)

Joseph Banks vests in Thomas Chaplin of Blankney, co. Lincoln and William Gilby of Grays Inn, co. Middx, esq., in trust for Banks and his heirs by the marriage.

Details of the trusts; and of all the properties.

MXD1206   Printed Act   **1748**

– for vesting the settled estate in London, late of Joseph Banks, the elder, deceased, in trustees

MXD1207-   Conveyance (lease and release) and bargain and sale   **13-14 Jun. 1748**
1211

Robert Banks Hodgkinson of St James, Westminster, esq. and Thomas Wallis of the Middle Temple, esq., trustees of the settled estates of Joseph Banks, deceased, to the Rt Hon. Thomas, 2nd Earl of Effingham

> House and stables, etc., as above, on the east side of St James's Square and in Charles Street

The premises are conveyed to Lord Effingham for £1,830, subject to the annual payment of a rent of £5 as part of a £30 rent, and subject to liability to a quarter share of the maintenance of the paving in the stable yard and gateway to Charles Street.

Includes releases signed by both parties, an enrolled copy of the bargain sale and a declaration by Francis Tregeagle of New Inn.

MXD1212   Declaration   **14 Jun. 1748**

– by Lord Effingham that Edward, Duke of Norfolk paid the purchase money of £1,830 above and that he, Lord Effingham will convey the premises to him when the Duke so wishes; and that the Duke will pay the £5 rent and other charges.

vi. Premises on the south side of Charles Street

MXD1215   Release and quitclaim   **30 Jul. 1710**

Edmond Poley of Badley, co. Suff., gentleman and Thomas
Fowkes of Bury St Edmunds, co. Suff., gentleman to the Rt
Hon. Henry, Earl of Portland

> Divers pieces and parcels of ground in the parish
> of St James

Recites the earliest development of St James's Square when
the Earl of St Alban granted the pieces of ground to trustees
Baptist May and Abraham Cowley to secure an £80 annual
rent; and that on 28 June last these were assigned to Messrs
Poley and Fowkes who now indemnify the Earl of Portland
against any claims from themselves in respect of the rents.

MXD1216   Grant for 30½ years   **18 Sep. 1710**

Philip Stotherd of St James's parish, gentleman to the Rt
Hon. Henry, Earl of Portland

> i) Parcel of ground 45 x 40 feet, part of the yard
> of Philip Stotherd; west on the yard of the Earl of
> Portland, south on ground partly in the tenure of
> Mr Barber and partly on that of Mr Gottyer, east
> partly on Minors Yard and partly on two coach
> houses late in the occ. of Sir Harry Dutton Colt,
> now in the occ. of Henry, Earl of Portland, and
> north on another part of Philip Stotherd's yard
> – as it is now set out and divided and intended to
> be enclosed with a brick wall (details and **plan**)
> ii) The two coach houses mentioned in i) above and
> the ground on which they stand (**plan**)
> and all ways, passages, buildings and easements
> belonging

Recites deed of 15 July last in which Edmund Poley and Thomas Folkes (as in 1215 above), executors of the will of Henry late Lord Dover, and Sir Robert Danvers of Rushbrook, co. Suff., baronet conveyed the premises to Stotherd, who now assigns them to the Earl of Portland for £400 for the remainder of their lease term.

MXD1217   Assignment   **1 Jun. 1722**

For a nominal sum Henry, Duke of Portland assigns the premises as above to the Rt Hon. Frederick, Lord Howard, one of the sons of Henry, late Duke, as trustee for the Duke of Norfolk.

vii. Ground between St Alban Street and St James's Square

MXD1218   Grant from King George II to the Duke of Norfolk   **8 Jun. 1738**

> Parcel of ground between St James's Square and St Alban Street, 45 feet in breadth at the west end and at its greatest breadth towards the east end, 60 feet 9 inches, and at the east end at St Alban Street, 9 feet; and in length 126 feet 10 inches; together with a passage or gateway in length from the east end of the said ground to St Alban Street 48 feet and in breadth in St Alban Street; abutting north on stables of the Duke of Leeds, south on the back of houses in Pall Mall, east on the said gateway and on buildings granted to Benjamin Timbrell, gentleman and Thomas Williams, esq., west on a freehold messuage of the Duke of Norfolk now in the tenure of *our Royal son and heir the Prince of Wales* the gateway being reserved as a common gate and passage way.

The ground is leased to the Duke for 48 years from Michaelmas 1740 at £3 15s. annual rent from 1740 on and at 12d. a year until then. Plan mentioned in the text is not present.

Fragmented great seal in tin box. Deed enrolled 29 June 1739.

MXD1219   Extension of the above lease   **15 Feb. 1764**

For a single payment of £30 King George III extends the above lease to the Duke of Norfolk at the same rent from 5 April 1789 for a further 24 years.

> Property description mentions that the ground now has a new kitchen, coach houses, stables and other buildings erected upon it and that the freehold messuage on the west is no longer in the occupation of *our dear honoured father*

Frederick late Prince of Wales but now of the Duke of Norfolk.

The great seal has been cut from its tag and the King's portrait has been cut from its cartouche. Deed enrolled 20 Feb. 1764.

MXD1220 Contract for sale **11 Nov. 1802**

Commissioners of HM Treasury agree to sell to Charles, Duke of Norfolk for £1,634

parcel of ground between St Alban's Street and St James's Square being the stable yard used and occupied by the Duke with his mansion called Norfolk House, with the use of a passage or gateway in St Alban's Street (abuttals given); situate on a field called Pall Mall Field or St James Field parcel of the bailiwick or manor of St James in the fields, formerly parcel of the possessions of the Hospital of St James, then of the Provost and College of Eton before being surrendered to the Crown; together with an annual rent of £3 15s. arising from the premises and payable until 1813

Plan with key.

viii. *House in John Street, south side of St James's Square*

MXD1221   Lease for 99 years at £21 annual rent   **14 Dec. 1741**

Anne Mettayer of St James, Westminster, widow and Samuel
Mettayer of the same, gentleman to the Most Noble Edward,
Earl Marshal and Hereditary Earl Marshal

House, now unoccupied but formerly in the tenure of Charles
Menonault on the E. side of Nott's Corner leading from Pall
Mall to St James's Square; north St James's Square containing
16 feet 8 inches north to south next to Catherine Street, east to
west on the south side 22 feet; abutting west Catherine Street,
south the backside of a house in Pall Mall also belonging to
Anne Mettayer, east on another house in Pall Mall in the occ.
of [blank] Thurett, jeweller
A **sketch plan** is inserted; schedule of fixtures does not
ennumerate the rooms.

MXD1222-   Conveyance (lease and release)   **5-6 Apr. 1810**
1223

Thomas and Lucia Maude of Great George Street, and others,
all beneficiaries of the will of Samuel Mettayer of Pall Mall,
deceased sell to the 11th Duke of Norfolk for £840

Messuage on E. side of John Street, heretofore Notts Corner,
abutting north on St James's Square and the family mansion
of the Duke in St Martin-in-the-Fields, west on John Street,
and south on property of Lewis Mettayer.   2 docs.

ix. Purchase of houses in Charles Street

MXD1224   Conveyance upon trust to sell   **23 May 1704**

Thomas Stoner of Stoner, co. Oxon., esq. and the Hon. Isabella
his wife, the Rt Hon. Richard, Earl of Scarbrough, Sir John
Talbott of Laycock, co. Wilts., knight, Henry Rodbourne of
St Andrews, Holborn, gentleman and Walter Compton, citizen
and goldsmith of London

> i) Five messuages in Charles Street in the several occs.
> of Thomas Guenault, gentleman, [blank] Fitzherbert,
> [blank] Martin, Samuel Whitton, and Ann Lucas
> ii) messuage in Wyld Street in St Giles in the Fields
> in the occ. of Richard Paxton
> iii) messuage in Queen Street in St Giles in the Fields,
> in the occ. of said Thomas Stoner

Thomas and Isabella Stoner also agree with the other parties to
strengthen their title by levying a fine during Trinity Term next.

Houses in Charles Street

MXD1225-   Copies to support Thomas Stonor's title: **[1689]-1704**
1227

– of the will of the Rt Hon. John, Lord Bellasyse, 1689; of
an agreement on the disposal of the Hon. Isabella Bellasyse's
property on her marriage with Thomas Stonor, 1695; and copy
of 1224 above.   3 docs.

MXD1228   Copies of fine as agreed to be levied in **MXD1224** above.   **[Trinity term 1704]**
2 docs.

MXD1229   Agreement for sale   **15 Jan. 1717**

Thomas Stonor as above to Sir Godfrey Kneller of Whitton in
Twickenham, co. Middx, baronet

> Messuage in Queen Street, St Giles in the Fields, as
> above, described as a 'great mansion' in the occ. of

the said Sir Godfrey, with the messuage and timber
yard late in the occ. of Richard Paxton; and stable,
stable yard, houses and outhouses adjoining

The parties agree that the premises will be sold to Sir Godfrey
within the next six months for £1,600.

MXD1230-1231	Bargain and sale, and copy	**15 Apr. 1732**

a) Thomas Stonor of Stonor, co. Oxon., esq., son and heir
of Thomas Stonor deceased, the Hon. Philip Howard, esq.,
youngest brother of the Most Noble, Thomas, Duke of Norfolk,
John Talbot Stonor of Etherope, co. Oxon., exors. of the will
of said Thomas Stonor deceased,   b) the Rt Hon., Richard,
Earl of Scarborough, son and heir of the Rt Hon. Richard,
late Earl of Scarborough, deceased,   c) Francis Loggin of
Middle Temple, gentleman and Henry Cranmer of Grays Inn,
gentleman

> Five messuages in Charles Street, as in **MXD1224**
> above

a) and b) convey to c), as trustees, for a nominal sum.
2 docs.

MXD1232	Copy decree	**[15 Jul. 1742]**

– in the case Thomas Stonor [aged about 10] eldest son of
Thomas Stonor, esq. against his father and Francis Loggin.

Reciting the marriage settlement, 14-15 April 1732 of the
plaintiff's parents, Francis Loggin is ordered to sell premises in
Oxon., Surrey, Sussex and Middlesex.

MXD1233	Attested copy of 'Mr Stonor's last Settlement'	**[16 Jul. 1750]**

– relating to the marriage settlement estates as above

MXD1234	Lease for 21 years at £60 a year	**7 Feb. 1750**

Thomas Stonor of Whatlington Park, co. Oxon., to Jeffrey
Henvill of St Martin in the Fields, tailor

> Messuage in Charles Street known as the *Academy*
> formerly in the occ. of [blank] Cowley; west on a
> messuage called the *Robinhood* in occ. of Joseph

Marston, east on [blank], north on Charles Street
and south on a stable yard

MXD1235-
1236
Conveyance (lease and release)   **22-3 Jul. 1751**

Thomas Stonor of Stonor, esq., son and heir of Thomas Stonor of
the same place, deceased to William Draper of Froyle, co. Hants.,
esq. and Robert Andrews of St George, Hanover Square, esq.

Five messuages in Charles Street in the several occs.
of Clare Amey, [blank] Scott, James Ramsay, Joseph
Marston and Jeffrey Henville, formerly of Philip
Stotherd, William Abdy, Mary Holmes, Richard
Tustian and [blank] Rambouillet, esq.

Reciting the marriage settlement above and subsequent decree,
etc., the premises are conveyed by Thomas Stonor [who is now
of age] and his trustee, Draper to Robert Andrews for £2,835.

MXD1237
Declaration   **28 Nov. 1751**

– by Robert Andrews that the £2,835 purchase money, above,
was the proper money of Edward, Duke of Norfolk on whose
behalf Andrews holds the premises as trustee.

MXD1238-
1239
Conveyance (lease and release)   **25-6 Feb. 1757**

Edward, Duke of Norfolk and his trustee Robert Andrews
convey the above premises absolutely to the Rt Hon. Thomas,
Earl of Effingham for £2,835.

MXD1240
Declaration   **15 Apr. 1757**

– by the Earl of Effingham that the purchase money, above, was
the Duke's and that he holds the premises in trust for the same.

MXD1241
Bargain and sale   **4 Aug. 1758**

Thomas Stonor the elder and his son and heir, Thomas Stonor
the younger, release to the Rt Hon. Thomas, Earl of Effingham
any rights they might have in the five messuages in Charles
Street.

MXD1242-
1243
Contemporary copy and abstract of **MXD1235-1237** above.
2 docs.

x. Purchase of ground rents

MXD1244-1245 Release of ground rents **23 Mar. 1771**

Robert Edward, Lord Petre of Writtle, co. Essex releases to Edward, Duke of Norfolk and trustees George Hobart of St James, Westminster and Thomas Berney Bramstone of Skreens, co. Essex, esq. of separate rents amounting to £30 a year on:

> i) the ground on which the northern part of the mansion house called Norfolk House, lately built by the Duke of Norfolk stands, with other buildings and structures, on which there lately stood another house, the estate of Joseph Banks the elder, esq., deceased. Ground rent £5
> ii) Five messuages on the south side of Charles Street (as in **MXD1246** etc. below). Ground rent £9 5s.
> iii) Capital messuage on the east side of St James's Square in which Francis, Earl Brook, Earl of Warwick lately dwelt which is now in the possession of the right Reverend father in God, the Bishop of London, all lying on the south side of and abutting north on the northern part of Norfolk House. Ground rent £6 10s.
> iv) Capital messuage which lately stood on the east side of St James's Square, formerly inhabited by Sir Thomas Webb and later in the occ. of the count of Selern late minister plenipotentiary from the Court of Vienna; which was conveyed by Sir John Webb (son of Sir Thomas) on 14 and 16 July 1770 to George Hobart who pulled it down and is building a new capital messuage on its site; all of which lies south of ii) above *and do make the north corner house* [sic] *from Pall Mall up to Charles Street*. Ground rent £9 5s.

Recites that the Duke of Norfolk is possessed of the premises in the names of his trustees the Rt Hon. Francis, Earl Brook and Earl of Warwick and George Hobart party to this deed. The

Duke now pays separate sums of £160, £296 and £296 making £752 in total for the release to him of all the above rents.
Two copies, each with the Duke's signature.

xi. *Leases of the Charles Street houses*

MXD1246   Lease for 200 years in trust   **23 Jun. 1773**

The Duke of Norfolk and the Earl of Effingham lease the five houses in Charles Street to Samuel Seawell of Mark Lane in the city of London, merchant, upon trusts relating to the leasehold premises of Hans Winthrop Mortimer in Surrey Street, St Clement Danes [see **MXD366-372** above]. The trustee holds the Charles Street premises as security for Hans W. Mortimer recouping his considerable costs in respect of the Surrey Street premises.

MXD1247   Draft of the above lease

MXD1248- Leases of premises on the south side of Charles Street
1251
by Thomas, Earl of Effingham on behalf of the Duke of Norfolk   **1757-1774**

1248   – to Edward Baron gent. for 21 years at £42 a year   **16 May 1757**

House in the occ. of the lessee; east Martha Scott, widow and west Sir Thomas Webbe, baronet

1249   – to Martha Scott, widow for 21 years at £45 a year   **16 May 1757**

House in the occ. of the lessee: east James Ramsay, sadler, west Edward Baron

1250   – to James Ramsay, sadler for 17 years at £45 a year   **14 Dec. 1761**

House in the occ. of the lessee; east James Piercy, victualler, west Lovell Stanhope, esq.

1251   – to Ann Baron, widow for 21 years at £52 a year   **13 Jun. 1774**

House in the occ. of the lessee; east William Roos, esq., west the Hon. George Hobart, esq.

MXD1252-1253   Lease by Lord Effingham for 23 years at £60 a year   **18 May 1776**

– to Charles Howard the elder of 'Graystock', esq. and Charles Howard the younger, his only son and heir apparent

House on the south side of the street, as above, late in the occ. of Mrs. Anne Freake, widow; west James Piercy, victualler and on a passage way leading from Charles Street to stabling, etc. at the back; east a newly built house in the occ. of Lord Galloway

Lease and counterpart survive with signatures of all parties

Endorsement, 1779 whereby the elder Charles Howard, now the [10th] Duke of Norfolk, reciting that he paid £1,000 to the previous tenant James Ramsay to obtain the lease, now, as Duke of Norfolk, assigns the remainder of the lease term to Vincent Eyre of Lincoln's Inn, gentleman, in trust for the said Duke.

MXD1254-1255   Lease by Lord Effingham, as above, for 21 years at £60 a year   **30 Mar. 1777**

– to James Piercy, victualler

House on the south side of the street, as above in the occ. of the lessee; east Charles Howard, esq. and west James Ramsay, sadler

With Piercy's bond in £500 for performance of covenants

MXD1256   Appointment   **22 Jul. 1782**

Delphy Piercy appoints William Seymour of St James's Square, gentleman, as her attorney to deal with the financial affairs of her late husband James.

MXD1257-1261   Leases by Charles, Duke of Norfolk and Charles, Earl of Surrey   **1778-1790**

1257   – to William Roos, esq. for 21 years at £60 a year   **15 Apr. 1778**

House in the occ. of the lessee; east James Ramsay west Mrs Williams

1258   – to James Ramsay, sadler for 21 years at £60 a year   **1 Oct. 1778**

House in the occ. of the lessee; east James Piercy, victualler, west William Roos

1259-1260   – to Edmund Burke of the city of Westminster, esq.   **30 Apr. 1779**

– for 9 years at £105 a year

House in the occ. of Henry Howard, esq.; west James Piercy, victualler, east a new house of the Rt Hon. George Galloway

Lease and counterpart each with a **room by room schedule** of fixtures and fittings endorsed

MXD1261   – to Alexander Grant of St Alban's Street, St James's Square, **7 Dec. 1785** Surgeon for 7 years at £90 a year,

House late in the occ. of Edmund Burke; east Robert Shand, victualler and west Lord Galloway and a coach way or passage way leading from Charles Street to coach houses and stable behind

MXD1262-   Lease by Charles [11th] Duke of Norfolk,   **25 Nov. 1790**
1263

– to [his agent] Vincent Eyre of Sheffield, co. York, esq., for 21 years at £50 a year

House in the occ. of Keane Fitzgerald, esq.; east Alexander Stewart, victualler and west Lord Galloway and to the messuage or gateway (partly built over) leading into the yard of certain backhouses and stables

Vincent Eyre's signature is absent

xi. St James's Square: various

MXD1264   Assignment of a £21 annuity   **1 May 1728**

Henry, Lord Viscount Palmerston and others (signatures and seals) to Thomas, Duke of Norfolk pursuant to an Act of Parliament to enable present and future inhabitants of the east, north and west sides of St James's Square to raise a rate *to clean, adorn and beautify the said square ...*

MXD1265   Common Recovery   **Michaelmas term 1814**

James Harting, gentleman [agent for the Duke of Norfolk] against Henry Silverlock, esq.

> 15 messuages, 10 tofts and 5a. land in the parishes of St James within the Liberty of Westminster and St Clement Danes

Great seal damaged beyond repair.

9. OTHER PROPERTIES

This part of the catalogue is a rag bag of odds and ends, among which lurk some significant jewels. The first three deeds of the collection of Clerkenwell Nunnery, relating to its foundation in the mid-12th century, are the oldest documents in the entire Arundel Castle Archives. The provenance of the Clerkenwell deeds is unknown, but there may possibly be a link to the Dacre family. The provenance of the 13th-century deeds relating to Knightsbridge is also unknown.

MXD1288 relates to a substantial property near St James Park leased by the Collector Earl of Arundel and Alatheia his wife in 1633. Though the lease does not say it, this was Tart Hall, for which an inventory of 1641 of the 'Pranketting Room' (Ref. IN 1) exists in the Castle archives. The house was much altered by Alatheia, which has attracted the interest of architectural historians as, for example, Diane Duggan, 'A rather fascinating hybrid' (*British Art*, IV, No. 3) and Juliet Claxton in *Journal of the History of Collections* (OUP 2009).

A very substantial late 17th-century copy deed on 17 parchment membranes relates to the development of what appears to be the Earl of Essex's property in the Strand, immediately east of the Duke of Norfolk's Strand Estate. It had presumably been obtained by ducal agents during the first stage of Strand Estate development as a quarry of information as to procedure.

The small collection of deeds relating to Richard Lechford's property in London are matched by a much larger group of deeds of his Surrey estates in the Castle archives. We have them through his widow Catherine (*née* Tattershall) who married Bernard Howard of Glossop, one of the many sons of Henry Frederick, 15th Earl of Arundel. By default of heirs male in the children of his older brothers, Bernard's descendants succeeded as Dukes of Norfolk, a succession which has endured to the present day.

i. The Nunnery of Clerkenwell

The deeds catalogued here relate to land in Clerkenwell and Tottenham, co. Middx, including Hanger Lane and Muswell (Hill). *Hewetone, Steple*, Wanstead and Stepney are also mentioned.

MXD1271 Royal decree: at Westminster **undated, temp. Hen. II (1154-89)**

a) Henry, King of England, Duke of Normandy and Aquitaine, Count of Anjou b) His justices and ministers in whose baili-wick c) the nuns of Clerkenewelle hold their lands and rents

283

> The church of Clerkenwelle and all the men (i.e. villeins), tenements and possessions of c)

The King makes it known to b) that c) and all their properties are under his protection as if they were royal demesnes. b) are ordered to guard, maintain and protect their church as well as the nuns themselves, to do them no harm nor permit any to be done to them. No one may impose any rents, customs or services on them or prosecute any pleas against them except in the King's own court.

Witnesses: Eustace son of Stephen the chamberlain
Seal: absent

MXD1272   **Grant in free alms**   (1152-1162)
undated, temp Richard Bishop of London
a) Jordan of Breies' and Muriel his wife   b) The Ven. Richard, Bishop of London, Hugh the Dean, Nicholas the Archdeacon, and all the Canons of the church of St Paul   c) the church of St Mary of Clerkenwell [*de fonte clericorum*] and the nuns serving there

> the ditch [or valley -vallis] with the fishpond and 3 perches next to the ditch to the north, along its length from the road which divides the nuns' land from Thurstan's land, as far as the bank of the Holeburne; and all the land which is between the said ditch and the nuns' church.

a) inform b) that they have granted this land to c) free of all temporal services on condition that one of their daughters may be received there if she wishes; but even if she does not, the grant is to remain in force.

Witnesses: Michael the chaplain and Roissa his wife, Rodbert of Murt', Mahald his wife [*sponsa*], Emma and Mahalle his daughters, John the chaplain, Alexander son of Roger, William Malet, Geoffrey his brother, Manasser his kinsman, Reginald Fount [or Well – *de fonte*], Helyas the chaplain, Geoffrey the chaplain, Roger of the Mynt', Richard the chaplain, William his brother, Walter the chaplain.
Seal: absent

MXD1273   Confirmation and quitclaim   **Undated (*c*.1160)**

a) Walter, servant of the Hospital of Jerusalem and Prior
of the fraternity who are in England. b) The monastery
of the Holy Nuns of Clerkenwell c) Jordan, the founder
of both houses

> i) 10 acres of land lying between the demesne of
> a) and the monastery of b)
> ii) 5 acres of land.

An argument has arisen between a) and b) regarding property
i), but it has been settled by c) giving property ii) to a); so that
a) now confirms b)'s right to property i) and he quitclaims
to them all rights he may have had in it.

This agreement was made in the presence of Ralph the Dean,
William, Richard, Richard the Archdeacon, Master Aubrey,
Hugh, Rodbert of *Auco* and other canons and the whole
chapter of the Church of St Paul in London.

Witness: Jordan, the founder himself.
Seal: absent

MXD1274   Confirmation   **Undated (*c*.1160)**

a) Alice who was dau. of Roger who was son of ?Fulbert
[*Fub'ti*]   b) The church of St Mary of Clerkenewelle and
the nuns serving God there   c) Lecia, sister of a)

> Land in Thothenha' [Tottenham], viz.: i) part held
> by a) ii) part formerly held by c) iii) rent of 24s.
> out of Lecia's part iv) all lands, meadows, pastures,
> ways, paths, woods and plains pertaining

a) confirms all to b) to hold of the Lord of the fee, except a
2s. rent out of property iii) which a) has since given to one
Walter. b) shall hold at 13s. annual rent, payable quarterly.

Witnesses: William of Warenne, Hosbert son of Harvey,
                 Geoffrey White [*albus*], Roger the Duke, Gilbert the
                 Dane [*le danais*], Richard, Ralph, ?Hernold, Gilbert,
                 John the priest, Gilbert Folioth, Benedict the priest,
                 Benedict of Blenford, Harvey the cook.
Seal: a fine oval seal of a), with impression and legend

285

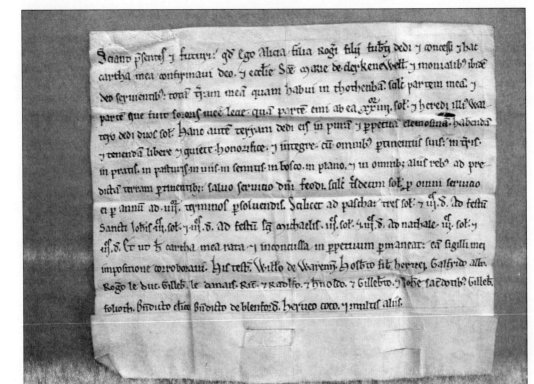

Fig. 17   Clerkenwell Nunnery.

The provenance of these early medieval deeds relating to the
nunnery at Clerkenwell is unclear. They may have come into
the Duke of Norfolk's archives from the Dacre family (via
Ann Dacre who married the 13th Earl of Arundel in 1571).
A wealth of detail about the landscape of early-medieval
Clerkenwell is contained in the property clauses, as this
catalogue shows. This deed is a rare example of one whose
seal has not been removed (long since, by persons unknown)
as a 'collectors' item'. (Ref. **MXD1274**.)

MXD1275   Grant   **Undated (*c*.1170)**

> a) Maurice of Toteha' [Tottenham] b) John, his
> son c) The church of the Blessed Mary and the Holy Nuns
> of Clerechenewelle

> > The land which Baldewine held; the land which
> > Wlfstan held; the land which Gill(bert) the clerk
> > held; the small headland in Godman's field in Great
> > Toteha' [Tottenham]; in all 30 acres.

> Recites that a) previously gave the land to c) in perpetual free
> alms for the good of his soul and the souls of his wife and his
> ancestors; he now grants it to b) and his heirs to hold of c); b)
> shall pay a) the ann. rent of 12d. in lieu of all services except
> the King's service.

> **Witnesses:**   Gilbert of Mustiers, John Folefant, Ric. le Palmer,
> Gilbert son of Mabel, Geoffrey English [*le engleis*],
> Jocelin, and Henry his brother, Ailwin the baker,
> Randolph of Pasci', Michael of Munten', William
> son of Guy, Walter of Wrtel, Alexander son of
> Guy, Alexander the chaplain, Robert the parson,
> Henry the clerk of Meldon.
> **Seal:**   absent

MXD1276   Grant in free alms   **Undated (*c*.1172)**

> Parties as above.

> > Land in Great Toteham (no details)

> a) now grants to c) the 12d. rent formerly payable to
> himself

> **Witnesses:**   Alexander the chaplain, Robert the parson of
> Toteham, Henry the clerk of Meld', Roger son of
> Maurice, Michael of Munten', Ailwin the baker,
> Henry brother of Jocelin, Randolph of Pasci,
> Walter of Wrtel, Laurence the clerk.
> **Seal:**   absent

MXD1277   Grant in free and perpetual alms   **Undated (*c*.1175)**

> Parties a) and c) of 1275 above.

Advowson of the church of Totham with the lands, tithes, income, pastures and work services pertaining to that church.

For the salvation of his soul and of the souls of his ancestors and his heirs, a) grants to c).

Witnesses: Alexander the priest, Muriel wife of a), Letia her daughter, Roger and John, sons of a), Michael of Munteinni, William son of Guy, Harvey son of Geoffrey, Gervu', Gocelin, Laurence the clerk
Seal: absent

MXD1278   Confirmation   **Undated (c.1195)**

a) Richard, minister of the Church of London   b) his beloved daughters in Christ, the nuns of Clerkenwell

A sum of [missing ?5 marks], from the offerings to the altar and from the small tithes of the church of Great Totham.

Cites deed of Maurice of Totham [presumably 1277 above] which was executed in the time of Gilbert, predecessor of a) [Gilbert, Bishop of London, 1163-1187]. Now a), having inspected and verified that deed, confirms the said revenue to b) because their honesty and diligence in serving God has brought them intolerable poverty; with contingencies to ensure the income if these revenues are insufficient.

Witnesses: A., Archdeacon of London, William of Ely, King's Treasurer, Alan ?the bargeman [*berengarius*], Richard the chaplain, John of Garland, Master Alexander, Hugh of Winton, William of Wald', William of Hedfeld, clerks.
Seal: absent

[This deed is dated principally through party a), Richard, bishop of London 1189-98]

MXD1279   Final Concord, Sunday before Ss. Philip and James, 1 May,   **1197**
            8 Ric. I

a) Lecia of Monteni, formerly wife of Henry Foliot b) Hermeniard, Prioress and the convent of nuns of Clerkenwelle   c) H[ubert Walter], archbishop of Canterbury, R[ichard Fitzneal], Bishop of London, G[odfrey of Lucy], Bishop of Winchester, Ralph Hereford, Richard, archdeacon

of Ely, Master Thomas Husseborne, Richard of Heriet, Osbert
his son, Simon of Patishulle, Giles son of Giles (or Fitz Giles),
justices   d) Emma of Monteni, sister of a).

Two virgates of land in Clerkenwelle, viz.:

> i) 14 acres of land on which the 'Priory' of the same
> nuns was founded; which lie both inside their court
> and which surround it outside on all sides of the
> curtilage and extend as far as the land of the Hospital
> of Jerusalem. And the land which is inside the court
> of the nunnery includes the ditch [or valley – *vallis*
>] in which there used to be the great fish pond, and
> it is the valley in which Skinnereswelle lies; and
> three perches of land beyond that ditch to the north,
> running along the ditch as far as Holburne; with
> the fishpond itself if it is still there. And the land
> which lies between that ditch and Godewelle, below
> the road all the way into Holburne; and across the
> road to the east as far as the embankment [*fossatus*].
> Three perches of land beyond Godewelle below the
> road and across it to the north. Five acres of land
> next to the said ditch lying along towards the middle
> and towards the north. And the land and meadow
> which lies between Holburne and the embankment,
> which goes from Holburne to the mill of the said
> nuns; and the embankment itself and the site of the
> said mill And the curtilage next to the said mill; and
> the land, meadow and garden which lie between the
> said mill and the garden of the hospital of Jerusalem
> which is upon Holburne. And the lands and houses
> [*masagia*], rents and gardens which lie between the
> said garden of the said Hospital and the 'bar' of
> Smethefeld upon the stream of Fackeswell towards
> the north. And the lands and houses which the said
> nuns hold of the fee of said Lecia between the said
> stream and Chikennelane. A messuage or house
> which Robert of Foleham used to hold; 2 acres of
> land next to the street which leads from the bar
> outside Aldredesgate towards Iseldon, next to the
> garden of the hospitallers of Smethefeld; and all the
> head (?headland) which is between Witewellebehe
> and Farncroft; and all Farncroft and the small
> ditch next to Farncroft to the north, that is, along
> Farncroft and the embankment beyond that ditch
> to the north. And all the land which ?William [*Wll*]
> the clerk of Smethefeld held from the same Lecia
> next to the curtilage of the said Nuns towards the

east. And all the land which Wig(?frid) Ricce held of the fee of the same Lecia in Hewetone. One acre of land in the same fee in Steple and one ? mark in rent of the third part of Wannestede; and the service pertaining to that third part of the capital messuage of Wannestede and payable to the same Lecia and her heirs as a sixth part of a knight's fee. And one virgate in Stebenee which Saloman used to hold.
ii) All the land which lies between that land which d) gave to the same nuns and the land which they held from a)

In a case between a) and b), heard before c), the King's Justices, it is agreed that a) shall grant property i) to b) and quitclaim to them all her and her heirs' rights in those lands; b) shall hold them free of all service dues except foreign service; a) also grants that the nuns may ?improve their conduit [*emendare conduct'u' suum*] on a)'s land and that the heirs of a) shall not impede it; and she gives property ii) so that her daughter Roesia may be received as a nun. For all this b) pay 10 marks of silver to a)

Witnesses: none
Seal: absent

MXD1280   Grant in free alms   **Undated (?c.1200)**

a) Robert son of Sewin of Northacu'   b) The nuns of St Mary of Clerkenwell

> i) 27 acres of land in Hangre in Totham
> ii) half a river meadow which Engelr' formerly held himself
> iii) 4 trees for firewood from the wood at Totheham
> iv) 10 grown pigs released from pasturage there [*quietus a pasuagio*]

Recites that a) was given i) by Malaculumb [Malcolm IV], King of Scotland which he held in the outpastures of London [*quas hutrediis de Lond' tenuit*] and that he held it free of all services except to the King of Scotland. a) now grants to b) on the same terms.

Witnesses: Hugh son of a), Edward White, the kinsman of Wilfrid the clerk, Sewin son of Robert, Ralph Malba, Nicholas of Fale, Wesley, William of Peri,

William son of Geoffrey, Geoffrey of Huntendune,
Ralph of Palerne, Reginald le Rus, William the
chaplain, Alex. of the Well [*de fonte*], Ralph the
clerk, Benedict, Laurence, Robert of Kingestun and
Reginald of ?Foliote [*fo"te*] who wrote this deed.

Seal: absent

MXD1281   Grant   **Undated (*c.*1200)**

a) Gilbert Folyot   b) John Folyot, brother of a)

The messuage that Brithena holds in Little
Thoteham; the croft that Ranulph the obedientiary
held in the same vill' at Brunebure

a) grants to b) to hold of himself at ann. rent of ½lb of
cummin payable at Michaelmas, free of all services except
Royal service, in token of which b) gives a) one measure of
yarn [*bilancium*]

Witnesses: Lord Michael of Munteny, Philip of Verly, Roger
Folyot, Peter Folyot, Robert son of Harvey,
Nicholas of Hadham the writer of this deed

Seal: part broken but impression intact.

MXD1282   Acknowledgement   **Undated (?*c.*1250)**

a) Peter son of Alan   b) The nuns of Clerkenwell   c) the
Warden of the Hospital of Claiaung

Land in Toteh' called Coppedhallefeld

a) acknowledges that the land is in the hands of c) who is
his sub-tenant, but that it is he himself who owes the annual
rent of 2s. 6d. to b); and that it is lawful therefore for b) to
distrain him for the rent.

Witnesses: none
Seal: fragment with good impression

MXD1283   Grant and Quitclaim   **Undated (?*c.*1275)**

a) Robert son of Hamund of Ponde   b) Ralph son of Simon
le Bouer

2 acres of arable land in the vill' of Thot'ham

291

Recites that a) had a reversionary interest in the land following the death of his father Hamund; he now quitclaims it to b)

Witnesses: John of Oveseye, Richard of Gibecrake, Bawale of Lamore, John of Shireburne, Michael son of Brice, John Herde, Robert Cuteler, Robert le Chaluner, Simon Sweriere

Seal: damaged with part impression and legend

MXD1284   Grant in free alms   **Undated (*c.*1275)**

a) Nicholas son of Gilbert of Totham   b) God and the Church of the Blessed Mary of Clerkenewell and the nuns serving there   c) Thomas son of James of Totham

Certain land in Totham

An annual rent of 4d. is payable by c) to a) for this land but a) now grants it to b)

Witnesses: Richard of Purl', then warden of the said house, Robert of Uleham, Bawal son of Luke, Richard Gibcrake, Gilbert of Totham, Nicholas the clerk, Geoffrey the clerk of Clerkenwell, Elyas of Soelle

Seal: absent

MXD1285   Grant   **Undated (?*c.*1300)**

a) Margery of Watvile, prioress of Clerkenwell, and the convent of the same   b) John Gerard of Hole Weye

A certain plot of land at Mosewelle with the buildings on it, five perches both in length and breadth, lying between land of a) on the east and land of Godfrey Patfot on the west

a) grants to b) to hold at 4d. annual rent, payable quarterly

Witnesses: Richard Digun, John Pas, William of Dunstapele, Walter le Puleter (?poulterer), Ralph le Torthur (? confectioner), John the smith of Iseldone, John the skinner, Matthew the carpenter.

Seal: ecclesiatical seal with impression and legend

MXD1286   Order concerning tithes   at Westminster   **3 Jun. 1307**

a) R[alph Baldock], Bishop of London   b) Master William of Halsted, venerable father of God   c) The prioress and nuns of Clerkenwell

a) instructs b) re payment by c) of their biennial tithes due to the Abbot of Westminster on their goods both temporal and spiritual.

Witnesses: none
Seal: absent

MXD1287   Memorandum   **(16th-cent. copy of 14th-cent. original)**

a) G[ilbert Segrave] Bishop of London   b) The Church of St Mary of Clerkenwell and the nuns serving there   Land outside the bar of Smethefeld, viz. the lands once of Reginald of Gynges and Emma his wife, Maurice of Totham and Muriel his wife and Henry Foliot and Lecia his wife

a) gives notice that he has granted b) perpetual parochial rights in the property

Witnesses: none
Seal: none

MXD1288   Acknowledgement of receipt the day after Easter 43 Ed. III
                                    16th-cent. copy (1369)

a) Idonea Suter (or ? Luter), Prioress of the House of the Blessed Mary of Clerkenewell and the convent there
b) John Herewode

The farm of Le Hangre in Totenham

a) acknowledges receipt from b) of 8 marks sterling for 2 years rent.

Witnesses: none
Seal: absent

MXD1289   Lease: in the common chapter house at Clerkenewell outside   **24 Jun. 1380**
London St John the Baptist's day, 4 Ric. II

a) Katherine Braybrooke, Prioress of the House of the Blessed
Mary of Clerkenewell and the convent there   b) William
Bredon and Elaine his wife

> A certain plot of land at Mosewelle, co. Middx, 64
> perches in length west to east from the highway as far
> as the field of a), and south to north 48 perches.

a) grants to b) for 1000 years to hold at 2s. annual rent payable
quarterly, to the intent that b) shall erect a house on the plot
within the next two years.

Witnesses: written in the presence of the prioress and
convent
Seal: small seal of b)

MXD1290   Copy of earlier deed viz.   **16th-cent.**

In the chapel of Mossewell outside London in the Diocese
of London:

Complaint concerning loss of privileges of the said chapel
to the Prioress and convent of St Mary of Clerkenwell …
[incomplete with omissions from text]

MXD1291   Order for restoration of tithes   26 July 5 Pope Sixtus IV   **(1476)**

a) Thomas Ian of the Consistory Court of the Bishop of
London   b) The Prioress of the nuns of Clerkenwell in the
suburb of the City of London, patrons of the Church of
Great Totham in the Diocese of London   c) Lord Robert
Stuard, vicar of the said church   d) Lord Richard Skykard,
rector of the said parish church of St Laurence of Devenge
Hundred of the same Diocese concerning tithes of:

> 50 acres arable lying on the west side of a boundary
> called Le Dole, stretching from a certain bush called
> the Blacke Busshe through a certain manor called
> Westnewland to a street called Lakstrete; a croft
> called Inescroft; a parcel of land called Twenty Acres;
> another called Doggeshille; another called Piehille
> adjacent to the said Manor of Westnewland; parcel
> of land called Sawers; two crofts, one commonly

called Mochmores, the other Litelmores; a croft called Townokes; a field called Uckfeld (or ?Vakfeld) within a certain island called Ramynsey, all in the parish of Totham.

Reciting that the great and small tithes of the parish church of Tottenham properly belong to a), b) and c) but that d) has taken tithes to the value of 4 marks, a) now decrees that d) shall restore to b) and c) the amount he took; and a) reaffirms the entitlement of b) and c) to the tithes.

Witnesses: the Venerable Master Humphrey Howard, Dr of Law, Nicholas Collys, Procurator General of the Court of Canterbury, Richard Spencer, notary.
Seal: absent

Addendum contains notary's mark (Nicholas Parker), clerk of Norwich Diocese

MXD1292   Assignment of lease   **2 Oct. 1530**

a) Isabel Sackvile, prioress of the nuns of Clarkenwel
b) Brother Thomas, Doctor, Prior of the Hospital of St John of Jerusalem in England, and his fellow brothers
c) John Reve, scrivener, 2 Oct. 1530

One tenement and the garden adjoining in Tremylstrete co. Middx *viz.* between the close of b) called le Bocher Closse on the east and the highway called Tremylstrete on the west; the tenement of b) in occ. of John Ap Gillam, carpenter on the north and the hospice "Brassmen" called Le Rose on the south

Recites lease from b) to a) on 7 July 1524 for 50 years at 7s. 8d. annual rent. a) now assign the remainder of the term to c)

Witnesses: none
Seal: absent

MXD1293   Brief account   **3 & 4 Philip and Mary (1556-7)**

– of the farm of the site of the former Priory of Clerkenwell, taken by William Burnell, gentleman, collector and farmer.

ii. Land at Knightsbridge

MXD1294   Gift   **Undated ?*c*.1250**

a) William Bisel and Ascelina his wife   b) Agnes their daughter

> 1½ a. land with appurts. in Knyttebrigge lying in one piece in Allescroft in the place called Brokefurlong betw. the land of William the smith of Knyttebrigge on the west and the land of a) on the east, its south head abutting on the ditch of the Abbot and convent of Westminster, the north head on the stream of Knyttebrigge

a) grant to b) and her heirs to hold of themselves and their heirs at 6d. annual rent

Witnesses: Simon of Kensingtone, William le Yungeman, John Atte Wodetone, John of Karduyl, Adam of Belegrave, John of Nottele, Walter the merchant (le Marchaunt) of Knyttebrigge, William the smith, William Walberd, Wm. Hod, William Brun

Seal: two, each with impression and legend, slightly damaged

MXD1295   Gift   **Undated ?*c*.1250**

a) William and Ascelina Bisel as above   b) Walter their son

> 1 acre of land with appurts. in Knyttebrigge, lying in Allecroft in the place called Brokefurlong between land of Margery, daughter of a) on the W. and land of William Hod on the east, the south head abutting on the ditch of the Abbot and convent of Westminster, the north head on the stream of Knyttebrigge

a) grant to b) and his heirs to hold as in **MXD1294** above, but at 4d. annual rent

Witnesses: as in **MXD1294** above.
Seal: as in **MXD1294** above, Asceline's seal nearly perfect, with a squirrel impression

MXD1296   Gift   **Undated ?*c*.1250**

a) William and Ascelina Bisel as above   b) Margery their daughter

½ a land with appurts. in Knyttebrigge lying in Allescroft in the place called Brokefurlong between land of Agnes, daughter of a) on the west and land of a) on the east, the S. head abutting on the ditch of the Abbot and convent of Westminster and the north head on the stream of Knyttebrigge

a) grant to b) and her heirs to hold as in **MXD1294** above, but at 2d. annual rent

Witnesses: as in **MXD1294**
Seal: as in **MXD1294-1295** above, but poor fragments

iii. Howard family: various properties, 1587-1887

The following deed perhaps relates to the house the family owned in Lothbury in the life time of Henry Frederick, 15th Earl of Arundel, who died in 1652

MXD1297   Final Concord   **Trinity 1587**

> John Ryche, plaintiff, against Christpher Myers, deforciant messuage and appurts. in parish of St Margaret in Lothburye

[Tart Hall]
MXD1298   Assignment of lease   **11 Oct. 1633**

> a) William Warden of Westminster, yeoman and Alice his wife, lately the wife of William Brown of Westminster, yeoman deceased   b) John George of St Martin in the Fields, yeoman, and John Browne of Westminster, vintner exors. of the said Wm. Brown deceased (his uncle and brother respectively)   c) Thomas, Earl of Arundel and Surrey, Earl Marshal of England of the Noble Order of the Garter, knight, one of His Majesties Privy Council and the Lady Alatheia his Countess

>> Piece of ground 100 feet in length by 50 feet in breadth; with the tenement or stable on it, enclosed with a brick wall in St James Street near or opposite St James Park wall parish of St Margaret, Westminster; adjoining the yard and ground of Sir John Byron, knight north west, house and garden in the occ. of Barnard Watmore south east; together with a passage or watercourse on the premises running into the land of the first lessor, Alphonsus Fowle

> Recites that on 27 Feb. 1625 Alphonsus Fowle of Westminster, esq. and Walter Alexander of St James in the par of St Martin in the Fields leased the premises for 31 years to William and Alice Brown of a) above. They and the other members of a) now assign the remainder of the lease for £160 to c). Annual rent not specified

MXD1299   Grant of the custody   **14 Mar. 1745**

– of Mary Howard, of Hammersmith, co. Middx, widow, a lunatic, to Charles ?Jernegan, of St James, Westminster, doctor of physick, and custody and management of her real and personal estate to Robert West of par. of St George the Martyr, Westminster, esq.

House in Soho Square

MXD1300   Declaration by Francis, Earl of Effingham   **24 Jul. 1741**

> Parcel of land on the west side of Soho Square, parish of St Ann 24 by 115 feet (approx., abuttals given), in the occ. of Charles Howard, esq. and valued at £70 a year

Recites that the premises were leased three days previously for 58 years by William, Duke of Portland to Jane and Elizabeth Strudwick, who have today assigned the remainder of this term to Charles Howard. The Earl declares that the purchase money of £1,150 for the assignment was the proper money of Charles Howard of Greystoke in Cumberland, esq., for whom he is acting as trustee.

Signature of Lord Effingham is endorsed

MXD1301   Lease for 6 years at £140 a year   **29 Jul. 1765**

Thomas Burrough of St Martin in the Fields, esq. to Sir Christopher Bethell of St George, Hanover Square, esq.

> Messuage on the west side of Albemarle Street, par. of St George, Hanover Square, being the fourth house southwards from Stafford Street, formerly in the tenure of the Rt Hon. Countess Dowager of Kildare, deceased, and since of the Rt Hon. Lord Bertie; north James Gressett, south Lieut. General Huste. **Room by room schedule** of fixtures and fittings.

MXD1302   Exemplification of a common recovery   **8 Jul. 1767**

Richard Heron, demandant; John Buckle, tenant; Charles Howard the younger, esq., vouchee

Ten messuages with appurts. in the parishes of St James in the liberty of Westminster and St Clement Danes
The premises are recovered in freehold by Richard Heron.

Very poor example of Great Seal

MXD1303   Lease for 10 years at £265 a year   **11 Apr. 1814**

Robert Peter Dyneley of Grays Inn, esq., Thomas Parry of East Burnham House, co. Bucks., esq. and Elizabeth his wife to Bernard Edward Howard of Fornham, co. Suff., esq.

Messuage or dwelling house, no. 27 Lower Brook Street [Mayfair], co. Middx, late in the occ. of Thomas Berington, deceased, having a frontage of 20 feet and 22 feet 6ins. (coach house) towards the street by 200 feet in depth; with the stables, coach house and buildings; with use in common with Davies Davenport of no. 28 lower Brook Street, of: i) a plot of land 10 x 6 feet at the north west corner of the coach house ii) the stair case and passage way leading from a mews or stable yard on the north side of the coach house which lead to the rooms over the coach houses of nos. 27 and 28 and iii) a 10ft square plot of ground, abutting west on the coach house of no. 28, east and south on the mews, and north on a public house at the entrance to the mews.

Room by room schedule of fixtures and fittings

MXD1304   Assignment of the above lease   **31 Dec. 1818**

Bernard Edward, now as [12th] Duke of Norfolk, assigns the remainder of the lease term at the same rent to John Rae Reid of Broad Street, city of London, esq.

Room by room schedule as above.
Ducal signature

MXD1305-1306   Lease for 21 years at £110 annual rent   **25 Mar. 1824**

Bernard Edward, 12th Duke, the Hon. Charles, Earl of Shrewsbury and others [names] as trustees of the Bavarian

Chapel in Warwick Street, Golden Square to Josiah Turner
of Vine Street, Piccadilly

> No. 23 Golden Square formerly in the occ. of
> Mr Griffen, then of the Misses Douglas and now
> of the present lessee

Signatures of the trustees including the Duke and the Earl
of Shrewsbury

Endorsed: assignment of the lease to John Ludwig Rapp of
No. 22 Clarges Street, Piccadilly, gentleman following the
death of Elizabeth Turner, widow of Josiah.

Annotated catalogue of James Coleman, Heraldic and
Genealogical Bookseller, 22 High Street, Bloomsbury shows
that this deed was purchased in 1863 for 12s. 6d.

11 Carlton House Terrace

MXD1307   Assignment of lease and mortgage liability   **22 Apr. 1856**

14th Duke of Norfolk to Rt Hon. William Ewart Gladstone,
MP

> Messuage known as no. 11 Carlton House Terrace,
> Pall Mall

Preamble contains earlier site history. The Duke, then as
Earl of Surrey, obtained a 99-year lease of the premises on
23 Dec. 1844 for £12,315 from Sarah Frances Crockford, widow
of William Crockford deceased. He at the same time raised a
mortgage for £4,500 on the premises from Hugh Parker late
of Woodthorpe near Sheffield but then of Tickhill co. York,
esq. He now assigns the remainder of the lease to William
Ewart Gladstone of Carlton House Terrace, MP for £6,000,
and the mortgage liability of £4,500 is also transferred to
Gladstone.

Good signature of Gladstone.

Building land at Kilburn

MXD1308   Sale for £5,000 and covenant to produce deeds   **3 Nov. 1874**

The United Land Company sells to John Quinn Dunn of 26
Wellington Road, St John's Wood, Middx, gentleman

53 plots of land at Kilburn in the parish of Chelsea, part of an estate called the Kilburn and Harrow Road Estate, with all buildings and rights pertaining

Coloured plan shows plots numbered 247, 256 and 288-338 in two rows of back to back house plots in Herries and Lancefield Roads between Mozart Street south and Dart Street north.

Schedule lists deeds relating to the premises 1764-1869

MXD1309   Declaration of trust   **9 Dec. 1874**

J.Q. Dunn acknowledges to Henry [15th] Duke of Norfolk and Augusta Mary Minna Catherine, [dowager] Duchess of Norfolk that he holds the above premises upon trust for them, as well as a further six plots purchased from the same company for £540 on 8 Dec. 1874.

MXD1310   Conveyance   **24 Jul. 1876**

J.Q. Dunn, with the agreement of the Dowager Duchess, conveys the 53 building plots as above to the Duke. Coloured plan endorsed.

Premises at Notting Hill, part of the Portobello Estate

For a plan of and report on the Kilburn and Notting Hill estates, 1881, see ACA/MD51; for rentals and accounts 1877-1878 see ACA/MD837-838

MXD1311   Conveyance for £1,600   **11 Aug. 1877**

Sir Charles Nicholson of The Grange, Totteridge, co. Herts., Bt. and William Nichol of Victoria Street, Westminster, esq., at the direction of the Land and House Investment Society Ltd., to the Rev. William Manning, the Rev. Robert Butler and the Rev. Francis Merrik Wyndham, of St Charles College, Ladbroke Grove Road, clerks in Holy Orders

Twelve parcels of land in the parish of St Mary Abbotts, Kensington having a frontage of 221 feet on Merchison Road to the south and 72 feet 6ins. on Portobello Road to the west.

Plan shows 11 small house plots and a large central plot as part of a triangular development with Worthington Road on the east.

MXD1312   Deed of covenant for production of deeds   **11 Aug. 1877**

Relates to the original purchase of the Portobello estate for £15,000.

Schedule mentions deeds of November 1875 between H.C. Blake, B.G. Lake and the said Society.

MXD1313   Conveyance for £1,800   **5 Dec. 1879**

The Revs. Butler and Wyndham as above (Manning having since died) convey the above 12 plots of land, with all buildings, etc., on them, to Henry [15th] Duke of Norfolk. **Plan**.

MXD1314   Conveyance for £215   **8 Jan. 1880**

The Liquidators of the Land and House Investment Society (names given) to Henry [15th] Duke of Norfolk

> Plot of land having a frontage of 17ft 6ins on Portobello Road, numbered 326 on the Society's plan of their Westbourne Park Estate, with all buildings, etc. on it.

The plot lies next to (north) of the block previously purchased by the Duke; sold with liberty to connect to the sewer in Portobello Road.

MXD1315   Lease for 21 years at £100 annual rent   **19 Jan. 1878**

William John Thompson of No. 9 Surrey Villas, Upper Norwood, gentleman to Henry [15th] Duke of Norfolk

House on the north side of Mortimer Street, no. 22, in St Marylebone; subject to the tenancy on sufferance of Mr Charles Melin and to the rights of the Duke of Portland or other superior landlords.

MXD1316   Assignment of the above lease for 4½ years at the same rent   **7 Nov. 1883**
The Duke assigns to Robert Alan Hoghton of No. 9 Colville
Mansions, Bayswater, merchant.

MXD1317-   Surrender of the above lease   **11 Jun. 1887**
1318

The Duke surrenders to Lewis Myers of 3 Woburn Square,
esq., assignee of the executors of the will of William John
Thompson, deceased. With a covering letter from Few & Co.,
the Duke's solicitors.   2 docs.

iv. *Sir Richard Lechford's house in parish of St Margaret, Westminster*

MXD1321-   Final concord   **Hilary 1634**
1322

Martin Bradley, gentleman, plaintiff against William Jones,
gentleman and Dorothy his wife

> messuage and appurts. in parish of St Margaret,
> Westminster

MXD1323   Inspeximus of conveyance dated 14 Nov. 1611   **16 Jul. 1635**

By the 1611 deed, John Warkehouse, citizen and grocer of
London, conveys to William Kewe, citizen and victualler
of the same and Rebeccah his wife

> messuage once known as the *Maidenhead*, then
> the *Castle* and now the *Globe* in Kinges Street,
> parish of St Margaret, Westminster

Text has flaked off in several places

Fragment of Great Seal

MXD1324   Final concord   **Hilary 1638**

William Weld, esq., Thomas Bursty, gentleman and Robert
Abbott plaintiffs, against Ann Alexander, widow and Charles
Alexander, gentleman, deforciants

> 2 messuages, ?three cottages, one barn, 5
> gardens and ?10a. land in parish of St Margaret,
> Westminster

Text very flaky and much is illegible

MXD1325-1326	Conveyance (two copies)	**1 Dec. 1637**

Sir Richard Lechford of London, knight, for reasons of fatherly affection, conveys to Richard Lechford of London, esq. his son

> premises called the *Fountain* in Kingestreete, in occ. of Thomas Andrew, vintner (as in 1329 below).

Signature, Richard Lechford; **seals** (one whole, one in pieces)

MXD1327	Delivery of monies	**8 Aug. 1660**

Mark Coe, esq. late Receiver General for recusants' estates for the County of Middlesex delivers money due on estate as in below to Sir Richard Lechford, knight

MXD1328	Conveyance to trustee	**4 Feb. 1661**

Sir Richard Lechford conveys premises as in 1329 below to John Woolfe as trustee to uses

MXD1329	Marriage Settlement	**5 Feb. 1661**

a) Sir Richard Lechford of London, knight   b) John Woolfe of London, gentleman   c) Edward Edwardes of London, gentleman and   d) Mary his wife who is the daughter of a)

> messuage, mansion house or tenement formerly known by the sign of the *Globe* but now of the Fountain, in King Street in St Margaret's, Westminster, formerly in the occ. of William Jones then of Edward Baker and now of William Traughton, with all rooms, houses, buildings, yards and backsides and all rents and profits

a) conveys to b) as trustee to hold the premises to the use of c) and d) for life of each of them with remainders first to Richard their eldest son, then to the younger children (not named)

Signatures: of a), c) and d) and seals with their crests

v. Premises in various parishes 1628-1769

Holborn

MXD1330-1333   Lease for 20 years, and assignments of residues of term   **1628-1635**

John Lee, esq. to Richard Hooper, tailor

> Messuage in High Holborn, between the messuages of James Gentleman on the east and of Edmund Wilmott on the west, abutting north onto the King's highway, par. of St Giles-in-the-Fields.

And later assignments from Humphrey Bailey, tailor and Susan his wife, late wife and exectrix of Richard Hooper, to John Clarke, citizen and merchant tailor of London; then John Clarke to Margaret Wiltsheir, widow; and John Clarke to Dorothy Mansell of Woodford in Essex, widow.

Assignment charge from £15 to £50 and annual rents from £10 to £19 per annum.   4 docs.

St Clement Danes and elsewhere

MXD1334   Copy bargain and Sale   [day and month illegible]   **1683-1700**
This deed has suffered from water damage and large parts are illegible. It seems to be a copy of an original and it relates to a substantial package of housing developments in London, perhaps related to the Essex House development. It was presumably obtained by the 7th Duke's agents for use with his own development plans.

The parties names are illegible on the first two membranes but can be picked up later when payments are cited, viz.:

In consideration of £3,500 paid by Bernard Turner, Felix Calvard and John Wilson to Sir James Ward, £3,500 paid by the same to Samuel Rawstone, £3,500 paid by the same to Nicholas Barbon and John Parsons and 5 shillings apiece paid to Sir James Ward,

William Morris, Samuel Rawstone, John Parsons, Nicholas Barbon, George Bradbury and Edward Noel, Turner, Calvard and Wilson sell to Sir Richard Haddocke, Samuel Dashwood, Anthony Sturt and Rowland Ingram:

> Well Close with all houses on it; all the buildings on or near Little Tower Hill in St Botolph without Aldgate, St Mary Whitechapel and Stepney, co. Middx, belonging to the manor of East Smithfield, and premises in the parishes of St Martins and St Clement Danes, co. Middx

Schedules of premises (not all entirely legible) mention Devereux Court, Crosse Lane between Temple and Milford Lane, Great Essex Street, and land on the east side of St Martin's Lane, etc. (illegible).

Authority is granted to build and set up new houses upon the same.

Extensive clauses containing fire policy provisions.

Endorsements to 1700 record the transfer, sale or inheritance of various rents and leases within the estates.   17 membranes

MXD1335   Bill for legal expenses   **1638-1639**

Costs incurred by [illeg. – ? Harte and another] on the part of William Tirrell in his defence against Roger Mallacke, citizen of Exeter. (Found with London deeds but the connection is unclear.)

MXD1336   Answer to bill of complaint (incomplete, court not given)   **Undated, *c*.1650**

James Webster answers the bill of complaint of William Johnson concerning:

> Messuages and tenements in Chancery Lane, St Dunstans in the West, London

Parish of St Giles

MXD1337   Lease for 5 years at £40 annual rent   **3 Mar. 1681**

Humphrey Weld of Weld House, parish of St Giles leases to Henry Kenge of the same parish, vintner messuage and yard in Weld Street, St Giles, in the occ. of the lessee, between a messuage in the possession of the Marquesse of Winchester and a tenement in the occ. of Widow Holden, with a right of way by a door in the yard of the premises into a piece of ground owned by the lessor, for the lessee, his family and servants to hang out clothes to dry; and also with the right to use the privy in the said yard

St Mary Abchurch

MXD1338   Lease for 21 years at £40 annual rent   **5 Sep. 1764**

Elizabeth Tracey of Newington Butts, co. Surrey, widow of Samuel Osborne late of Abchurch Lane, tallow chandler, deceased, William Nichols of Camomile Street, Allhallows in the Wall, London, gentleman, Mary Bickerstaff of Christ Church, London, spinster, Hannah Headach of Knightsbridge, widow to Stephen Huntley the younger of Threadneedle Street, London, hatter

> Messuage divided into two dwellings, formerly in the occ. of Edward Popplewell and lately of Thomas Shoutes, in Abchurch Lane, St Mary Abchurch, London.

Includes clauses re the division of the rent between the various recipients and a room by room schedule of fixtures and fittings.

MXD1339   Assignment of the above lease   **1 Jan. 1769**

Stephen Huntley's estate in the premises were assigned to Thomas Cable Davies of Abchurch Lane, hatter, in 1767 who now, for a down payment of £105, assigns again at the same rent to Ann Pringle of Sherborn Lane, London, widow.

Westminster

MXD1340   Lease for 7 years at £50 annual rent   **22 Mar. 1769**
William Barrett of Old Palace Yard, gentleman to Richard Knight of the same place, stable keeper

Messuage, livery yard, stables, coach houses etc. in the occ. of the lessee in Abingdon Street, St John the Evangelist, Westminster, known as *the Horse and Groom.*

The lease is made on condition that the lessee puts the buildings into good tenantable order.

By endorsement, 13 May 1769, Knight assigned the lease for the remainder of the term at the same annual rent to Robert Reignolds, of St Marylebone, dealer in horses for a down payment of £105. By further endorsement 8 Feb. 1875 the remainder is assigned at the same rent by Catherine Reignolds, residuary legatee and executrix of the will of Robert, to Thomas Collier of Marylebone, coachman for a down payment of £40.

APPENDIX I

After we had finished renumbering this collection and just after we had sent the whole draft to the publishers, we found that the following leases had escaped the net. Fortunately there was still time for them to be included in this appendix.

6th Duke's leases: Strand
(see MXD181-193 in the main catalogue)

MXD1341   – to Thomas Alderman, bricklayer   **2 Jan. 1678**

> Parcel of ground 16 feet (frontage) by 60 feet in depth next to ground leased to John Gumley; with the liberty of the passage or alley leading out of the Strand by the *Maidenhead* to a back tenement belonging to the premises hereby leased [The last clause is interlined.]

Leased for 41½ years at a peppercorn rent for the first year then £32 a year for the rest of the term. An endorsement, witnessed by Thomas Langford and Richard Audley, reaffirms the interlined clause.

MXD1342   - to John Hodge, carpenter   **13 Jan. 1680**

> Messuage now in the occ. of the lessee and the parcel of ground on which it stands, in Angel Court, 13 feet (frontage onto the Strand) x 115 feet in depth, x 6 feet in breadth at the south end; west Angel Court and ground of John Barton, east on ground leased to William Williams, glazier and Thomas Gamon, carpenter, north on the yards of two of the Duke's houses leased to Edward Richards, haberdasher of hats and [blank] Wearge, south on a passage leading into Howard Street in which Joseph Hickes, joiner was granted the liberty to pass and repass

Leased for 39½ years at £6 annual rent

7th Duke's leases: Strand
(*see* **MXD194-204** *in the main catalogue*)

MXD1343   – to Bartholomew Parsons, spurrier   **12 May 1699**

> Messuage in Arundel Rents formerly in the occ.
> of Edward Richards, with the yard that lies
> behind it, as it is now divided and enclosed with
> a brick wall; now held by the lessee and formerly
> leased to Bartholomew Parsons, father of the
> lessee, now deceased; east Anne Moore, west
> Mr Templeman

Leased for 7 years at £30 annual rent

MXD1344   – to Anne Moore, widow   **12 May 1699**

> Messuage in Arundel Rents 11 feet (frontage) x
> 43½ feet in depth in the occ. of the lessee, as the
> same is now divided and enclosed with a brick
> wall from another in the occ. of Bartholomew
> Parsons [above], with the house of office, 4 feet
> x 3 feet, made out of the yard of Parsons' house;
> west Bartholomew Parsons, east Mr Sands

Leased for 7 years at £30 annual rent

MXD1345   – to John Tipping, woollen draper   **8 Sep. 1699**

> Messuage with liberty of passage as in **MXD1341**
> above; abutting east on John Gumley button seller
> and west on [blank] Taylor

The premises were previously assigned by Thomas Alderman
to Tipping. The Duke's trustees now ratify that arrangement
by granting him the remainder of the term at the same
annual rent.

Charles Mawson's leases
(*see* **MXD593-594** *in the main catalogue*)

MXD1346   Mortgage by assignment of rent   **28 Jun. 1710**

Charles Mawson of East Barnet, co. Herts., gentleman to Sarah
Paunceforte of St Andrews Holborn, co Middx, widow

A ground rent of £16 10s. arising from:

> Parcel of ground leased to John Prince on the east side of Norfolk Street, 22 feet (frontage) x 70 feet in depth; north William Blackwell, south John Greene

For a loan of £50 the rent is assigned to Mrs Paunceforte for the remainder of a 39-year term beginning in 1678, to secure repayment of £53 by 1711

Mawson's signature and seal. Receipts are endorsed with signatures and a full settlement in 1713, witnessed by Rachel Bruce and Anthony Wilkes

The 9th Duke's leases: east side of Surrey Street
(*see* **MXD363-364** *in the main catalogue*)

MXD1347-1349 21-year leases (all water damaged) **10 May 1762**

– to John Salkeld of St. George the Martyr, bricklayer

> i) Messuage in a plot 17 x 54 feet in the occ. of William Owen, tailor, being the 4th house from the corner of Howard Street
> ii) Messuage being the corner house next to Howard Street [dimensions and other details illegible]

– to Joseph Stevenson, tailor

> Messuage and yard in the occ. of the lessee, 21½ feet (frontage) x 54 feet in depth, being the third house from the corner of Surrey Street

The separate premises are leased at £8, £20 and £18 respective annual rents. The down payments are waived on condition that the lessees to do substantial repairs within the first 15 months of their tenancy.   3 docs.

MXD1350 21-year lease (water damaged) to Thomas Moore, blockmaker **12 Nov. 1762**

> Messuage in the occ. of the lessee (abuttals illegible)

Annual rent £22 without a down payment, on same covenants as above

The 11th Duke's 60-year leases: Arundel Street west
(*see* **MXD772-788** *in the main catalogue*)

MXD1351	– to Thomas White of Aldgate High Street, London, oil and colour man	**20 Jul. 1786**

Parcel of ground with two messuages on it, formerly leased to John Gumley on the west side of Arundel Street, 16 feet in breadth (onto the Strand) x 60 feet in depth

Down payment £300; annual rent £27

The 12th Duke's leases: east side of Norfolk Street

MXD1352	Lease for 15½ years at £100 annual rent – to David Russell Lee of Norfolk Street, esq.	**1 May 1835**

House (no. 27) in a plot 20 feet x 71 feet, in the occ. of the lessee

Joseph Hodskinson's properties on the east side of Water Street
See **MXD807-808** *in the main catalogue*

MXD1353	Assignments of leases	**12 May 1835**

Edward Christian the elder formerly of Princes Street, Leicester Fields, co. Middx now residing at Calais in France to John Boykett Jarman of Roseneau House in Datchett, co. Bucks., esq.

Two parcels of land each with stables, coach houses, lodging rooms and buildings lately erected by Joseph Hodskinson, being the 5th, 6th, 7th and 8th coach houses from the north east corner of Water Street [cited as nos. 8, 9 and 10 Water Street on the front of the doc.]

Recites former leases to Hodskinson on 7 Sep. 1789 and 1 Jun. 1790, sublet by him to Isaac Heaton and Thomas Bolton of Norfolk Street, gentleman). Hodskinson died in Feb 1812. Now Christian, acting as his executor, assigns the original lease terms for a nominal sum to Jarman

APPENDIX II

Other Sources at Arundel Castle
relating to the principal London estates

The references below relate to the four published catalogues, *Arundel Castle Archives*, vols. I-IV by Dr Francis Steer (West Sussex County Council, 1968-1980) and there are also references to the box lists of further material in Arundel Castle Archives, for which a fuller list is available on application to the Archivist at the Castle. This appendix provides a reasonably comprehensive list, although other references to the Strand Estate and Norfolk House may also exist in more general series of accounts and correspondence in the Duke's archives.

Existing catalogues: The Strand Estate
Acts of Parliament

Cat. 1,p. 150

AP 11	22 & 23 Car. II (1670)	for rebuilding Arundel House and tenements thereto belonging
AP 13	1 Wm. & Mary (1688)	for building into tenements the remaining part of Arundel Ground as now inclosed
AP 16	10 Geo I (1723)	to enable Thomas [8th] Duke of Norfolk to make leases for 60 years of the houses and ground in Arundel Street, Howard Street, Norfolk Street and Surrey Street
AP 35	23 Geo III (1783)	– to enable Charles [10th] Duke of Norfolk to grant building or repairing leases of certain tenements, house and grounds in St Clement Danes, co. Middx, and in or near Arundel
AP 85	25, 26 Vic. (1863)	– for the embankment of the north side of the River Thames from Westminster to Blackfriars Bridges

Cat. II, p. 194

AP 159	– re sewers in the City and Liberty of Westminster, 1847

Cat IV, pp. 29-30
FC 331, 526, }
FC 598, 638   } Draft papers re Thames Quay Bill, 1824-6

FC 641   Bills, and papers re proposed Thames Embankment road and railway, 1853-1860

Deeds: inc. copies and drafts
Cat II, p. 70
MD1241   Draft conveyance to trustees, 1680
MD1305   Copy deeds 1622

Cat IV, pp. 29, 66
FC 115   Draft release re premises in Milford Lane, 1817
MD2708   – re mortgages on premises in Surrey Street, 1695

Leases and rentals
Cat II, pp. 70, 71
MD665   Agreements for leases, 1676-168
MD666   Rental particulars, 1728
MD439   Rental 1737-1738
MD443   Part rental, c.1792
MD671   Licence to sublet, etc., 1840-1851

Cat. IV, pp. 6, 86
MD 689   Rental 1777
MD 277, 278, 374,
    2392, 2576   Various 18th-cent. leases

Cat IV., pp 108-110, 114
A 1956,1949, 2138   Rentals 1742-1746, 1763-1765, 1798-1799
A 1937   Rental 1827
A 2078, 2170   Rentals 1840-1842

Accounts, surveys and valuations
Cat II, pp. 10, 71
MD810   Receipts for carpenter's work 1677-1680
MD667   Survey and valuation, before 1724
MD668-669   ditto, late 18th-cent.

Cat IV, pp. 1, 68, 75, 108-115
FC 653   Accounts kept by Anthony Wright of London (?re Strand Estate)
FC 2391   Accounts for building work in Strand Estate 1791-1793
FC 2322   Reports on property, including Strand Estate, late 19th-cent.
A 2079, 2085   Accounts, inc. for building work 1782-1795
A 1936   Accounts of Robert Watkins, agent, 1817-1818
A 1938   Arrears, 1827
A 1939, 2080   Accounts of Robert Abraham, 1841, 1845

Various

<u>Cat II</u>

p. 10	MD17	Joseph Hickes, building covenant, Surrey Street
p. 54	MD1121	Fire insurance policies, 19th-cent.
p. 55	MD840, 911	ditto
pp. 70-73	MD	(Various refs) – consult catalogue

<u>Cat. III</u>

p. 27	MD1889	History of Arundel House site
	MD2138	Articles, etc. about the Arundel Marbles, 1972

<u>Cat IV</u>

p. 30	FC 632-634	Case against King's College re their proposals, affecting Surrey Street, 1847-1849
p. 74	MD691	Photographs of properties on Strand Estate
p. 76	MD2228	Photographs of various properties including Strand Estate, late 19th-cent.
pp. 89-91	MD	(Various refs) correspondence and papers 17th- to 20th-cents.

Plans and drawings

A box list is available at Arundel of further architectural plans of hotels and other estate developments, *c.*1880-1930, ref. Acc 48

<u>Cat I</u>

pp. 70-1	H1/49, PM 190	Plans of 'Arundel Buildings' 1724 and 1836
	H3/2, P5/66	Thames Embankment: plans for appropriation of reclaimed land, 1861-1862

[Not in catalogue] P5/51, P5/53   Strand Estate plans c. 1860 (Robert Abraham)

<u>Cat II</u>

p. 12	MD1209	Plans etc. re 6 Norfolk Street 1852
p. 70	MD1110	Photos of 1724 estate map
p. 71	MD1221	Plans of houses, 1820-1825, 1859
p. 72	MD685	Plans and elevations, mid-19th-cent.
	MD450	Plans (with surveyor's working papers), 1851-1863
p. 73	MD689	'River View' of the Arundel estate, 1864

<u>Cat III, pp.26-8</u>

MD	(Various refs) plans and elevations, 19th- and early 20th-cent. including an earlier engraving of Arundel House

<u>Cat IV, pp. 90-1</u>

MD2680, 2682	Elevations of houses 1820s
MD2679, 2681	Plans of properties by the Thames, 19th-cent.
MD2641, 2622	Hotel and other development 1967-1971

Existing catalogues: Norfolk House

Household bills and other papers also exist, (Box List 3, ref MXE and GH); and a small series of 1930s correspondence (Box List 4, Boxes 177-9)

Cat I p. 150

AP 17 6 Geo II (1725)	Act of Parliament to enable the inhabitants of St James's Square to raise a rate to improve the Square

Cat II, pp. 11, 12, 71-74

MD18	Accounts for interior decoration, inc. of Jean Cuenot 1751-67
MD1308-1311	Vouchers re repairs, 1814-1819
MD1470	Engraving re drains, 18th-cent.
MD813, 814, 882-884	Estimates and accounts re interior decoration etc., inc. of Charles Nosotti; and correspondence 1869-1885
MD438	Rental of houses in Charles Street, 1762.
MD452	Tax vouchers
MD457	Papers re alterations and repairs, 1904

Cat III, pp. 26-27

MD	(various refs) Abstracts of title 17th- to 18th-cent.; estimate from Charles Nosotti, 1875; building plans and correspondence 1910-1914

Cat IV

p. 26	FC 592	– inc. sketch of the evidence room, 1828
p. 29	FC 4,5, 139, 411, 495	– re building work at Norfolk House
	FC 624	Plans of stable and offices at Norfolk House, 1813-1816
p. 69	FC 2674	Estimates for repairs 1904-1905
p. 75	FC 2322	Reports on property including Norfolk House, late 19th-cent.
p. 83	MD2583	Papers re insurance policies, mid-19th-cent.
pp. 90-1	MD	(Various refs) papers re drains 1750-1808 (consult catalogue) – and correspondence 1832-1864 and 1879-1915
p. 108	A 1955	Household accounts 1767-1777
p. 109	A 2010-2015	Vouchers for expenses in London (?inc. Norfolk House)
p. 114	A 2109-2110	'London bills' 1835
p. 130	IN 76	Silver plate at Norfolk House, post 1777

Introduction to the indexes

A publication such as this contains a disproportionately large number of personal names relative to the overall text. Indexing has therefore been tackled in the following way. There are two indexes which between them have aimed to include every personal surname in the catalogue. As well as the indexes, readers should consult the Contents page at the start of the catalogue in order to understand the context of the references.

The first index contains the 'key players'. These are members of the ducal family and their agents, as well as other gentry and nobility who acted as parties to deeds or leases. Members of City of London crafts guilds have been included here because many of them had a major role in the building of the Strand Estate. Other craftsmen who were among the first builders have also been included; as are those tenants whom the indexer recognised as having shone in their professional field. They include, for example, the mathematical instrument makers and the map and book sellers in the Strand. By contrast, many of the esquires and gentlemen who belonged to the various Inns of Court in and around the Strand and Chancery Lane and who acted as lawyers in the execution of deeds and leases have been omitted here, but their surnames will be found in Index II.

Places in the first index relate both to the locations mentioned in the deeds and leases and to the parishes or neighbourhoods in which the people who were involved in the transactions resided. However, the residential parishes of people living in St Clement Danes itself, and in its neighbouring parishes, have not been included as they are too numerous. The places flagged up are further distant areas of London and out-county parishes and seats. Country esquires and gentlemen generally did own or rent a London house, but it is often difficult to discover where they were located. It is hoped that this index may help.

The second index has been generated more simply as a surnames only index. For the aid of genealogists and family historians it brings in all the other persons not mentioned in the first index, to include all the under-tenants, occupiers and near neighbours mentioned in the leases and deeds.

Index I: People and Places

Index II: Surnames

Killingworth, 126
King, 29, 50, 59, 60, 87, 113, 122, 203
 Sir Peter, 123
Kingestun, 291
Kingrove, 205
Kinsey, 116
Knatchbull, 214
Knight, 130, 148, 207, 261, 309, 310
Knott, 137
Knox, 213
Knowlis, 27

La Terriere, 229, 230
Lacy, 161
Laidlaw, 224
Lamore, 292
Lance, 128
Lander, 154
Lane, 145, 147, 211, 212
Langford, 311
Langley, 119
Lany, 129
Launder, 52
Laurence, 155, 156
Law, 159
Lawley, 21
Lawrence, 210, 215, 234
Lay, 212, 229, 235
Leaver, 116
Ledge, 138
Lee, 307, 314
Leech, 188
Levett, 213
Levile, 112
Levy, 215, 220
Lifford, 185
Lingham, 169
Linle, 99
Locks, 106
Lockwood, 145
Loddington, 142
Lodyhame, 4
Lodyon, 4
Loggan, 122, 128, 134, 136, 188
Loggin, 130
Loggins, 120
Long, 17
Longbottom, 160, 161
Longland, 81
Longueville, 175, 176
Lovell, 15
Lovis, 147
Lowe, 212
Loyd, 52
Lucas, 273

Luddington, 141
Luders, 195
Luile, 96
Luke, 71, 73, 74, 292
Lushington, 216
Luxford, 137
Lyle, 4
Lyndraper, 13
Lyne, 21
Lynley, 16

Macartey, 129, 130
Macarty, 146, 153
McCarthy, 137
McCarty, 125, 126, 131, 186
McCurdy, 237
McKinnon, 186
Mackworth, 110, 111
Madge, 246
Madocks, 167
Malba, 291
Malet, 284
Mallacke, 308
Mann, 3, 80
Mansell, 307
Marchant, 138
Marquois, 94
Marriott, 121, 132, 181
Marryot, 127
Marsh, 115, 121
Marshall, 64, 129, 134, 189
Marston, 275
Martin, 104, 124, 139, 273
Martindale, 50
Martine, 81
Mason, 29
Massey, 217
Mather, 218
Mathews, 27, 113, 175
Matthews, 112, 178, 182
Maurice, 155
May, 50, 268
Mayer, 235
Mazarine, 163
Meakings, 188
Meakins, 29
Mearyweather, 156
Medlicott, 145
Meggy, 237
Meld', 287
Meldon, 287
Melin, 303
Menonault, 272
Merchant, 296
Merge, 52

Michell, 27
Middlehurst, 10
Middleton, 205
Milbourne, 74
Miles, 189
Millan, 104, 105, 172
Miller, 68
Millington, 7
Mills, 28, 96, 101, 155, 168, 172, 176, 181, 184, 186, 187
Milnes, 216
Minchall, 138
Mines, 54
Mockett, 261
Moland, 16
Mone, 15
Monington, 21
Monteni, 288, 289
Moore, 72, 106, 312, 313
Morgan, 27, 115, 116, 163, 211, 215
Morley, 131, 132
Morris, 308
Mortimer, 176
Moryell, 2, 3
Moseley, 209
Mosse, 261
Mountney, 134, 135, 136, 189
Muchall, 151
Mundy, 145
Munteinni, 288
Munten, 287
Munteny, 291
Murt', 284
Mustiers, 287
Myers, 298, 304
Mynt', 284

Nash, 102, 105
Neal, 106
Nedys, 4
Neild, 177
Neilson, 100
Nevill, 163
New, 128, 129
Newman, 235, 238
Newport, 140
Newsom, 211, 224
Newton, 18, 162, 163, 164
Nicholl, 238
Nicholls, 21, 22, 24, 106
Nichols, 221, 309
Nield, 172
Nixon, 119
Noel, 308

Norcliff, 156
Norris, 179, 182
Northope, 4
Northopp, 4
Norton, 204, 208
Nott, 89, 100
Nottele, 296
Novello, 216, 242
Nutt, 101
Nutthall, 139

Obbard, 216
Okely, 145
Oldnar, 131
Oldner, 125
Orwell, 17
Osborne, 309
Osboston, 2, 3
Overton, 116
Oveseye, 292
Owen, 313

Paine, 55
Palerne, 291
Palfrey, 18
Palfreyman, 234
Palmer, 212, 287
Palser, 211
Paris, 126
Parker, 89, 295
Parks, 126
Parry, 216, 300
Parrys, 20
Parson, 287
Parsons, 93, 155, 307, 308, 312
Partington, 168
Pasci', 287
Patfot, 292
Patishulle, 289
Paunceforte, 312, 313
Paxton, 273, 274
Pearce, 125, 126, 152, 160
Pearkes, 79
Pearse, 112, 129, 131, 132, 135, 183, 187
Pearson, 70, 75, 76, 77, 113, 167, 190
Pease, 27, 28, 29
Pecock, 17
Peele, 154, 162, 164
Peirson, 73, 81
Pember, 51
Pennington, 115, 116, 182
Peri, 291
Perkes, 61